Why Crucial Decisions
Can't Be Made in the Blink of an Eye

Th!nk

MICHAEL R. LEGAULT

THRESHOLD
EDITIONS

New York   London   Toronto   Sydney

THRESHOLD EDITIONS
Rockefeller Center
1230 Avenue of the Americas
New York, NY 10020

Copyright © 2006 by Michael LeGault

All rights reserved, including the right of reproduction
in whole or in part in any form.

Threshold Editions and colophon are trademarks
of Simon & Schuster, Inc.

Designed by Jan Pisciotta

Manufactured in the United States of America

10   9   8   7   6   5   4   3   2   1

Library of Congress Cataloging-in-Publication Data

LeGault, Michael, 1959–
    Think! : why crucial decisions can't be made in the blink of an eye /
Michael R. LeGault.—Threshold editions
        p. cm.
    ISBN-13: 978-1-4165-2378-9
    ISBN-10:   1-4165-2378-2
    1. United States—Intellectual life. 2. Creative thinking—United States.
3. Thought and thinking. I. Title.

E169.1.L498 2006

153.4'20973—dc22   2005054336

For information regarding special discounts for bulk purchases,
please contact Simon & Schuster Special Sales at 1-800-456-6798 or
business@simonandschuster.com.

To my mother and father

Contents

CHAPTER 1

Don't Blink, Think

The company, a medium-sized automotive supplier based in Ohio, was already spinning in the upper regions of a vortex heading directly down the tube. What the company did sounded simple enough. It took glass windshields, put a strip of rubber around the perimeter, and shipped them to major automotive manufacturers. An operator placed the glass into a machine, and the machine injected melted rubber around the edge, then quickly cooled it to make it stick. The problem was this: The glass was breaking. The scrap rate mounted—10 percent, 20 percent. Little bar graphs posted in the cafeteria illustrated the amount of money the company was losing each week. Employees blinked uncomprehendingly when the figure reached a million dollars. Was anyone doing anything?

The company was doing all it could, or at least it felt it was. It hired a young, dynamic, university-educated plant manager. Intuition their guide, the plant manager and his team of floor supervisors and engineers attacked the problem. They pulled the dies—large steel molds into which the glass was placed—

from every machine and scanned them with lasers to confirm dimensions to a thousandth of an inch. They ran quality control checks on all shipments of glass they received from other companies. They installed new process control software on the machines to continuously monitor the internal condition of each machine. Day and night, one or more engineers paced the factory, poring over printouts, making adjustments to the machines. Some days, on a few machines, there appeared to be progress, then just as quickly, things spun out of control and it seemed every other windshield was being devoured by mad machines determined to put the company out of business. Hunches about the cause of the problem were getting the company nowhere.

The head office called an emergency meeting. They were giving the plant one last chance to fix itself. They slid the plant manager the business card of a guru. His fee was $1 million. It seemed cheap.

The guru asked for the scrap rates of each machine operator. The company had the scrap rates for each machine, but not for the operators, who were rotated on machines on a daily, or even hourly, basis. The guru spent one month gathering the data. He spent an equal amount of time plotting and analyzing the numbers. Engineers at the plant still intuitively believed the problem was somehow related to the equipment, but the guru, examining the plots and data, noticed something odd—the women operators had much higher scrap rates than the men. But there was an anomaly: Two male operators also had high scrap rates. He asked to meet the two men. They were both slightly built and on the short side. A million-dollar light went on inside the guru's head.

The windshields weighed twenty to forty pounds, depending on the model. The operators had to lean over and into the machines to place the windshields into the molds. The workstations were set up in a one-size-fits-all mode. The guru watched one woman strain to place the heavy windshield in the mold so that it would line up properly with the guiding pins. The machine closed and the windshield shattered. The woman loaded the next part and the guru told her to wait. He ran his hand along the top edge of the windshield. The part seemed to be loaded properly between the guiding pins; however, he noticed one edge rode out a little farther on the pin than the other. He gave the edge a push. He told the woman to run the machine. The large steel jaws clamped together, then opened to reveal a gleaming windshield looking for all the world like a Van Gogh.

The company modified workstation ergonomics, redesigned the die guiding pins, and trained staff workers. Scrap rates fell below 5 percent. The guru was feted and paid. A sigh of relief was heard around the plant. Only the plant manager was somewhat chagrined. He was embarrassed he had to rely on the critical thinking skills of someone else to fix his plant.

He could, if he wished, console himself. Sharp, incisive, clever thinking is steadily becoming a lost art, more and more the domain of specialists and gurus. The trend is troubling and raises the question, Is America losing its ability to think? If, for argument's sake, we define thinking as the use of knowledge and reasoning to solve problems and plan and produce favorable outcomes, the answer is, apparently, yes.

Consider the sober assessment of John Bardi, a lecturer at Penn State who has been teaching university students a variety of philosophy and cultural study courses for over twenty-five years. In a 2001 essay about the decline of critical thinking, Bardi states, "The intellectual qualities I see displayed in my classes . . . are getting worse every year, with the current crop [of students] being the worst." Critical thinking is a cognitive skill that permits a person to logically investigate a situation, problem, question, or phenomenon in order to make a judgment or a decision. Bardi argues that the collapse of critical thinking skills in this country may be "systemic and historical, even inevitable," although he allows that many of his colleagues have a simpler explanation—that the problem is not history or culture, but today's students, who, for whatever reason, "lack the critical thinking skills necessary for higher learning."

Certainly our universities, especially the upper tier, still attract many diligent, gifted students who can knock off a set of differential equations as if they were a connect-the-dot drawing. If Bardi's and his colleagues' harsh assessment annoys some, think of it as applied "on average." Of course, this still means that the critical thinking skills of even the top college students have, on average, declined. If this is the case, it is not surprising, as independent testing on our schoolchildren has confirmed deteriorating performance in reading, math, and science for many years. The Organization for Economic Cooperation and Development's Program for International Student Assessment (PISA) conducts a triennial evaluation of the math, reading, science, and problem-solving skills of fifteen-year-olds living in the primary industrialized countries. In PISA's 2003 assessment, American students ranked twenty-eighth out of forty countries in problem-solving ability. The performance was on par with that of students from Serbia, Uruguay, and Mexico, and well below that of fifteen-year-olds from Japan, France, Germany, and Canada. The most recent National Assessment of Educational Progress has measured some improvement in the reading and math scores of fourth- and eighth-grade students since 2000. Overall, however, the unvarnished results show that more than two-thirds of our nation's fourth and eighth graders are not performing at their grade levels in either math or reading.

If a decline in thinking skills were limited to unmotivated or hungover university students hell bent on frittering away their parents' money, we could probably muster a shrug, perhaps in the naive belief that the stringent standards of academia will inevitably weed out the deadwood. Poor thinking and nascent idiocy, according to this optimistic view, will be nipped in the bud, contained safely on campus, before they reach the real world. It is obvious, however, that this cannot be the case. Many of these students have become adept at muddling through their curriculums, finding a smorgasbord of courses they can pass, and picking up their degrees. One by one these graduates are transporting their limited knowledge and deficient thinking skills into the fields of their chosen professions, as the next generation of teachers, nurses, sales representatives, and company managers. Thus we have teachers, health care workers, and managers with historically inferior critical-thinking skills teaching, caring for patients, and managing businesses.

At least one high-level automotive executive, General Motors' Robert Lutz, has lamented the inferior problem-solving skills of U.S.-trained engineers. Other refined mental skills crucial to workplace performance also appear to be deteriorating. A 2004 report released by the National Commission on Writing, a panel of educators assembled by the College Board, brought to light the growing disgruntlement of businesses with employee writing skills. The report, *Writing: A Ticket to Work . . . or a Ticket Out*, included a survey of chief executives from the nation's top corporations. The results were not pretty—about a third of the companies said only one-third or fewer of their employees knew how to write clearly and concisely.

Predictably, as if filling a growing market niche, a new-age, feel-good pop psychology/philosophy has sprung up to bolster the view that understanding gleaned from logic and critical analysis is not all that it's cracked up to be. This outlook, which sounds especially appealing after a couple of beers in a loud bar, suggests that the rational model is often unnecessary, and may even be obsolete. Malcolm Gladwell has recently set the high-water mark for this philosophy with his book *Blink—The Power of Thinking without Thinking*. In *Blink*, Mr. Gladwell argues that our minds possess a subconscious power to take in large amounts of information and sensory data and correctly size up a situation, solve a problem, and so on, without the heavy, imposing hand of formal thought.

As a demonstration of the omnipotence of instantaneous, Blinklike snap judgments, defined as an understanding arrived at "in the first two seconds," Mr. Gladwell relates a story about a forged Greek statue purchased by the J. Paul Getty Museum in Los Angeles in 1984. The sculpture was a nude male youth, claimed by the art-dealer-seller to be one of the stylized statues known as a *kouros* produced in ancient Greece.

Officials at the Getty were apparently suspicious of the origins of the statue from the start, as it radiated "a light colored glow" not typical of ancient statues. Nonetheless, after extensive scientific tests showed that the marble from which the statue was carved came from an old quarry in Greece, and also verified that the statue was covered with a fine layer of calcite—a substance believed to be formed over thousands of years by natural processes—the Getty purchased the *kouros* for many millions of dollars.

Then, as Mr. Gladwell describes it, things began to unravel. One by one, a host of art experts were led to the statue, with each expert, to a person, instantaneously experiencing the same feeling that there was something "not right." The Getty became so concerned it had the statue packed up and shipped to Greece to be examined by the country's leading authorities on ancient Greek sculpture. One of the experts, the director of the Benaki Museum in Athens, felt a wave of "intuitive repulsion" the moment he laid his eyes on the statue. With alarms going off, the Getty launched a full-scale investigation, uncovering a trail of fabrication and trickery, and ending with the unhappy discovery that the statue had been made in a forger's workshop in Rome in the 1980s.

Boiled down, the Statue That Didn't Look Right is a cautionary tale about the limits and failure of applauded scientific methods and rational analysis, and the far-reaching power and success of homely, undervalued gut feelings and intuition. (*Blink* unpackaged being, by any other name, intuition.) But how meaningful is the story in proving the author's thesis that quick snap judgments often yield results equal to or better than those produced by thoughtful critical analysis?

First, the scientific testing did not fail. The dolomite marble of the statue was covered in a thin layer of calcite. The ingenious forger had apparently used potato mold to induce calcite formation in a couple of months. Other initial evidence had corroborated the apparent authenticity of the *kouros*, including records of ownership that turned out to be phony.

Second, if you read the story carefully, it is clear there is something else going on in the experts' minds other than just out-of-the-blue hunches and intuition. Laying eyes on the *kouros*, the first word that popped into the mind of Thomas Hoving, former director of New York's Metropolitan Museum, was "fresh," that is, too new-looking to be several thousand years old. The director of Athens' Acropolis Museum, George Despinis, said he "could tell that that thing has never been in the ground." The Benaki Museum director's "intuitive repulsion" was apparently informed by his observation of a contradiction between the statue's style and the fact that the marble had come from a specific quarry on the Greek island of Thasos.

In other words, lying behind these "snap judgments" are educated impressions formed by years of study, thought, and analysis. And these educated hunches were confirmed by further analysis, which established, for instance, that the Greek statue was "a puzzling pastiche of several different styles from several different places and time periods."

One of the appeals of *Blink* is that we all have intuition and rely on it to help us make decisions and get through the day. There is a sort of mythology that has sprung up about the power of first impressions. But mythology is not scientific. In a section on "speed dating," a tightly organized event in which a group of men and women have a few minutes to talk to each other and decide if they want to go out together, Mr. Gladwell taps into the power of the belief that first impressions are the best validation of people's characters and personalities, especially as they relate to male-female relationships.

> If first impressions are so important in modern society in establishing close relationships, why is the divorce rate so high?

But how cut-and-dried is this truism? If first impressions are so important in modern society in establishing close relationships, why is the divorce rate so high? Indeed, we have no inclination to track or know how often our first impressions and snap judgments fail us. Upon hearing that a serial killer lived in their community, people are often surprised. "He seemed a nice, regular guy," is a statement one commonly hears on the news. For thousands of years, humans' first impression of the earth was that it was flat. When, looking through his newly improved telescope at the sun, Galileo saw dark spots, the Church brought heresy charges. The first impression of the sun was that God had made it uniformly bright.

In essence, Mr. Gladwell is making a case for one-half of a classic false dichotomy. A false dichotomy, sometimes also called "the fallacy of the excluded middle," is an either-or proposition presented in such a way as to make us think only one, not both of the choices, can be true. The ruse is often used in politics, as in, "Will you reelect Congresswoman Smith, or face the prospect of more jobs going overseas?" In this case the false dichotomy is intuition versus stepwise analysis and critical reasoning. Mr. Gladwell not only separates and distills intuition as a mental power unto itself; he promotes it as a potential source of unbounded, utilitarian good: "What would happen if we took our instincts seriously? I think that would change . . . the kinds of products we see on the shelves, the kinds of movies that get made, the way police officers are trained . . . and if we combine all of those little changes, we would end up with a different and better world."

He allows that our biases can lead automatic judgments astray, but provides no definitive insight on how to improve our snap-judgment ability other than "practice." In fact, critical scientific reasoning almost always involves a component of intuition, and intuition is almost always informed by experience and hard knowledge won by reasoning things out. When Einstein was working on his theory of special relativity, he had a "hunch" that energy and matter were different versions of the same thing. Not until he worked out the equations using his astounding powers of critical reasoning, arriving at the famous $E = mc^2$, was his hunch worth a damn.

The technique by which we make good decisions and produce good work is a nuanced and interwoven mental process involving bits of emotion, observation, intuition, and critical reasoning. The emotion and intuition are the easy, "automatic" parts, the observation and critical reasoning skills the more difficult, acquired parts. The essential background to all this is a solid base of knowledge. The broader the base, the more likely one is to have thought through and mastered different concepts, models, and ways of interpreting the world. The broader the base, the more likely all the parts will fit together. Yet, just as intuition is possessed by each of us, so is the ability to think and reason critically. One of the fundamental principles of the Age of Enlightenment, a period of discovery in which evidence for the great power of human reasoning came to full light, was that *all* people have the ability to shake off dogma and superstition and think for themselves. Much of modern twentieth-century philosophy also largely rests on the assumption of man's basic freedom and his ability to create his own destiny through reason, free will, and personal responsibility.

This is the point where *Think!* and *Blink* diverge: the assumption that in contemporary life the public is somehow wary of making snap judgments; that our tendency by nature or cultural custom is to methodically research and analyze data before reaching any conclusion. If Mr. Gladwell were limiting the scope of his book to select research labs and corporate management teams, his assertion might have weight. In wider society, however, a society bombarded by a glut of information, spin, marketing messages, and demands on one's time, snap judgments have become the norm. We are living and, in some cases, dying by snap judgments. Many people resort to paying someone else to think for them. We have become a society dependent on the views of experts—psychologists, landscape designers, financial advisors, even parent coaches. The realm in which we are permitted to entertain, play, and puzzle over life's everyday mysteries has narrowed. In the absence of a habit of mind conditioned by careful, unbiased observation and applied critical thinking, snap emotion-based judgments have come to predominate. Snap judgments may account for "A nation divided," the tag line that got so much play in the media during the Bush-Kerry election. We've become a "gut-level" society, relying more and more on instinct to make our way through life. We're very comfortable with what we already believe and know. Change, even of our opinions or thinking processes, has become the great anxiety for most people.

As naturopathic medicine taps into a deep mystical yearning to be healed by nature, *Blink* exploits popular new-age beliefs about the power of the subconscious, intuition, even the paranormal. *Blink* devotes a significant number of pages to the so-called theory of mind reading. While allowing that mind reading can "sometimes" go wrong, the book enthusiastically celebrates the apparent success of the practice, despite hosts of scientific tests showing that claims of clairvoyance rarely beat the odds of random chance guessing.

Although it is completely unverified by any rigorous scientific test, Mr. Gladwell's premise has an air of legitimacy thanks to the groundwork laid by several generations of academic "postmodernists" and activists who zealously attempt to deconstruct each and every certainty of nature or society into an underlying set of bogus cultural assumptions. The same method is used to cast doubt on the very method of critical reasoning. These groups argue that rational, reductionist thought is sexist and repressive because it is based on assumptions already compatible with a power structure's values and outlook. As a result, the status of scientific ideas derived from skepticism and rational thought has waned, while the standing of whole hosts of faith-based views and trends has correspondingly risen. *Blink* not only assures us that making snap judgments is good practice, it implies a compatibility with the new-age paradigm of mental acuity based on instinct, emotion, and intuition.

I am certainly not out to bury intuition, "ah-ha" moments, or emotion. As I've noted, these elements of the human psyche are all indispensable to critical and creative thinking. But as far as delivering results, that is, favorable outcomes, critical thinking and its main elements, observation, logical reasoning, and skepticism have a demonstrably better track record. This fact is also why *Think!* differs structurally from *Blink*. It is not the aim of this book to be a compendium of case studies proving the superiority of critical thinking over intuition. In this respect, I, along with many others, need simply note there is nothing to prove. The case is closed. As documented in books such as Michael Lewis's *Moneyball*, statistics and analysis almost always beat instinct and guessing. That's why managers study tendencies of batters and pitchers and "play the percentages," that's why blackjack players good at card-counting methods do better than players who wing it, that's why companies employ systematic analytical tools such as design of experiment and Six Sigma to solve problems and improve efficiencies. Yet, if the case is closed about the overall superiority of critical thinking to improve decision-making, the mystery remains why subjectivity, emotion, and instinct have come to predominate in the lives of people and the wider society. This, then, is a book analyzing the causes of the decline of logic and reasoning in American life, and also a book proposing solutions for stopping and reversing this slide. While the analysis is made with America in mind, it is not strictly limited in scope to American society, as many other industrialized countries appear to be suffering from a similar malaise in thinking, for similar reasons. There are political connotations to some of these conclusions and recommendations, but this is not the book's main point. The book's aim is not macroscopic, it's microscopic—not changing institutions, but changing thinking and habits that have often led to institutionalized dysfunction. If some writers focus on the value of the "bricks" of society and culture, my attention is directed to the importance of the "molecules"—the way we think and how it shapes our lives, destiny, and society. And surely, as it inevitably plays out in millions of decisions made each day, there is a direct connection between the way we think and the society we get.

In reality, the only thing being created by the swelling desire for the easy and thought-free is a critical mass of bad outcomes:

- Blunders in planning and emergency preparedness that led to the catastrophe in New Orleans in the wake of Hurricane Katrina
- Big and small American companies that seem to have "plateaued," with declining prospects for dynamic growth in a changing world economy
- Worsening science, math, reading, and problem-solving skills across all levels of American education
- Growing numbers of teachers who cannot even clearly explain a class assignment, let alone effectively teach difficult subjects such as math and English
- The strident, automatic alienation of Americans along ideological lines on any given issue or problem
- The alarming decline in health of millions of Americans whose bodies are merely following the decline of critical capacities of their minds

These are all, to be sure, complex situations. When the facts are all tallied, however, the root cause for each of these problems must ultimately be traced to hazy, nonrigorous, institutionalized, faulty thinking: faulty thinking in government planning and execution, defectively conceived corporate strategy, an indifferent attitude to the value of knowledge and its power to fulfill our daily existence.

THE CONTINUING DETERIORATION in thinking ability of students emerging from the nation's education system also naturally raises the question of how to account for it. As many studies have shown, much of a person's ability to learn is fostered through parental nurturing and instilled values that create the desire and work habits leading to good thinking skills. If the vast majority of the so-called Y or millennial generation has strictly a utilitarian interest (or lack of interest) in intellectual pursuits, and an impatient, even hostile attitude toward the formal work involved in mastering thinking methodologies—logic, research, analysis, deductive reasoning—it seems reasonable to assume that the psychology behind these habits has been "picked up" from their surroundings. Surroundings can be taken to mean the milieu of moral, ethical, and practical values found in contemporary society. Young people mainly encounter and absorb those values through social interactions with family, friends, and mentors.

The chapters that follow will track down and record the increasingly debilitating effects of the marginalization of thought and intellect in our society. This quest will be informed by a no-holds-barred look at some of the historical and cultural trends contributing to this mental malaise. In spirit, and perhaps at times in tone, the assessment may appear harsh, overly grim, and unfair. So be it. Americans possess a strain of stamina, perhaps arising from this country's particular style of democracy, that allows them to absorb, digest, and exploit the most scathing of criticism—criticism that would demoralize and wound other societies, many of which have far more serious and intractable problems than the United States. The history of our drama, cinema, and literature is one of unceasing, self-lacerating examination and criticism. From Theodore Dreiser's *An American Tragedy* to Allan Bloom's *The Closing of the American Mind*, America and its writers and artists have been compelled to look deeply into our souls and tell us they do not like what they see. The news has been stinging, but somehow bracing, regenerative. In America the dark truth, stirred up and examined, is always a fresh air that lets us forgive ourselves and strive even harder.

Having mentioned Bloom, I need to acknowledge the importance some of his ideas have had in inspiring and framing the arguments in this book. When Bloom's acerbic critique of American higher education, *The Closing of the American Mind*, was published in 1987, it struck a nerve because it released a pent-up pressure arising from years of declining student performance and institutionalized political correctness. Some of the ideas in his book remain central to the core argument presented here. Bloom, a professor of political philosophy, was irritated by the moral relativism of the day's students and their galling indifference to the heroic elements of life. The relevance of Bloom's critique to this book is clear: If there is no such thing as good or bad, there is no meaning, no will to achieve, and no need for knowledge and inspired thought. The point will be taken up in more detail in several chapters, most prominently in Chapter 11, Hearing the Harmony of Reason: Embracing Objectivity, Thinking Critically. Whereas Bloom traces this apathy toward noble pursuits, knowledge, and the life of the mind to a perversion of moral values, mostly as a result of the introduction of foreign ideas into American society, I assign culpability to numerous social, cultural, and historical trends. These are, in their most immediate guises, trash culture, marketing, reliance on therapy, aversion to risk, the self-esteem industry, lack of standards in the workplace and classroom, and lax, hands-off parenting. Taken together, these habits and fashions have institutionalized mediocrity and glorified mental indolence, leading to the documented decline in critical-thinking skills.

Perhaps the main difference between my analysis and Bloom's is in the way we identify primary and secondary causes. I would argue, though, that Bloom's philosophical take on the decline of the American mind-set, while brilliantly lyrical and thought-provoking, is too far removed from everyday experience to do the average American much good. Bloom, no doubt, preferred it that way. He felt no strong identity with mainstream, bourgeois America. However, I disagree with Bloom's dark take on the professional and working-class segments of America. I have run into engineers studying French at night with their wives and known intellectually inspired shop supervisors, cab drivers, and security guards. My view of America and Americans is more in line with those of Emerson, Whitman, and Ginsberg—an America with an infinite, if sometimes flawed, impatient, distracted yearning for experience and knowing. Yet it seems obvious, if we are to re-move the obstacles preventing Americans (and people every-where) from achieving what they want in life, that the best way is to first identify and attempt to mitigate the effect of direct, immediate causes.

I challenge the view that the decline in critical-thinking skills and the cheapening of intellectual life in American soci-ety is in some way the result of free will, and thus historically inevitable. Rather I believe it is the result of a flawed, passive way of perceiving the world, reinforced by the consensus of ever-present and powerful social forces. Further, with the aging of the Baby Boomer generation, I believe we are possibly seeing evidence, for the first time in our history, of a new na-tional mind-set more appreciative of reflection and ideas. The new attitude, born in part through disgust over mass market-ing and trash culture, may in turn help foster a new idiom, one in which books, science, and the arts are as much a part of everyday conversation as sex, jokes, homespun anecdotes, and braggadocio.

But why are critical-thinking skills still important in the day of the computer, the Internet, television, and the DVD? For it is this book's most basic premise that clear, rational thinking and its fundamental nourishment, knowledge, both broad and specialized, are crucially important. Superior think-ing is important not only to our jobs, community, and na-tional interest, but to our identity as humans, our happiness and fulfillment in our professional and personal lives. Think-ing is literally power, sexy and inspiring.

One way of illustrating this is to consider the work of the man many consider history's best thinker, Albert Einstein. Einstein, who was great at sound bites, once mused: "The most incomprehensible thing about the universe is that it is comprehensible." In our age of conflict, spin, counterspin, and information overload, the view that the world and its puzzles will yield to creative insight and the light of reason may seem a quaint, overly optimistic outlook. Yet Einstein, who as a young man was no obvious genius in grooming, had proof it would.

Using no more than a pencil, some paper, and his brain, Einstein unlocked the deepest secrets of the universe (see Chapter 8, Great Thinkers). Today, of course, Einstein is recognized as one of history's most brilliant and creative scientific thinkers. Yet perhaps his grandest achievement was, ultimately, his demonstration of the wondrous might of the human brain and its astounding cognitive capabilities. His discoveries are so elemental, so beyond the perception of everyday, commonsense experience, that one is reminded of the line from *Hamlet*: "What a piece of work is a man, how noble in reason, how infinite in faculty!"

ON THE SCALE EXPRESSED by immortal poetry, $E = mc^2$ pales in comparison to the power of the human mind. The splitting of an atom of uranium will release a huge amount of random, destructive energy. But only the mind can observe, reflect, analyze, and deduce truths about reality, then put those conclusions into useful (or, sadly, harmful) action through the arts and various forms of civic, private, and personal enterprise. Aristotle, among other philosophers, considered the mind the only thing that separated man from the beasts, all other parts and functions of our bodies being the same.

We don't need to think as well as Einstein did, but in order to achieve a useful, fulfilling life, in order to realize our personal and professional ambitions and goals, we need to think as well as we can. Yet, despite its practical uses and seemingly limitless potential, human brainpower is largely untapped, neglected, even ridiculed. Everyday experience confirms that the life of the mind is not doing well. It is, in fact, ill. With the rise of reality shows, content on television has reached an all-time abysmal low. (The television sitcom, with its dialogue and conflict resolution, at least has roots in a type of comedy invented by the Greeks.) Why do niggling problems in our companies or towns never seem to be solved? Why are the lives of so many people seemingly out of control, overwhelmed by tribulations involving money, relationships, and drugs? When was the last time a person mentioned a book he or she was reading? A local newspaper in my parents' town recently polled passersby during a cold snap, asking, "How do you fight cabin fever?" Three people said by shopping, one by snowmobiling, one by rabbit hunting, and another said by drinking and watching sports on television.

No doubt there are mental nuances involved in each of these activities; however, for me, as a die-hard football fan, these reflections usually consist of observations along the lines of "kill him" or "what the hell kind of call was that on third down?"

Full disclosure: I am not always thinking well, and sometimes not thinking at all. Like many, I suppose, I often find myself pulled toward a pleasant, soothing unreflective state of unfiltered daydreaming, a state I call "is-ness." In its most refined form, is-ness is a simple running mental account of our sense perceptions (the air is chilly, the stars are bright), although this register is usually overlaid by personal commentary (I need to call Dave, fix the faucet, or [my present favorite] make more money). Such reflections, while useful or fun, if overindulged, actually work as a block to higher appreciation and understanding of life. As the philosopher George Santayana once observed, in imagination, not perception, lies the essence of experience. Is-ness is pure perception uninformed by memory, knowledge, or critical evaluation. You might remember the street-savvy query, "What it is?" The right answer, it would appear, is that is *is* nothing special, a sort of universal condition of being.

Which brings me to an important point: The decline in the quality of critical-thinking skills, and waning appreciation for knowledge and the power of the intellect in general, is not strictly an American phenomenon. I lament Michael Moore's disparaging, fatuous remark, "Americans are possibly the dumbest people on the planet." It is a natural, healthy reaction to get angry when someone calls you stupid. The most appropriate reaction to Moore's opinion, however, is neither rage nor contempt, but pity. For Moore, who uttered these words in front of a fawning French audience, was essentially acknowledging his own low self-esteem, as well as his ignorance of history.

Americans are not stupid. No economic, cultural, political, and military superpower, be it Greece, Rome, or Victorian Great Britain, has ever been built by a citizenry of half-wits and morons. The citizens of the British Empire, or say Spain under King Ferdinand and Queen Isabella, in some ways have more in common with twenty-first-century Americans than the people of present-day Great Britain and Spain have today. Superpowers are arrogant, pushy, vigorous, physical cultures, preoccupied with commerce, trade, and the protection of their empire from invading armies (or, in the present world, terrorists). Superpowers have always been fascinated with themselves; the ancient Romans seem to have invented celebrity culture and its absorption with success and power. This basic axiom reads: The cultural and political influence of an imperial power on other nations always exceeds the influence of other nations on it. The smug insularity this often creates is partly a consequence of power, not ignorance. Bordered by oceans on its east and west, the United States is also largely geographically isolated from the influence of foreign cultures, languages, and societies.

Moore falls for the temptation, quite common throughout history, of assuming the superiority of cultures or great civilizations that came before current ones. Europe, with its magnificent museums and opera houses, its generations of renowned writers, artists, and composers, is the caretaker of what many scholars consider the pinnacle of human reason and intelligence, the classical order. The classical order, with its emphasis on humanistic issues and speculative reasoning, was actually revived from the Greeks in fourteenth- and fifteenth-century Italy by writers and philosophers such as Petrarch, Boccaccio, and Pico della Mirandola. With the Greeks as their guides and inspiration, the Italians and, later, other Europeans, produced one of history's most prolific periods of virtuoso artistic creativity and scientific inquiry, the Renaissance.

Does it follow that modern individual Europeans are better critical thinkers than Americans? European students test higher in math, science, and problem solving than American students, but many educators argue the results are skewed by greater ethnic, social, and economic diversity in the United States. So it is largely a rhetorical question, but given recent political disagreements that emphasize the differences between Europe and the United States, one that nonetheless fascinates. My answer? *Non, mes amis.* With the exception of linguistic ability, which is more a consequence of geography and historical conditions, I do not think Europeans, on average, are either more intelligent or better critical thinkers than Americans. Europeans, on average, possess perhaps more abstract, "book-based" knowledge, but Americans know more about the practical and the real. Having traveled frequently to Europe, I can verify that Europeans are equally enthralled by celebrity gossip and scandals, if not more so than Americans. In Europe, even in the midst of an abundance of culture, there exists the same great pull toward a life of easy mindlessness, soccer games, and countless hours spent drinking and daydreaming in cafés substituting for football and shopping. While the average European may be slightly more aware of us than most Americans are of them, this awareness often takes the form of stereotyped notions about American culture and society received through the media and movies. (The inspiration for Danish film director/writer Lars von Trier's *Dogville*, a portrayal of a neanderthal-like America, was apparently his own research-void, mythologized view, as von Trier admitted in an interview to having never set foot in the United States.) Moreover, the average European's critical thinking is often undermined by the same gaps in knowledge, prejudice, and flawed logic that often afflict the critical thinking of Americans. (A British acquaintance once lectured me on a bus for forty-five minutes about the environmental sins of the United States, apparently oblivious that this country's environmental regulations, as embodied in the Clean Air Act, Clean Water Act, and numerous other pieces of legislation, are the most stringent of any industrialized nation.) There is also an adverse political influence on the quality of critical thinking in Europe. Indeed European critical thinking and analysis appears to have stagnated, hemmed in by a few sacrosanct postmodern, left-of-center principles that seem to dictate all modes of logic and all possible outcomes. Looking for solutions to festering problems such as rising unemployment and how to pay for the skyrocketing costs of the welfare state with a declining population, Europeans are in effect barred from a truly rational, free-thinking inquiry by the entrenched political special interests of their societies.

America, on the other hand, is becoming more and more dependent on a class of elite thinkers produced at our nation's top universities. Many of these graduates are filtered off into high-paying professions such as law, medicine, and investment banking. In a global economy based more on knowledge than muscle and practical know-how, America needs all hands on deck, so to speak. We need smart teachers, smart nurses, smart sales representatives.

If I can make one broad generalization, the European decline in critical thinking appears to be mainly a product of political forces, whereas the quality of intellectual debate and critical analysis in America has wilted under the onslaught of a number of social, historical, and cultural trends. The pervasiveness of these trends, and the apparent inevitability of falling reasoning and thinking skills, has given birth to an entire service industry designed to both soothe and profit from the ignorance of the unwashed masses. Parents routinely agree to psychological or pharmaceutical intervention on their children at the first sign of difficulty in the classroom. Whether you're a TV producer, marketer, or product designer, the home run is a no-brainer, something so obvious its meaning slaps one across the face before the message can be absorbed into that perilously unpredictable mental processing unit, the human mind. Markerers invite us to celebrate our state of cluelessness. "Life is Random" is the slogan used by Apple to promote its iPod Shuffle. A commercial now widely seen on television plays on both our sense of having less time and our aversion to doing messy details. The commercial shows various people in the office who make a difficult situation go away by pressing an "easy" button. If only real life were so easy!

Faulty thinking is a result of two distinct but interwoven factors—the inability to think critically and a lack of will to think clearly. Often, the ability may be present, but the will or power to do so may be lacking or formally restricted. For example, critical and creative thinking at the level of a large organization, say a corporation, university, or government department, is most often the result of a collective will or consensus. There may be good analytical and critical thinkers in the organization, but their opinions can often be stifled. Thus, we must also be aware of the role played by institutionalized censorship of truth, ideas, and ingenuity in the social patterns we may take to be direct evidence of declining thinking skills.

This theme will be examined in more detail throughout the book. In passing, however, I propose that modern America has evolved into a complex bureaucracy increasingly preoccupied with mastering rules and staying out of trouble, rather than one engaged by knowledge, progress, truth-seeking, and clear, innovative, analytical thinking. It is a society anxious about perceptions, directed by a sort of neurotic interplay of competing ideologies, political spin, commercial and marketing interests, and litigation concerns.

A type of neurosis, or perhaps more succinctly a paralysis, involving competing governmental, legal, and bureaucratic interests, seems to have played a role in the breakdown in decision-making before, during, and after Hurricane Katrina hit New Orleans. First, there was a failure to upgrade the city's levee system even though a study conducted by Louisiana State University researchers several years before had concluded that the levees would not be able to contain a tidal surge generated by a storm the size of Katrina. And Katrina was not a surprise: Officials and experts had long acknowledged it was not a matter of if, but only when, such a storm would arrive. Second, when the water did breach the levees and flood the city, it touched off a communications blackout among city officials and emergency crews. A $7 million grant to improve emergency communication had apparently disappeared, according to a *Time* magazine report. "We didn't expect the water," Louisiana governor Kathleen Blanco was quoted in the report. Evacuation plans were plagued by similar lapses in anticipating and being prepared for the worst. Most astoundingly, one of the biggest causes of the catastrophe appears to have been official timidity and an aversion to taking legal risks or stepping on someone's political toes. The *Time* report harshly concludes, "At every level of government, there was uncertainty about who was in charge at crucial moments. Leaders were afraid to actually lead, reluctant to cost businesses money, break jurisdictional rules or spawn lawsuits." The only response one can muster to this is the one-word, universal euphemism for disgust, "unbelievable."

We have become a society in which the first instinct is not to think clearly, it is the protection of one's backside.

Today, paralyzed by various cultural, political, and social trends from any meaningful use of critical thinking in the search for truth, we have largely turned to emotion-based "analysis" of any given situation or issue. For ours indeed has become the Age of Emotion. It is an age typified by strident, pointless, bombastic screaming "debates" seen on television journalism and talk shows, and increasingly between politicians, family, friends, and neighbors. Or, by contrast, it is an era of simmering spite and tight control, clamming up and staying "on message." Needless to say, these inarticulate, politically charged screes and scrums have more to with the glands than the brain. They are the antithesis of rational inquiry, which is barred by the rules of this sport, as it might lead to a second thought, a concession of point, an admission of error, a boring nuance of agreement or (worse case) a gloating reproach. The defining idea and strategy in the Age of Emotion is to stake out a position, to arrive at a belief, even if it has to be pulled out of the air, and then to filter in only the type of information that would tend to confirm the position.

Emotion and subjectivity, not critical thinking, have become the overwhelmingly popular method of evaluating our world and making decisions. It is quite possible that books such as Daniel Goleman's 1995 book *Emotional Intelligence: Why it can matter more than IQ* have played a part in the mistaken perception that emotion is identifiable with intelligence. Goleman is not necessarily to blame; many of his points are valid—emotion is very much an essential *part* of intelligence. Researchers in artificial intelligence, for example, have found that emotions, especially feelings associated with memories, play an important part in intelligence. It is this component of intelligence that AI researchers have found difficult to mimic in their quest to build machines with intelligence comparable to a human brain.

The ascendancy of emotion over critical thinking and reason may be either partly a result of, or partly a cause of, increasing political polarization of the nation. Entrenched outlooks and positions are emotionally high maintenance. Arguably music, especially rock and roll, has played a large role in creating the perception that raw, artistic passion and emotion are superior to reasoning and formal learning. Three generations of post–World War II Americans have grown up enthralled by that emotion (today's poetry) and by artists and music that seem to capture the essence of their dreams and disappointments. Emotion is associated with bohemianism and creativity. Yet, this view is something of a conditioned myth. Few fans would be inclined to think of Mick Jagger, Bono, or Bruce Springsteen as well-read and thoughtful, but that's exactly what they are. High intelligence and critical thinking are not incompatible with their creativity; they are the essence of it.

Rock and roll culture has helped to glorify a number of

macho, monosyllabic myths about education and intelligence in general. As Pink Floyd sings:

> We don't need no education
> We don't need no thought control.
> ("Another Brick in the Wall," 1979)

Multiply the above anthem by a thousand variations and you begin to get the picture. Thinking and learning are for boot-licking conformists destined for lives as cubicle mice.

Or another twist on the theme, provided courtesy of a famous action-movie actor:

> No one I know reads books.

So who's the conformist?

Or one more common take found in the tough-guy world of many adolescents, including grown-up ones: To read, reflect, and think is to be an egghead, a genius. Here we also detect that hint of social ostracizing that awaits the unsuspecting egghead: "You're intelligent. That's pretty uppity and pretentious of you, buster."

Yet the consummate egghead, Al Einstein, was neither pretentious nor obedient nor conventionally bright in his youth. In her memoir, Einstein's sister, Maja, writes that by the time he had reached high school Einstein "had formed a suspicion against every kind of authority."

But ultimately we need to think critically and seek knowledge, whether it's considered cool or uncool, because it fulfills a deep practical and even spiritual human need. If we can only evaluate the world through the lens of our mercurial emotions, if we grope our way through the day using snap judgments and our instincts as guides, if we let ourselves gravitate toward and settle into is-ness, we really are much worse off than the beasts—dumb and aware of it. As Bertrand Russell wrote in an essay on mathematics, it is only through knowledge and critical reasoning that we are able to possess "the true spirit of delight, the exaltation, the sense of being more than man." I think Bruce Springsteen would agree.

CHAPTER 2

Analyze What?

Should you ever be drowned or hung, be sure to make a note of your sensations.

—EDGAR ALLAN POE

You don't have to be an Einstein or a manager of a company to appreciate the importance of critical thinking. When problems arise in everyday life people are not looking through the Yellow Pages for someone to give them a snap judgment or best guess. They want the top critical thinking for their dollar.

THE PIPE THAT WOULDN'T WORK RIGHT

A personal experience of a friend proved the value of the time-honored critical approach to problem solving. His mantra on the home front is "low maintenance," so when he moved into his current house, he was surprised to find how much technology went into keeping a backyard pool operating. The pool is an "old style" design, lined with a type of concrete and dug deep into the ground. Piping under the pool deck runs into the house to a small room in the basement where a pump keeps the pool water circulating and fresh. One piping line carries the water in, where it is passed through a filter, and another piping line carries the water out and back into the pool.

When he started the pool up in late spring this year, he noticed, as did everyone in the house, that something was wrong. There was a loud rattling sound coming from the basement. The sound stopped as soon as he turned the pool pump off, so it was something to do with the pool water circulating through the pipes. The sound was the loudest in a small downstairs storage room where pipes passed through an open ceiling before tunneling out to the pool. As he stood in the room listening to the noise, he heard what sounded like the ping and grind of small particles inside the pipe. Hunch number one: When he repaired the pool deck earlier in the year, sand and gravel had somehow gotten into the lines.

When the man from the pool maintenance company arrived he noticed the pump was working at only about 75 percent of its capacity. A little sand and gravel couldn't cause this, he said. The problem, in his view, was either hunch number two, a blocked pipe, like a plugged sink drain, or hunch number three, a collapsed pipe, most possibly as a result of the reconstruction of the pool deck.

My friend felt his body sag. A collapsed pipe sounded intuitively correct. He had had heavy equipment rumbling over the yard where the pipes were laid a few months before. He now faced the prospect of paying thousands of dollars to dig up the yard and find the source of blockage. Before proceeding, he called in a plumber for a third opinion. The plumber was following the course of pipe from the pump room through the downstairs bathroom when he noticed a bit of mold in the corner of the ceiling. Looks like you've got some moisture there, he said, and as he pressed his screwdriver against the drywall, it slid in like a knife through butter, releasing a small torrent of water.

Three snap judgments, all seemingly plausible, all wrong. A small crack in the plastic inlet pipe was causing the pump to suck in air. The air caused the pipe to "cavitate," making the loud pinging sound as turbulent water banged around inside the pipe. It cost a few hundred dollars to fix the leak (insurance covered the water damage), but if he had blindly followed his hunches he would have paid much more.

Critical thinking is critical because it avoids jumping to conclusions. It holds judgment at bay until all the evidence is in; indeed one of its objectives is to obtain the evidence needed to prove or disprove a hunch. But what makes critical thinking more important or special than any other type of thinking? Indeed, what exactly do I mean by the imperious imperative Think! Be they computer specialists, government employees, executive assistants, stockbrokers, accountants, plumbers, shop supervisors, retail clerks, nurses, engineers, or insurance salespeople, every prospective reader of this book spends a great deal of the day engaged in some species of concentrated thought. On whose high horse did I ride into town proclaiming, in effect, that people need to go back to school? Where am I coming from when I implore America (and the world) to think more, better, and to practice the skills upon which the intellect breathes and grows? What exactly do I wish we'd think more about, and how do I propose this would help us?

Every person thinks. It is the fundamental nature of our brains to produce thoughts. Sometimes these thoughts occur randomly, with no apparent connection to the moment we're living in; sometimes spontaneously in response to the stimulation of our immediate surroundings; sometimes in a detached, reflective, stepwise form of an internal "dialogue," registered in our acquired native language. The challenge we face is not producing thoughts, it is producing *useful* thoughts. These are thoughts that are capable of analyzing the formidable but fascinating complexity of the world in order to guide actions to yield the most appropriate or best result. I call this critical and creative (C&C) thinking. Critical, because it requires the gathering and processing and evaluation of information; creative, because we ultimately use this information to produce a result that would not have happened without our effort. Henceforth I will simply refer to critical thinking, leaving the creative element implied, not stated.

To some people the word "critical" may have a negative, judgmental connotation, as in, "Whoa, you're in a critical mood today." The perception is imprecise. Critical thinking, as applied to evaluating a person's work performance, for example, may yield a negative assessment, but it can also find much to praise. It is in the most general sense simply a method of investigating and arriving at meaning and understanding. Very often, the understanding is a new one, which makes critical thinking exciting—it is a quest. As historian Bert James Loewenberg notes, "Criticism is the leaven of creative thought."

Intuitive, creative "leaps" that bypass conscious reasoning, such as the chemist August Kekule's discovery of the ring structure of the chemical benzene in a dream, are well documented. More times than not, as studies have shown, years of research and critical thinking about the topic have laid the mental groundwork for such leaps. Because the creative usually derives from the critical, the front half of critical thinking is the key to releasing all the mind's higher cognitive powers. The political economist and sociologist William Graham Summer gave this definition of critical thinking: "[It] . . . is the examination and test of propositions of any kind which are offered for acceptance, in order to find out whether they correspond to reality or not. . . . It is our only guarantee against delusion, deception, superstition and misapprehension of ourselves and our earthly circumstances."

We are all born with the ability to think critically, but, like any skill, it is one that is honed and perfected by practice. Critical thinking requires an intellectual infrastructure that must, like the steel framework of a building, be built up over time in order to give it a definitive shape and power. In his book *Beyond Feelings: A Guide to Critical Thinking*, Vincent Ryan Ruggiero says the three basic activities involved in critical thinking are finding evidence, deciding what the evidence means, and reaching a conclusion about the evidence. It follows that keen observation, both wide-ranging and specialized knowledge, memory, good information, and analytical tools will all be important in boosting critical thinking. In the pool-pipe problem, one key piece of information was the discovery that the pump was working at 75 percent of its capacity, which eliminated one of the hunches.

Admittedly, I come to praise critical thinking, as well as the life of the mind in general, but there are a couple of caveats to that praise. Critical thinking is not always perfect. It errs, as we err, because it is the product of imperfect humans. The world is complex and is miserly with its secrets. Our perception or memory can be faulty. Instant replay exposes faulty perception on the part of umpires and referees at sporting events quite frequently. Or we could lack key information. Likewise, even the most diligent, original, and virtuoso of thinkers, say Sir Isaac, is not always thinking critically. (Newton, in fact, had a fondness for alchemy, the most discredited of witchcrafts, which attempted to turn lead and other metals into gold.) Because we are human, emotions, superstitions, and prejudices sometimes have their way in even the best-trained mind. Finally, there is not one cookie-cut shape of critical thinking, but many. For instance, there is critical thinking applied to evaluate situations and problems (are energy and matter equivalent?), critical thinking applied to argumentation (we should cut spending, not raise taxes), and critical thinking used to persuade (developing the city's waterfront will create jobs and pay for itself in five years). Even these variations, however, have things in common.

We can think we're thinking critically when we're not. True, we all think. Some of us, perhaps even many of us, think very well, thank you. I would argue, however, on the basis of evidence, that the vast majority of people do not even get near to thinking critically or creatively on a consistent, life-changing basis. Instead, we've mostly fallen into a habit of cruising on a number of default brain modes. These range, at the low end, from a state of pure sensation or is-ness to the high end, a condition when we're sharp and mentally focused on accomplishing specific tasks.

Task-driven thinking is not ineffective. Indeed it, along with intuitive insight, is one of the gold-card mental processes carried out with apparent humdrum efficiency by the human mind. Nonetheless, it is a pale shadow of critical and creative thinking.

There is a major difference between specific task-related thinking, say planning your department's budget, and critical-thinking skills and problem-solving ability in general. The former, task-driven thinking, can often be learned by rote, sort of like mastering the steps of a recipe without having to consult a cookbook. We can become better at it, perhaps by combining or rearranging steps to make the operation run more efficiently, but the type of thinking we do is dictated by the task at hand. It is a method of thinking that is less critical, analytical, or creative than it is organizational, predetermined by routines and pragmatic realities. For example, in order to accurately calculate your travel budget for the upcoming year, you need to know the number and types of business trips you'll be taking. Planning your business trips may require you to project marketing initiatives, prioritize client needs, research important trade shows, and so on. This type of thinking is almost entirely straight-line or linear thinking.

Critical thinking is a product of the most highly evolved hardware in the human brain, the cerebral cortex, the surface of the brain's largest region, the cerebrum. The cerebral cortex occupies the uppermost region of the brain, a geography that gives it a biological and symbolic significance. Think of the human brain as evolving upward from the most primitive features of the nervous system, such as the brain stem, various glandular portions of the brain, and the cerebellum—parts of our brain we have in common with animals further down the evolutionary tree. The farther we traverse upward toward the cerebrum, the more uniquely human our brain becomes. As humans ascended the evolutionary ladder, our brains grew to be about 250 percent heavier than the brain of our nearest relative, the chimpanzee, with almost all of that extra gray matter packed into the cerebrum.

Critical thinking combines and coordinates all aspects of cognition produced by our biological supercomputer—perception, memory, emotion, intuition, linear and nonlinear modes of thought, as well as inductive and deductive reasoning. It's no surprise then that we're willing to hire "gurus" and pay for expert opinions produced by this mental and evolutionary incendiary.

At its best, critical thinking can assess a multitude of variables, say all the factors affecting the time it takes your company to build and ship a product, and pick out a pattern—in-house inventories are highest on Wednesday. From this pattern a person can make conjectures about the cause of the circumstance, or design a model of how a system works, or propose how the system could be improved to work better. Such thinking often requires analytical tools, such as statistics or data analysis, to cull out patterns. Often, but not always, such "patterns" are hidden from us in plain sight. For example, applying one method of critical analysis called Enterprise Value Stream Mapping to its operation, a client of a consulting firm, Lean Advisors, Inc., uncovered a major operational flaw that was delaying shipments and costing the company thousands of dollars a week. The culprit? It was nothing more than a complicated, unclear form creating unnecessary paperwork, confusion, and errors.

Neither is critical thinking directly associated with widely promoted new-age or "breakthrough" types of thinking, as epitomized in Gerald Nadler's and Shozo Hibino's *Creative Solution Finding*. This book, which reads like an expanded list- and jargon-filled PowerPoint presentation, mostly reduces "creative solution finding" to a task-driven method, with a few wrinkles. Some of the wrinkles, such as studying the solution, not the problem, merit consideration. Yet this book and many others like it promote pie-in-the-sky expectations that exceptional reasoning and problem-solving skills can be learned as a sort of package deal, as a process or method distinct from any other factors in a person's life. Nowhere is there mention of the importance of wide, general, nontechnical knowledge, reading, serendipity, or nonlinear, horizontal thinking.

Author Ruggiero offers several defining characteristics of critical and noncritical thinkers. Critical thinkers acknowledge what they don't know, whereas noncritical thinkers pretend they know more than they do; critical thinkers regard problems and controversial issues as exciting challenges, whereas uncritical thinkers regard problems and controversies as nuisances and threats to their egos; critical thinkers base judgments on evidence rather than personal preference, whereas noncritical thinkers base judgments on first impressions and gut reactions.

Keeping one's emotional, impulsive reactions under control is absolutely essential for good, clear thinking. Broad, wide-ranging knowledge is also important. It endows us with a discerning intellectual framework in which to evaluate incoming or new information. The information or knowledge obtained through reading (or listening) allows us to make "annotated observations," which can pave the way to lateral thinking and improved problem-solving ability, even though the specific knowledge may not be directly related to a given problem. Stephen Jay Gould, the late Harvard paleontologist, relied on a lateral type of critical thinking to discover an alternative interpretation to the standard adaptationist view of evolution while studying the spandrels under the dome of the cathedral of San Marco in Venice. Gould, who was fascinated by architecture, noticed that triangular spaces (spandrels) appear automatically between the areas where arches connect for no apparent planned reason. Gould proposed it was likewise futile to speculate about the biological "purpose" of every physical feature of an animal or plant, as if natural forces could predict all the uses a specific design, for example, the large human brain, might have millions of years down the road.

The ability to comprehend what is written is a great help in the development of good critical-thinking skills. Literacy in turn depends to a large extent on a culture that supports the value of reading and the information and knowledge it imparts about society, culture, and the world. It is hardly a surprise then that we are seeing evidence of declining problem-solving and high-end thinking skills as we move inexorably from a literate culture to a visual and, increasingly, digital culture. According to researchers at the University of California, Berkeley, Americans spend 170 minutes a day on average watching TV and movies. By contrast, a forty-year-old

American spends about 35 minutes a day reading; a thirty-year-old allots even less time to reading, only 28 minutes.

The relationship between television, school performance, intelligence, and literacy has been extensively studied since the 1960s. Television has been the official bugbear and whipping boy of several generations of educators and many parents who fret about the corrupting influence of the "idiot box" on young, impressionable minds. The reputation of TV has sunk, deservedly, to new lows in recent years; so much so that it is a cliché to say that it is a cliché that TV is bad for the brain. Naturally, the very fact that TV is assailed by the elders and the establishment makes it fatally attractive to the young and some not so young. I recently spotted one kid wearing a T-shirt bearing the image of a TV with the words "anything that kills brain cells can't be all bad."

Yet, obviously, some of this is bombast. Television can provide useful and insightful information and inspire people, through stories about their own heroes, to take action. In the form of educational programming, it can even have a salubrious effect on language development and critical and creative-thinking skills. Drinking two glasses of wine a day is good for you; downing two bottles, not as good. As with anything, the key is moderation, balance.

Still, America has become a TV-addicted society, and some of the bad publicity about television, cliché or not, is rooted in reality. While some researchers have found little or no correlation between time watching TV and literacy, the majority of researchers come down on the side of "displacement"—that is, the more TV watched, the lower the literacy-related skills. For example, a study conducted by the National Opinion Research Center from 1974 to 1990 found that "television watching is negatively correlated to vocabulary" while "newspaper reading is positively related."

The decline in vocabulary and literacy skills has resulted in the gradual dumbing down of textbooks and other reading materials over the years, which of course further dilutes literacy skills. Reading specialists have found that the average American daily newspaper is written at the reading comprehension level of an eighth grader—an assessment that, for some metropolitan dailies I've seen, could be on the high side. The trend also means that, inevitably, growing numbers of people are losing their ability to understand and follow ideas, reasoned arguments, and technical information presented in a written, narrative form. According to the National Institute for Literacy, only one in twelve seventeen-year-old white students can read and gain information from specialized texts. These literacy ratios are much lower for Hispanic and African-American students.

More will be said about the influence of TV and the computer on thinking skills in subsequent chapters. Yet the crucial question for some people here may be this: If ideas, information, stories, knowledge, and work functions are more frequently being conveyed and carried out by visual and digital media, why should we care about reading?

Because, in a nutshell, even in a world that is progressively visual and digital, the written word is still the best way of passing on and obtaining detailed, deep, primary technical and social knowledge about the world. As Donald A. Norman observes in his book *Things That Make Us Smart:*

One of the strengths of serious literature is that alternative interpretations are possible. The reader's understanding of the characters and the societal issues being addressed by the work is enhanced by exploring alternatives to the possibilities suggested by the author. This requires time to stop and reflect upon the issues, to question and explore. This is difficult to do when watching a single performance of a play, movie or television show.

It's also a matter of bits and bytes, the currency, ironically, of the wired set that would have us mothball the written word. One of the most tedious and oft-quoted conventional wisdoms holds that a picture is worth a thousand words. This may be, but a thousand words is still one-tenth the content of a typical *New Yorker* feature article, or one-hundredth the information contained in a smallish novel. Think of words as pixels or dots, the grains of light and color that make up a picture. Obviously, a twenty-thousand-dot (word) article about a town paints a much higher-resolution and clearer representation than a still image of the town.

Movies project a far greater amount of information about a subject using sequences of hundreds of moving images and dialogue to create a story line. Yet if we relied only on movies for our knowledge about life, society, and culture, the intellectual framework needed for critical and creative thought would look a bit like a piece of Swiss cheese: a bizarre to-

If we relied only on movies for our knowledge about life, society, and culture, the intellectual framework needed for critical and creative thought would look a bit like a piece of Swiss cheese.

pography lacking any solid continuity. The critically acclaimed movie *Sideways*, for example, contained a lot of information about the intricacies of winemaking and wine appreciation—types of grapes, wine types, tastes, aromas, and so on. Walking out of the theater, however, a typical moviegoer (myself) could truthfully claim to know only a trivial amount more about wines than when he walked in. To acquire the level of wine expertise portrayed in the movie I would have to learn for myself, which would most likely involve some combination of tasting, instruction, studying, and reading about wines over many years.

A movie is built on a progression of interconnected scenes. Through flashbacks, cutaways, dialogue, voiceovers, and other filmmaking particulars, we can gain a sense of context for the subject, say a teacher, and some aspects of his circumstances. In a 120-minute movie such digressions, if overindulged, become labored. The story must move forward, quickly, fleetingly, somewhat like life.

A written form of narrative, however, is more fluid. It moves easily into the past, present, and future. It can flick into and out of characters' thoughts, be subjective or objective, first-person minor, first-person major, or third-person with full or partial omniscience. It can dwell on nuances of setting, digress into history, finely delineate sensations of smell, touch, and taste, or draw in a completely different story, all in the space of a few pages. This is why a high percentage of people often say they liked the book compared to the movie. Indeed there's a reason many movies are based on books, or ideas and stories cribbed from them. The history of movie-making is about the attempt to selectively re-create on film what a writer is able to fully articulate in prose narrative.

Movies mimic the stream of consciousness we experience mentally and visually. A word narrative slows this stream down. Movies are great at making us feel. I feel great walking out of a movie because in two hours I have lived through dozens of emotional experiences and come out unscathed. I have felt, through the struggles of the characters, that life has meaning. Movies are a compressed art form, a sort of visual poetry. Like poetry, a movie is based on architecture, rhythm (beat), allusion, and symbolism, and less on literal, free-ranging expression. As they aspire to, and work like, a cinematic play-poetry, movies are uniquely expressive, often enlightening and frequently entertaining. Still, because they must adhere to certain rules, movies can provide us only with a limited (increasingly so, some critics say) range of information about society, culture, and the inner life of humans.

Currently, there is the common complaint that movies are becoming less and less like cinematic poetry-plays built on fine acting and dialogue and more like video games—sequences of digitally generated special effects created for emotionally arrested males of all ages. This may account in part for the decline in movie attendance: 48 percent of adults say they are going to movies less often than they did in 2000, according to a CNN/Gallup/USA *Today* poll conducted in 2004. Casting the largest shadow over contemporary filmmaking, however, is money. A movie is a huge, risky investment. This overriding commercial aspect imposes a largely artificial but universally adhered to structure on movies. At its most harmless, perhaps, this structure limits a story to a cast of arche-typal characters—hero, mentor, shadow, trickster—archetypal plot intrigues (girl meets boy) and archetypal endings (happy). At its most intellectually odious, the formula relies on stereo-typed conceptions about the world in order to reach the widest audience with the least offensive, most politically palat-able message—strong, smart, idealistic women; stupid, snivel-ing, greedy, violence-prone men. Writing in an issue of the magazine *Scriptwriting Secrets,* a top Hollywood script consult-ant, Richard Krevolin, codified a version of this rule of thumb as follows: "Most people don't identify with the rich, mean or stupid. So, in general, main characters tend to be well-meaning characters of the working class trying to better them-selves." The insinuation that the rich (or the successful, or the smart) are really the archetypically mean, greedy, heartless, and stupid (Hollywood establishment excluded, of course) is one more strand in the popularization of an anti-intellectual mythology that cuts through all strata of American society. It is a theme that will be revisited and analyzed throughout this book.

The visual and digital media exist by and large to stimulate our eyes and our emotions, not our thoughts. For these there's language, in both written and spoken forms. Many psycholo-gists believe that the evolution and development of language opened the door to all higher thought and cognitive powers. The importance of language, the written word, the spoken word, and reading to critical thinking is indisputable. As Cur-tis White writes in his book *The Middle Mind,* "But without the self-consciousness that reading provides, we cannot think our culture, we can only be thought by it. In short being able to read is a large part of what it means to be human as opposed to being a mere social function."

The implication is clear: Americans need to increase the amount of time we spend reading and to improve our reading skills. I expect this news will be received in some quarters much as Ebenezer Scrooge received the news that he would be visited by three spirits. Perhaps the premonition of Scrooge here is apt. For, as the black-shrouded spirit foretold in that story, I also believe we do face dire consequences unless we change our ways and pay greater attention to the life of our minds.

LET'S CONSIDER THE IMPORTANCE of critical and creative thinking to something damn important: our jobs. Maybe there once was a time when we could rely on an elite to do our thinking for us. This swaggering group of fat-cat managers, researchers, and entrepreneurs could always be counted on to have their fingers on the pulse of the economy and market. Unerringly, it seemed, they could always guess what we wanted, make the right decisions and, just when the market was getting a little flat, produce something out of nothing: hula hoops, Slinkys, cooler, faster, and bigger cars, gas-fired backyard grills, bar-code scanners, elite stereos, better medicines and drugs, desktop computers, Walkmans, PDAs. The researchers invented and tweaked, the entrepreneurs invested, and the managers oversaw and produced. The products and the processes changed but you could be damn sure that whatever the hell it was, it was going to be made by an American company, on American machines, by American labor, on American soil.

There'd be a job for the manager's nephew, his niece, and his neighbor's son. There'd be more jobs than you could shake a stick at.

From his corner office, on a mythical day in this mythical time, the manager might have pushed back in his chair, happy with his productivity and satisfied with his quality, contemplating the ride home in his new company car. As he gazed out the window, a small, frail-looking vehicle might have caught his eye as it pulled into a parking space reserved for visitors. The manager might have remarked the car was no bigger than his son's toy roadster powered by push pedals. The man might have laughed derisively at the tiny, Japanese-built car, as many did. He had no idea, of course, that the building he was sitting in would some day be razed to the ground in order to build cars and trucks made by the Japanese company that had made that car. He had no idea his son, his nephew's son, and his neighbor would some day work for that company.

Over the past two decades, the American business and academic community has produced hundreds, perhaps thousands, of management-type business books prodding and showing Americans how they can work smarter, get better results, and compete with those wily Asians. From Tom Peters's *In Search of Excellence* to Ken Auletta's *The Art of Corporate Success* these books span the globe to find examples of best-practice management techniques. By and large they all urge companies and managers to aspire to greatness by listening to their customers, championing innovation, fostering empowerment and leadership, and ratcheting up quality. Many companies have done very well following the advice contained in these books. Others have faltered. Such inconsistency is a result of two apparent flaws with many of these best-selling tomes. The books, with few exceptions, are mostly geared for managers and mostly preach using techniques based on task-driven thinking, not critical thinking.

As I will argue in the next chapter, we've taken these task-driven practices as far as we can. Or, as it's captured in a phrase often heard at business conferences, "All the low-hanging fruit has been picked." Today, Japanese and other foreign "transplant" companies are welcomed with delirious happiness to compensate for all the millions of jobs lost over the years at American companies forced to shut plants or split to lower-cost countries. There are very few bosses or managers at these transplant companies. Employees are empowered and taught to make decisions on their own. Companies everywhere are now harangued to "build the knowledge base" and urged to turn their companies into "perpetual learning organizations." Such an organization can learn only as quickly and as well as its members. In a sense, we have all become inventors, entrepreneurs, and managers. The most sought-after labor commodity is no longer a muscular hand that can crank a wrench, but a pumped-up brain that can think creatively, critically, and out-of-the-box.

But even a Dilbertlike automaton employed in one of those increasingly rare jobs that require only that one sit calmly in front of one's computer screen meditating in subliminal, task-driven thought would still have plenty of good reasons to seek more and better kinds of knowledge.

Trash culture, sleaze, sex, sensationalism, graphically portrayed violence, and vulgarity have been around since the Greeks. Yes, the human mind has a fondness for the low. Yet the human mind also has a fondness for art, poetry, history, music, and science. As Oscar Wilde once said, "We are all in the gutter, but some of us are looking at the stars."

Yet trash culture, and its financiers, appears hell-bent on tightening its grip and closing off even those few unobstructed views of the sky. I'm writing off 90 percent of TV, and watching that slim 10 percent with modest intellectual aspirations evaporate before my eyes. With some time to kill late at night in a hotel recently I turned on the Discovery channel to find it running a two-hour episode on abused pets! After fifteen minutes of pet abuse, I was ready to drive to the nearest bar.

The proliferation of trash culture is not a zero-sum game. Books, philosophy, art, and theater are still out there. Through the Internet, the ideas of great writers, modern philosophers, award-winning columnists, and brilliant scientists are more accessible to more people than at any time in history. It is clear, however, that the ascendancy of low culture, mainly through the outlets of the mass media, is not as harmless as many cultural critics would have us believe. Its pervasiveness and immediacy has diminished awareness of higher culture, of refined ideas, and of the importance of critical and creative thinking to our health, well-being, and democratic institutions. And, as we are sometimes reminded by the aphoristic dose, perception is reality.

A true libertarian, it could be said, would favor individual choice at all times and would hesitate to advocate imposing personal views and choices on others, even if he or she believed these might better friends or neighbors. The charge is strictly true, up to a point, and in this sense perhaps I fail the test for libertarian purism. It seems to me that this strict definition, however, must also come with some fail-safes or suicide pills. One of these would allow for prescriptive, hectoring stances when individual choices begin to limit or restrict the choices of other individuals, or more seriously, when these choices begin to undermine our freedom and the quality of life upon which our liberty depends. This is the compelling force behind *Think!* Ultimately, I trust that my libertarian instincts will ring true with the reader. I am only arguing that my views be considered on their merits, by free-thinking individuals, not that they be imposed by a higher authority.

For the most part it is liberals, not libertarian conservatives, who have taken up the cause of fretting about the declining intellectual abilities of Americans. Certainly there is cause for concern about the quality of thinking on both sides of the political fence. Liberals excoriate the fundamentalist wing of conservatism for questioning the validity of evolution and Big Bang theory, and conservatives are driven to drink over liberals' tacit support of politically correct causes that undermine the basis of the American political and economic system—the concepts of personal responsibility and reward based on merit.

In general, extreme political ideology and critical reasoning make a strange cocktail. But ideology is not the only cause of unclear, lazy thinking among smart people. Many people who are curious, well-read, and intelligent have built their views on unfiltered, gullible acceptance of information and knowledge. Often there is a connection between ideology and passively received information, as when a newspaper article seems to confirm their beliefs. Yet just as often there is no clear ideological connection. I'll often hear someone say something like "Did you hear that drinking green tea reduces risk of heart disease?" after reading a report of a research study in the morning newspaper. The studies, and many like it, usually prove only a correlation, not a cause. Drinkers of green tea may simply lead a lifestyle more conducive to lower cholesterol. Skepticism, not merely open-mindedness, is required for effective critical thinking.

Today, ideology, received knowledge, and platitudes account for much of the flawed thinking and poor results observed in the workplace, school, government, and home. Writing on the dignity of the late Arthur Miller's drama, David Mamet noted how Miller was able to avoid those platitudes that ". . . inform us of what we already know—the infirm have rights, homosexuals are people too, it's difficult to die. . . ." Mamet, of course, is exactly right: We cannot expect to build a critical, creative life of the mind around the obvious, or expect anything brilliant to be made from the mundane. The higher functions of the mind are for probing the hidden, the nonintuitive, and for building a refined sense of observation and appreciation for everyday life based on knowledge.

Neither, however, is critical thinking merely an abstract search for meaning. Instead, it plays a significant, even necessary role in our physical and mental well-being.

Even better, using the brain makes the brain stronger. A study conducted by researchers at London's University College found that the hippocampus—a part of the brain crucial to long-term memory and decision making—of London's taxi drivers was enlarged compared to those of control subjects.

The results suggest that the effort to build a detailed mental map of the city had added neural circuitry to this region of the drivers' brains.

Improving critical-thinking skills and tapping the enormous capacity and potential of the human brain is our final frontier. Not only is it needed to secure our jobs in a world where the most highly prized and valued good is knowledge. It is indispensable to the healthy functioning of an open, democratic society, and to the restoration and reinforcement of the pillars on which our country is founded: individual liberty and personal responsibility.

Americans could perhaps once count on an elite group of thinkers, entrepreneurs, researchers, and managers to innovate, create wealth, and keep jobs in this country. Undoubtedly, America still has millions of elite critical and creative thinkers in its midst. Indeed, it is a beacon for such people. However, as I said earlier, we can no longer count exclusively on them for our jobs, standard of living, or sense of self-worth or self-esteem.

More troubling in the long term, perhaps, is the effect that a decline in critical thinking is apparently having on public debate, discourse, and democracy in this country. The net result is an increasingly radical political partisanship that seems to preclude meaningful discussion and debate from public and private life.

How did this come about? As our intellectual framework for perceiving and assessing the world becomes more stunted and fragile, we rely more on ideology, received knowledge, conventional wisdom, and blind faith to make our way through life. The psychological effect of this is a tendency to build shells in order to protect our identities, which are based on things we've been told and beliefs these things have engendered about the world. We tend to shy away from discussion about "unpleasant" things. The Gestapo-like, motherly dictum "Never talk about politics or religion" has expanded to a more encompassing "Never risk venturing beyond matter-of-fact observation and common anecdote."

Yet people need to talk and debate ideas. As the scientific philosopher Karl Popper once observed, "If we ignore what other people are thinking, or have thought in the past, then rational discussion must come to an end."

Ironically, this trend of clamming up does not eliminate the desire for an intellectual debate or resolve conflicts we seek to avoid—it merely buries them. When these repressed mental energies do find their way to the surface, as they must, they are likely to do so in a violent, uncouth manner. A society of slow-burners and ranters is consistent with a society that has lost its intellectual self-confidence. It is a measure of a culture that is retreating into an increasingly narrow comfort zone, avoiding risk and cutting itself off from the renewing lifeblood of ideas. The cure is not anger management, it's a history or biology course, a discussion, a piano lesson, or a book of Hemingway's short stories.

Critical thinking is a prerequisite for the continued prosperity of America, a country in which a great deal of power is constitutionally entrusted in the hands of the people. As Jamie McKenzie observed in a recent article published in the *Education Technology Journal*, "Democratic societies require citizens capable of challenging conventional wisdom, the propaganda of zealots and demagogues, as well as the platitudes and bland assurances of those in office who would like us to suspend critical judgment when systems break down."

Today the zealots we must dissuade and face down are not just in our own country, they're scattered across the globe. Since 9/11 and the start of the war in Iraq, a fresh wave of anti-American hysteria has swept the world. Even in Canada, a country dependent on trade with the United States for 50 percent of its gross domestic product, over two-thirds of the people say the United States is a negative influence in the world. Two-thirds! This is the same nation that has a love affair with Cuba, a country that has not held a democratic election in fifty years. The opinion of Canadians is not based on critical thinking or research, but on myth and balderdash dished out by the country's legions of left-leaning scholars and pundits, as well as, ironically, by Hollywood and the U.S. media. Still, it is not enough to scream "Hypocrites! Ingrates!" Unless America can engage the world on an intellectual level, it is doomed in the war for the hearts and minds of people. The country needs a new generation of leaders, diplomats, and citizens trained in the arts of critical engagement, debate, and argumentation. American education needs to devote a higher portion of its curriculum to the study of politics, language, and the history of other countries.

Perhaps this itinerary seems a tad too ambitious. But don't cash out your ticket yet. You can enter this journey at any level, at any time. Life is sufficiently long (although not long enough) and abundantly strange, and certainly a brain, finely tuned and nurtured, can come in handy. Just Think! Of the benefits, that is: a healthier body, a more secure job, new and improved interest in life and a stronger, safer country.

And it doesn't cost a penny.

CHAPTER 3

Thought, American Style

Every democracy which has enjoyed prosperity for a considerable period first develops through its nature an attitude of discontent towards the existing order.

—POLYBIUS, GREEK HISTORIAN (200–118 B.C.)

A century or so ago, a group of American scholars got together for drinks to discuss an important new discovery. They had realized, not all at once, that the social and intellectual differences between the United States and Europe were not a historical hiccup that would eventually go away if Americans drank in so much French wine or British wit, but something profound, real, and permanent. In order to communicate and investigate the full meaning of this insight, they founded a new school of philosophy called, fittingly, pragmatism, often acclaimed as America's contribution to world philosophy. As interpreted by author Cornelis De Waal in the book *On Pragmatism*, the bottom-line significance of pragmatism meant "We (humans) fix our beliefs by having external realities guide our thoughts, as opposed to having our thoughts guide themselves."

Hold it right there. Houston, we have a problem. Consider, if you will, that last statement: We fix our beliefs by having external realities guide our thoughts. Did I hear that correctly? Am I a native of the same country as William James, one of the founders of pragmatism, who after many years of careful observation and reflection about the nuances of American thought must have leaped from the chair in his study and shouted something to the effect: "By George, I think I've got it. America and Americans work from the outside in, rather than from the inside out!"

So much for Mr. James's eureka moment. Obviously, those were very different times. Today, American society would appear to be anything but pragmatic. Dogmatic (my way or the highway), didactic (let me tell you how it is), frenetic (I don't have time to think, let alone read), solipsistic (reality: it's all about me!), relativistic (whatever)—there's a troubling validity to every one of these generalizations about the modern American cultural landscape. But pragmatic? A society that carefully and thoughtfully examines factual evidence before forming and expressing its views? "It depends on what the meaning of the word 'is' is," President Bill Clinton once intoned under oath. Here was a perfect illustration of thoughts straining to conjure reality rather than reality naturally inspiring thoughts. It was (at the time) the high-water mark of evidence for the country's drift away from pragmatism as a national philosophy. It signaled that our public life and its institutions had become so immunized to lawyerese and twisted, illogical rhetoric that even the president would publicly question the meaning of one of the first verbs an infant learns to speak, without any apparent fear of ridicule.

We have become a society so accustomed to the most surreal rationalizations of behavior or viewpoints given instant credibility that many Americans come to view truth as something manufactured, as a car tailpipe or iPod would be, according to some set of predetermined specifications. Or perhaps people simply no longer believe there is a thing called truth. Even in cases where specific information is available and known (Our sales are falling and our sales staff spends most of its time in the office—maybe there's a connection?) the equality of subjectivity with objectivity usually takes precedence, requiring schools, businesses, and other organizations to proceed as if all viewpoints are valid (Sending sales staff on the road is expensive—it is just a slow market).

So it goes. The first responsibility of a manager on any project these days is to consult. "Seeking input" and "building consensus" have largely replaced the effort that once went into analysis and decisive management. No doubt, getting input and striving to reach solutions that everyone can live with is worthwhile, as long as they form the basis for analysis rather than replacing analysis. I call seeking knowledge, not for knowledge's sake, but for the sake of arriving at a solution that everyone can feel good about, "egalitarian intelligence." Egalitarian intelligence is the shaping of knowledge and education to fit an individual's brain, rather than shaping a brain to learn formal methods of problem solving, deductive reasoning, and factual knowledge. No child can be left behind, no person can be diminished, and (yikes, let's not even think about it) no one can be discriminated against.

The "intelligence" resulting from egalitarian intelligence should not be considered a consequence of democratic governance, which is the power to enact policies approved by the popular majority. Rather, egalitarian intelligence is a form of populism, the strongly felt presence of the needs, ideas, views, and behavior of the people. It is an outgrowth of crowd psychology and its reference point is the "collective consciousness." At the turn of the century, Emile Durkheim founded a new field, sociology, to study social psychology and its effects on individuals and also society. This new field's fundamental unit, which has been described as akin to the atom in the sciences, was the social fact. Like an atom, a social fact is devoid of context. Think of the little boxed surveys on the front page of USA Today that provide in graphical format "the top reasons people would never use a cell phone exclusively" and other such information. The idea is to study a social "situation," not a series of interrelated events. All situations being equal, like atoms, it follows that knowledge derived from, and decisions made on, this basis will usually be full of subjective "truths" and logical fallacies.

A brilliant case study of egalitarian intelligence in action is the design plans for Ground Zero. The plans have changed and shifted countless times as more people and organizations have delivered their input to the committee overseeing the plans. The striking, twisting wedge-shaped tower originally approved for the Freedom Tower has now apparently been scrapped, a victim of security concerns. Instead, a new design being favored for the tower is one built on a concrete pedestal, giving the building a fortresslike appearance. The building's design has been scorned by critics, who have called it a "nightmare." The fallacy in this decision is that, on the basis of one major terrorist attack in the city's history, security should be made the main concern in the design of a new tower. Yet, by far, the greatest risk, from a security or financial standpoint, is building a new tower in the first place. Letting the security issue override all logic, however, the committee is seriously considering approving a building that will mark Lower Manhattan, in perpetuity, with a horrid monument to fear.

An article in the *New York Times,* "At Ground Zero, Vision by Committee," by Benedict Carey, takes up the Ground Zero plans in order to explore the ways in which the decisions of committees are swayed by political factors or social group dynamics, not necessarily sound thinking. The article quotes Ralph Cordiner, the former chairman of General Electric, who once said: "If you can name for me one great discovery or decision made by a committee, I will find you the one man in that committee who had the lonely insight . . . that solved the problem that was the basis for the decision."

There are numerous indications that empirically based, critical reasoning is often being displaced by a mass-induced, consensus, egalitarian-style intelligence in American society:

- Since 1985, a fifteenfold increase in the diagnosis of attention deficit disorder in American students, who are often prescribed drugs for treatment, despite the lack of a single, peer-reviewed paper claiming to prove ADD has an actual medical basis
- A boom in the disability/therapy industry, where anything from gambling to stress to excessive shopping is widely,

and sympathetically, viewed to be a "disorder," thus label-
ing people and largely relieving them of responsibility for
their actions

- An increasing number of Americans who believe in superstition, paranormal behavior, and junk science (a 2000
poll found 43 percent of Americans believe in UFOs)

The spread of egalitarian intelligence is a boon for lawyers,
psychiatrists, and self-esteem consultants, but a big problem
for Americans. It means leveling down instead of up. It means
short-term gain for long-term pain. At its core lies a rejection
of the traditional empirical, pragmatic American mind-set
and values of a results-driven society. This was a society
groomed by its entire historical national experience, as well as
the temperament of its individuals, to believe there was a
thing called truth, and experience and evidence was its name.

Americans, by intellectual inheritance, training, habit,
and disposition, have always been prone to be empirical in
outlook and thought. *Empiricism* is a fifty-cent word for the
view that knowledge of the world, life, others, yourself is obtained exclusively through what you observe. An empiricist believes we live in an externally real world independent of our
lives or awareness, but one that is nonetheless accessible, to a
high degree of accuracy, through our senses. What is true is
what is experienced by our senses.

America's empirical, pragmatic intelligence has done
well. Early in the twenty-first century, the United States is an
economic, cultural, and military superpower on a scale unmatched in history. The country has the largest, most produc-

tive economy in the world. From the period 2001 to 2003 alone, American businesses increased manufacturing output per hour by nearly 20 percent, by far the largest productivity gain of any industrial country. Americans enjoy more disposable income than the citizens of any other country, have access to the most advanced health care, low unemployment, and some of the world's highest standards for environmental protection in the industrialized world.

Of course empiricism, the view that all knowledge is mainly assimilated from experience rather than derived from idealistic principles or subjective feelings, isn't the only factor that accounts for America's rise on the world stage. Historical circumstances, economic policy, and the idiosyncrasies of American political democracy have all played a role in creating a society that is naturally progressive, entrepreneurial, work-oriented, and abundant in opportunity. Indeed, empiricism by itself cannot accomplish anything. As German philosopher Immanuel Kant understood, the most important factor activating intelligence and accomplishment in anything is will power. "Enlightenment," he wrote in 1784, "is man's emergence from his nonage." This nonage, or immaturity, he went on, was not a result of "lack of intelligence, but from lack of determination and courage to use that intelligence without another's guidance. Have the courage to use your own intelligence!"

Americans have traditionally never lacked the courage to strike out on their own and use their intelligence to innovate and explore because they have always had the incentive. In his book *They Made America*, Sir Harold Evans posits that

America's unrivaled capacity to churn out innovators and inventors is due to a combination of the country's geography, economic structure, political and educational systems, and psychic make-up. From Samuel Morse (Morse code) to Thomas Edison and Sergey Brin (Google), America's legacy as a place of frenzied invention rests not so much on genius, according to Sir Harold, as on the dogged desire of individuals to make things work in the market. "Originality is not the prime factor," he observes, echoing Kant, "effectiveness is."

Or, as Madonna put it, "We are living in a material world." Critical, creative thinking is the key bridge between observations about the world and positive, effective outcomes. We want, we want, but first we observe, observe, then figure, experiment, draw, revise, calculate. Ascending civilizations have been especially good at connecting all the dots. The Egyptians worshiped the sun but invented astounding new engineering and construction methods, while managing the daunting logistics of organizing and feeding a workforce of thousands of men during the building of the pyramids. The Greeks, while best known for the mystique of their speculative philosophy, were hands-on types, inventing the water screw, the catapult, and the basics of geometry. Romans took such care with detail that their roads and bridges are still standing, and usable, two thousand years later.

By most outward signs the United States is at the zenith of its productivity and creative capacities. Historians, who enjoy dwelling on the fleeting nature of all power and glory, have recorded how internal changes, usually involving revision of traditional values and the indulgence of various types of superstition and irrational behavior, have often preceded visible deterioration of great civilizations. Could the decline of traditional American common sense and an objective outlook on life be the first signs of an America on the wane? Is the rise of consensus-seeking, egalitarian intelligence itself a by-product of a society with less incentive, interest, and aptitude to take risks, apply knowledge to practical problems and create innovation? Have marketing spin, political correctness, new law, obsession with appearance, and a feel-good culture diminished America's appetite for the effort and intricacies of learning and applying critical reasoning and factual knowledge?

There are certainly many signals that the transformation of America from an empirical, rational, results-driven culture to an emotional, complacent, "whatever" society is well under way. One telltale sign is the gradual but persistent lowering of standards and accountability, a prerequisite for egalitarian intelligence. It is worth noting that a decline in standards may be a cultural trend, not limited to learning: In the 2004 Olympics, dropped batons in relay races cost the United States two gold medals, and it was painfully evident that American basketball players have fallen behind the rest of the world in mastering the game's fundamentals—passing, defense, dribbling, and shooting. In education, the first recognizable declines are in those areas most dependent on critical and creative thinking—writing, math, and problem solving.

At the 2005 annual conference of the Society of Automotive Engineers, GM executive Bob Lutz gave a speech. "We're actually training our engineers to be managers while the rest of the world trains them to be doers," he said. Lutz, who has spent most of his career designing GM's vehicles, claimed engineers from other countries can arrive at more effective solutions to a problem more quickly than U.S. engineers. Lutz reported that U.S. engineers often need to call in specialists to do revisions to technical drawings, a procedure that may take weeks and add tens of thousands of dollars to the cost of a project.

Lutz's observation is noteworthy for another reason. It comes from a top manager at a company that has lost more than half of its share of the North American market in the past forty years, from 60 percent to about 25 percent, with 3.5 percent of that decline over the last three years. Almost all of that market share has gone to the Japanese automakers, in particular Toyota and Honda, which are building cars and trucks more efficiently, at lower cost, in makes and styles with high demand among consumers. Toyota surpassed Ford as the world's number-two automaker in 2004, and some industry analysts predict it is just a matter of time before it overtakes GM as the world's top auto producer. What's an objective measure of the value placed on this huge difference in performance? GM's bond rating has been recently cut to "junk" status by two rating firms. As I write, at current stock prices, you could buy all of GM's shares for a paltry $22 billion. The sum of all Toyota's shares would cost you nearly seven times that amount, $140 billion.

There once was a saying, often uttered with more than a trace of hapless, ironic truth, that what's good for GM is good for America. We can only hope that this is not the case any longer. What has happened to this venerable corporate American Goliath? If one was of the conspiratorial mind-set, one might fret that GM is being brought down by a backlash of worldwide anti-American sentiment, except that most of the new buyers of Japanese cars are Americans. Well then, there's the dastardly Japanese government and its low yen policy, which means the average Japanese citizen lives like an ant, but that the country's products are cheaper to

> There once was a saying that what's good for GM is good for America. We can only hope that this is not the case any longer.

sell abroad. And let us not forget about the curse of this Goliath's existence, as a recent *Economist* article details: "The main cause of their [GM's] problems is not in the factory or even the design shop. Detroit's carmakers are being strangled by concessions they made to the United Autoworkers . . . when times were good." With much higher pension costs and health care costs than the Japanese carmakers, surely no one can dispute that the UAW is the main cause of GM's demise. We're talking global macro- and microeconomics here, plain and simple. No one can claim, it might be supposed, that something as intangible as a decay of critical- and creative-thinking abilities has played anything more than a minor role in the decline and fall of a company that once employed nearly a million people across the world.

I cannot only claim that the deterioration of critical and creative thinking has been an ever-tightening noose around the neck of General Motors, it would be a dereliction of my journalistic duty if I did not state this exactly. In the mid-eighties, a freshly degreed eager beaver, I went to work at a General Motors facility that made a transmission so complex that only one person in the entire company understood how it

worked. At a time when foreign carmakers seemed to intuitively grasp the significance of Occam's razor (less is better),
GM was designing machinery that conjured the image of
Frankenstein. The 700R4, as it was called, went into the bel-
lies of many of the company's fast-selling trucks and cars at the
time. Every Monday morning, twenty or so managers and supervisors in suits and ties assembled in the boardroom anx-
iously waiting for a plaid-shirted Dave (an hourly worker on
permanent "special assignment") to arrive and evaluate, in his
calm Appalachian drawl, the likely causes of the latest fritz
out. "My God, it stalled in rush hour traffic on the Lodge for
the vice-president of corporate finance," I remember one executive wailing. It was telling, I and others thought, that they
made Dave, not the engineers who designed the 700R4, fly to
the far ends of the country to smooth over these snafus with
irate executives, dealers, and customers.

The 700R4 wasn't the only culprit in GM's ever-mounting
problems in the eighties and nineties. It was the corporate
mind-set that built the 700R4 that was hurting the company.
It was a mind-set incapable of or unwilling to learn new tricks,
a mind-set steeped in complacency and divorced from effective use of critical and creative thinking, operating for years
and years in a like-minded manner, that kept pushing the
door open wider and wider for the Japanese.

As part of my grooming, I was sent circulating through various departments for stints of a few weeks at a pop. The experience was my "Education of Henry Adams." In quality
assurance, I met Charlie, a man given to rambling, strident
monologues about the corporation's incompetence at every

level, all in earshot of his supervisor, who occasionally emitted a bored rejoinder, "You got it out of your system yet, Charlie?" It seemed to escape the supervisor's notice that Charlie did little, if anything, to earn the comfortable salary GM was paying him. In shipping/receiving I met an overweight, surly insurgent of an employee nicknamed "Wild Bill." Bill, a forklift truck operator with many years' seniority, was management's incarnation of the UAW employee from hell. My first day in the department Bill pulled me aside and boasted he had filed 365 grievances against management, one for every day of the year. When he had a day off, he filed two to make up. In every area of the plant I ventured into, in the attitude of nearly every person, there was a palpable undercurrent of derision and cynicism about the job, about the company, about life.

It wasn't as clear to me then as it is now that GM had committed the most grievous of sins in the business world. It had created and daily sanctioned a culture of unaccountability. As it had grown to dominate the industry, it had become the ultimate government project, insulated from customers, ideas, and the dynamics of the market. A culture of unaccountability is a culture without incentive, and a culture without incentive is the death of critical and creative thinking. To claim the company's loss of market share is the result of complex global economics and poor decisions made years ago is to simply state the obvious. It is impossible to imagine a Japanese or German carmaker tolerating one day of operation with a plant full of deadbeats such as Charlie and Wild Bill. Intelligence, Kant reminds, is not so much a result of genius, rather it is a consequence of a determination to use it.

The degree to which the culture at GM has become unaccountable, blithely cut off, as it were, from those difficult, headache-inducing consumers, is demonstrated by some remarks by Peter Davis, director of interior strategy and quality at General Motors. Speaking at the same conference as Mr. Lutz in 2005, Davis observed, "Customers are becoming more diverse. Minorities, women, and people under the age of thirty-five have unique needs and buying preferences." Mr. Davis was apparently alluding to the market for smaller, fuel-efficient cars, the one GM has handed over to the Japanese car manufacturers on a silver platter. It has been a huge market segment for at least fifteen years, but one that apparently is just coming onto the radar screen at GM.

In some ways the circumstances of contemporary America mirror the situation of General Motors. There are, of course, still high levels of accountability and incentive, as well as small miracles of efficiency and innovation built into the American economic system that, for the most part, still handsomely reward effort and effectiveness. But, like GM, America is being victimized by its own success. Its very size and wealth allow it to coddle, indeed reward, incompetence. As GM was once the biggest and baddest, America is today; as with the company, American society is rife with a passive, cynical, complacent acceptance of problems.

Ten years ago, you would have had a tough time reading one upbeat review of any GM car or truck in the automotive trade press. Today General Motors has made large strides in improving the quality of its vehicles, which receive ratings similar, and in some cases superior, to those given Japanese-built vehicles. GM is also acting to cut high overhead costs and has replaced its Byzantine hierarchy of divisions and departments with a decentralized "matrix" organization that is supposed to promote quicker, better decision making. It remains to be seen whether these and other changes at the company will provide its employees with the incentive to use and improve their critical- and creative-thinking skills, but it is certain that everyone knows that this is what the deal boils down to. As high-profile automotive consultant Dennis DesRosiers has suggested, the future of the automotive business is all about brainpower.

Ditto for the future of education, health care, banking, information technology, advertising, and filmmaking. As John Kenneth Galbraith predicted, the university has replaced the bank as the major supplier of the nation's most needed source of capital. Not only is knowledge the world's most valuable commodity, access to it is instantaneous and universal. The world is wired, and every company, institution, and enterprise is seeking to tap this interconnectivity to do more work for less money. The spoils in this post-industrial world will not go to the people, companies, and nations winging it and relying on snap judgments and gut feelings, but the ones sweating the details and doing the best critical and creative thinking.

THERE ARE MANY PEOPLE around the world who view America as an anti-intellectual brickyard and feel the country will have an insurmountable disadvantage in today's knowledge-based, global economy. It is a damning, demeaning assessment, of course, and it is meant to be. It is based partly on cultural observation and analysis, partly on fable, and partly on many various types of ill will and politically based resentment. But how much of the anti-intellectual label actually sticks? How much of this huge generalization about an entire country is rooted in reality and how much of it is a snap judgment or parody?

For starters, this damning appraisal overlooks or flatly ignores the central question: What is intelligence, or for that matter, an intellectual? Psychologists today recognize the virtuosity of the brain and its ability to produce many types of intelligence. Certainly, on a scale measured by definite outputs produced by mental activity such as creativity, invention, and prosperity, America ranks as perhaps the most intellectually well-endowed nation in mankind's history.

This anti-intellectual label also rings with the hollow sound of a false, either-or absolutism of the type expressed by truisms such as "You are either with us or against us" or "The enemy of my enemy is my friend." In the real world, people are often neutral and the enemy of your enemy may still hate you. American society and culture is no more anti-intellectual or hostile to the uses of intelligence than European society is antipragmatic. All intelligence, be it business, musical, or mathematical, must eventually be translated into the real and the concrete in the form of a venture, a song, or a set of solved equations. There is always a practical side to the intelligent and an intelligent side to the practical.

What then does it mean to say, as many do, that America is anti-intellectual? In his book *Anti-Intellectualism in American*

Life, Richard Hofstadter proposes that it is the egalitarian nature of America's founding, its history, and its contemporary society that has predisposed Americans to believe that plain common sense is superior to learned, formal, and abstract knowledge. Hofstadter's analysis, which won him the 1964 Pulitzer Prize in nonfiction, shed fresh light on America's tempestuous relationship with intellectuals and its low regard, often bordering on apparent hostility, for abstract concepts, knowledge, and reasoning too far removed from the realm of everyday experience. He reports how the Federalists attacked the acquisitive and erudite Thomas Jefferson for his lofty intellectual pursuits, something that would be inconceivable in England or France, then or now. Ultimately, Hofstadter's conclusion boils down to what is essentially a political point: Americans favor applied, everyday knowledge over highbrow intellectualism and erudition because they view the latter as a vestige of the elitism, class-based power, and hereditary privilege the country rebelled against.

This interpretation bears repeating. American anti-intellectualism is not directly anti-ideas, -knowledge, or -thinking. It is an opposition to or a calling out of the elitism often associated with learned, formal education and abstruse, abstract thinking. It is a reluctance to give credibility, and thus status and power, to someone simply because he knows a few things he has spent a lifetime studying. It is an aversion to being "talked down to," a repulsion from the feeling of having the sum total of one's life diminished or called into question in order to allow a few philosophers the privilege of dancing on the head of a pin.

Yet, a whole subculture of Americans is professionally engaged in high-level intellectual pursuits in primary education, academia, scientific research, and other fields. Another segment of the population is composed of "lay" intellectuals and experts on hosts of topics and pursuits ranging from chess and gardening to history and ornithology. Presumably these polymaths and connoisseurs are not pariahlike figures in their communities and families, compelled by their disreputable activities to keep their true identities secret. Within their circle of colleagues and relations, many of these intellectually inclined people are undoubtedly admired, respected, and even liked. The topic of anti-intellectualism in a book such as Hofstadter's refers to a broad cultural assessment. Hofstadter is talking about mainstream attitudes toward intellectuals and intellectual pursuits.

More current writing on the subject also reflects on the political angle to America's rocky relationship with intellectualism. In an essay in the online journal *Context*, Mark Crispin Miller suggests the ascendancy of George W. Bush and the Republicans can be accounted for by relentless pandering to the anti-intellectual undercurrent of American civic culture. Miller cites this quotation from Fox News chairman Roger Ailes: "What people deeply resent out there are those in the 'blue' states thinking they're smarter." In other words, many in red states are simply casting their vote against intellectual elitism. Miller's purpose in quoting Ailes is to support the claim that Democrats are smarter, and therefore are less electable in certain areas of the country. Yet the remark, carefully considered, and the evidence actually imply something entirely different. If the most significant political fault line in this country is formed around a gut-level dislike of elitist eggheads, the way swing votes swing probably has little to do with ideology, political stripe, or even bottom-line intelligence. A successful American politician must first and foremost project a non-egghead persona. He or she must simply connect with the public. Bill Clinton and George W. Bush win, Bob Dole, Al Gore, and John Kerry lose.

The theory that American anti-intellectualism is rooted in the masses' instinctive sensitivity to the social protocols of equality, while intriguing, ultimately leaves several questions hanging: Why does a significant segment of American society view a display of broad, arcane knowledge as elitist, but not the flaunting of excessive wealth? While foreigners, especially Europeans, fret incessantly about income inequality in the United States, numerous polls have shown the issue is a non-starter with most Americans. More relevant to this discussion, what is the cause of the intellectual-elitist link? How, specifically, has the cultural and social fabric of American life shaped this country's beliefs, mind-set, and attitudes toward intellectual endeavors and critical and creative thinking?

If America were a sentence it would be active, grammatically speaking, by default. This is a country of doers, built on the muscle, sweat, and ideas of more than a dozen generations of industrious individuals who awake each day, dust the sleep out of their eyes, and go out into the world to get things done. Americans judge others, and themselves, by results. Talk is cheap, we like to say, and we are naturally inclined to be skeptical about the good intention, the Big Idea, and the grandiose plan. Americans' tolerance of failure and personal reinvention is nearly infinite, their sympathy for deadbeats and the dissolute limited. It is no coincidence that the motto of a state in the center of the American heartland, Missouri, is "Show Me." An updated version of a motto reflecting the national attitude might be "Yeah, right."

Empiricism, in the form of organized observation, is one of the two pillars of the scientific method invented by Galileo, Bacon, and others in the fifteenth to seventeenth centuries. Science begins with a "direct appeal to the facts," according to the astronomer Sir John Herschel. "Seeing is believing," the convenience store clerk opines during a brief checkout conversation, unaware she is on the same page as Sir John in extolling one of the key ideas behind the development of Western civilization, one that also informed and shaped the early American experiment.

Other ideas and philosophies have played a part in shaping the cultural and political landscape of America. Transcendentalism, the original "turn on, tune in, drop out" social-philosophy movement, was popularized in the nineteenth century by writers such as Ralph Waldo Emerson and Henry David Thoreau. The work of many American writers and artists was swayed by European intellectual movements such as romanticism and existentialism. Socialism—another European invention—under various guises, has left its imprint in the political and social fabric of the country during the twentieth century. The population's awareness of some of these ideas has been widespread, but the effort to spread their acceptance was somewhat akin to trying to grow a palm tree in the north woods. No-nonsense, hard-boiled, show-me-the-money empiricism has really been the only moral, ethical "philosophy" to completely take root in native American intellectual soil.

Why is this? In an after-the-fact sense, empiricism certainly appears the best fit to both the American political and economic system and the national mood. This attitude was faithfully captured by the nineteenth-century American historian Richard Hildreth, when he wrote: "I pay no attention to what I have been taught, except so far as my own examinations confirm it." The importance of using objective fact to establish the truth of any statement, mundane or profound, was expressed in the Declaration of Independence when Thomas Jefferson wrote, "We hold these truths to be self-evident." The principles enshrined by the Declaration are a logical consequence, not of abstract ideas, but of touchable, seeable experience. They are not beyond dispute, but Jefferson and the fifty-six men who endorsed the document believed the evidence conclusive.

Jefferson and all the Founders were deeply influenced by the thinkers of the European Enlightenment, most notably the ideas of Francis Bacon, John Locke, and David Hume. The writings of Hume, a Scotsman and peripatetic bachelor who spent much of his life in Paris, have special relevance to the development of the American intellectual spirit and temper. Perhaps the most important and far-reaching implication of Hume's ideas was the notion that nations and systems of government purporting to have the best interests of their citizens at heart ought to take their cue from human nature, not from a menagerie of cooked-up ideals, no matter how good they sound. But Hume's empiricism could cut both ways. Not only should the ideas on which government is founded be based on experience, that is, evidence of the way humans behave, but the very ideas, concepts, and standards of judgment that people use to think, reason, and govern themselves were also shaped by experience and culture.

The notion that experience influences ideas and patterns of thought is a key to understanding the American intellect. What are these encounters that ultimately predispose Americans to a mainly empirical, practical, and skeptical outlook? The answer seems to be the uniqueness of the historical, social, and political experiences upon which the country was built.

Post–Native America was founded by intrepid Englishmen and women seeking adventure, profit, escape from religious persecution, or all of the above. The Puritans were certainly not empiricists, at least in the strict sense of the term. Like the ancient Greek philosopher Plato, the Puritans believed knowledge derived from sensory experience was an imperfect facsimile of eternal forms and ideas. For the Puritans, these ideas were present in the mind of God. Yet neither did Puritans advocate that humans stick their heads in the proverbial mud of ignorance. Just the opposite. They believed ideas and insights derived by observation and reasoning to be useful and a sign, ultimately, of the unity of faith and science. The Puritan leader John Cotton once observed, "Knowledge is no knowledge without zeale [faith]," and, "Zeale is but wildfire without knowledge."

Many historians have recognized that the Puritans played an important role, beyond just being the first on the scene, in setting the stage for the growth of American democracy. The Puritans were tolerant of other religious beliefs and respected and valued the uses of factual learning and reasoning. In his book *American History in American Thought*, Bert James

Loewenberg observes: "Pilgrims and Puritans crossed the ocean, fought the Indians, and wrote history with conscious purpose. Whatever assessments later generations made concerning the Puritan way of life, much of the American intellectual tradition commences with it."

The commercial nature of the first American colonies was another stimulus in shaping a mind-set that paid close heed to the immediate, real, and pragmatic. The Virginia Company and the Massachusetts Company were both joint stock corporations founded with the mixed mission of settlement and trade. In return for ships, food, and housing, the charter required planters and indentured servants to work for a set number of years for the company. At the end of the servitude (up to seven years), the laborer would be granted a piece of land and be free of obligations to the company. Jamestown, Plymouth, and other early settlements were no goodwill or research missions living free and easy off the king's pocketbook. Not only did they face the onerous task of fending for themselves in an uncharted wilderness, but they were expected to eventually turn a profit for their king and investors. From the get-go, the very earliest settlers in this country had to focus the totality of their mental and physical energies on the real and the present.

For a number of reasons—Indian raids, starvation, fire, ineptitude—the ventures got off to famously rocky starts. In the opinion of Thomas J. DiLorenzo, author of "How Capitalism Saved America," problems related to failure of crops and food shortages were mainly due to communal ownership of the land by the company for the first seven years. In 1611, four years after Jamestown was founded, the British government changed the system, permitting each man three acres of his own land and demanding no more than one month of his work as contribution to the company. Whether or not the change in the system helped directly improve agricultural productivity, there is little doubt it must have produced a profound shift in the mental atmosphere breathed in by the early colonists. Overnight, individual planters and laborers went from the condition of being regulated and dependent on others to being free to pursue their own ends in the way they wished, independent of the choices and work ethic of others. Crop production did improve after this change was instituted, so DiLorenzo's theory rests on a base of some solid, if circumstantial, evidence. But the claim is also consistent with Hume's view of human nature, as well as the research in modern psychology and economics that has found that people become better critical and creative thinkers in circumstances with a large potential for personal gain. The historian Charles Beard believed it was predominantly economic self-interest and opportunity that influenced the course of the country's history, from the earliest days onward. High motivation to succeed (and fear of the consequences of failure) spurred the first Americans to be good observers and diligent, ingenious practitioners of common sense and applied knowledge.

Yet the early colonial experience was only a prologue to the most influential event shaping the American intellectual temperament. The ideals embodied by the American Revolution, and the actions they aroused, have been the touch point of American moral, ethical, and intellectual life through two centuries of global upheavals, internal social crisis, and cultural/

ethnic change. The essence of the ideal is a radical faith in both man and the vigor of human reasoning.

America and its Founders weren't the first to espouse liberty and place a high value on the perfectibility of man and the capabilities of his mind. These ideals were essentially invented by the Greeks and rediscovered, modernized, and brought to the surface of social consciousness by the writers and artists of the Italian Renaissance and European Enlightenment. While Americans appropriated these principles, America was the first country to employ them as the foundation of a constitution and political commonwealth. "The genuine liberty on which America is founded is totally and entirely a New System of Things," wrote British colonial statesman Thomas Pownall in 1783.

Not only was critical reasoning expected to play a marquee role in making this new system of things work, it was indispensable to getting the entire concept off the ground. If there was ever a crowd that lived by its wits, it was the Revolutionary bunch. They spent as much or more time engaged in conflicts of ideas as they did packing muskets. "The Revolution was fought with words before it was fought with deeds," writes historian Loewenberg. Time and again, a new political or social issue would threaten the well-being of Americans or the cause of independence, requiring an empirical examination of the facts and a reasoned response. It was a time of manic writing, voracious reading, and vociferous, pointed debate. The pamphlet was the CNN of its day. Between roughly 1763 and the end of the war in 1783, some two thousand pamphlets were printed on the most divisive topics of the time. Books, diaries, letters, and newspapers spread the debate into all corners of the country.

Thomas Paine's forty-four-page pamphlet *Common Sense* used both evocative language and reasoned argument to stoke a highly distilled, potent strain of revolutionary fever in the minds of his readers. Paine rebuked those who believed America should reconcile with Great Britain because of its natural and permanent relation to the Mother Country. "Europe, not England, is the parent country of America," Paine wrote. "The first King of England of the present line [William the Conqueror] was a Frenchman, and half the peers of England are descendants of the same country; wherefore, by the same method of reasoning, England should be governed by France."

After the revolution, the unprecedented freedom of America's population and the country's westward expansion further ingrained an empirical, practical outlook into the national culture. In his influential book *The Frontier in American History* Frederick Jackson Turner argued that a continually expanding frontier was the greatest single factor determining the character of American life. Not only did grappling with a primitive environment require rugged individualism, it tended to level social distinctions of birth, class, and education. The West casts a long mythological shadow. Its remnants can still be seen in American values, patterns of behavior, and national psychology, especially in an egalitarian, nonelitist outlook and the demands it often places on our national discourse.

Today the West is East, represented in threats and opportunities posed by countries such as China and India. If, one hundred years from now, America hopes to be at the vanguard of innovation, quality of life, and political influence, it will need to slow and reverse the leveling down of standards that is leading to the domination of emotion- and intuition-based egalitarian intelligence. Good critical-thinking skills will be imperative for the continued prosperity of America in this new world, which comes nearer to us every day. The United States needs to rekindle belief in the value of the uniquely American outlook based on pragmatic values and an empirical outlook. It must also become more than just empirical and practical.

Good critical and creative thinking must begin with personal observations about the external world. But as Columbia University's John William Burgess, renowned as the founder of "scientific" history, argued emphatically, only when a person has constructed a conceptual framework do the facts, historical or otherwise, begin to acquire meaning.

Man cannot live on facts alone; probably never could, but especially can't today. The world is flat, is the way *New York Times* columnist Thomas Friedman characterizes the situation in the book of the same name. In this world the facts of your personal experience must be supplemented by the facts of other people's experience in order to acquire true value and meaning. These extra "facts," information outside the realm of one's own personal experience, can be obtained by discourse, digital media, or the old-fashioned written word. The people who succeed, find fulfillment, make a decent living under these new conditions will be the ones who understand that the fashionable dictates about the questionable relevance of formal, book-style learning and knowledge are themselves old-fashioned. This isn't about solving the conundrum of the Unmoved Mover or an expanding universe. It's about being able to express viewpoints and rationally debate important issues with family, friends, and colleagues. It's about winning a contract with a company in India by being able to recite a few lines of the Bhagavad Gita. It's about saving the rain forest by *proving* that trees and commerce can coexist.

Now *that's* practical.

CHAPTER 4

Feeding the Feel-Good Monster

Each day, in thousands of American schools, teachers ensure that thinking is made easier to swallow. As detailed in Lawrence Diller's *Running on Ritalin*, here's what it's like for students at an elementary school in a comfortable suburb:

> The lunch bell has just rung and the kids are noisily pouring out of classrooms to enjoy a brief recess in the schoolyard before mealtime. Inside, next door to the principal's office, the school secretary is arranging bottles of medication on a tray. Scotch taped to the tray are little photos of 14 children, labeled with their names and keyed to bottles. Though by now she pretty much knows who gets what, at the beginning of the school year, this system helped make sure she didn't make mistakes—that each of the children taking Ritalin at school received the right pill and dose. . . .
>
> At a nearby school of similar size, the kids getting Ritalin are organized in 10-minute shifts because their number ex-

ceeds 30. And this weekday ritual is carried out . . . at schools across the United States.

Ritalin is a psychotropic stimulant that works by increasing the amount of the neurotransmitter dopamine in the brain. It is prescribed for children (and adults) judged to be underperforming or hyperactive or both. Why would you give a stimulant to someone who is hyperactive? In children at least, a stimulant has been shown to have the opposite effect of reducing distractibility, known in pharmacological circles as the paradoxical effect.

While Ritalin helps "normalize" behavior, there are a few gremlins that come with the drug. There is no conclusive proof it improves a student's grade performance over the long term. One study found that students on Ritalin react more strongly to possible punishment than to potential reward, a finding that implies taking Ritalin actually reduces the incentive to achieve. Drugs, in general, usually do not increase motivation. There is also the messy issue of Ritalin's being a potentially addictive drug. The Drug Enforcement Agency classifies Ritalin as a Schedule II controlled substance, the same as the narcotics heroin and cocaine. Noted ADD critic Dr. Fred Baughman found that of the 2,993 adverse reactions to Ritalin recorded by the FDA from 1990 to 1997, 160 were what you would call worst-case—death. Last but not least, Ritalin is expensive. A prescription for one hundred Ritalin tablets can cost over $150.

An estimated 4.4 million American children ages 4 to 17 have been diagnosed with ADD or the related ADHD (attention deficit hyperactivity disorder), up from about a half-million twenty years ago. About 10 to 12 percent of all boys between the ages of six and fourteen in the United States have been diagnosed as having ADD. Fifty-six percent of children diagnosed with ADD have used Ritalin at one time or another. But who is doing the diagnosing? How did an ailment that essentially didn't exist thirty years ago become a problem, in the words of Dr. Diller, "of epidemic proportions"?

The answer lies in what must increasingly be viewed as a landmark moment in the history of American education. The momentous event, one seemingly destined to change the emphasis and objectives of American education, was a committee meeting of the American Psychiatric Association held in 1980. It was at this meeting that attention deficit disorder (ADD) was first defined and codified as a mental disorder. Here are some of the "symptoms" of ADD as listed in the association's bible, the *Diagnostic and Statistical Manual (DSM)*.

- Often fidgets with hands or feet or squirms in seat
- Often runs about or climbs excessively in situations in which it is inappropriate
- Is often on the go or often acts as if driven by a motor
- Often blurts out answers before questions are completed

There are five more symptoms, and if a child exhibits any six of them over a six-month period, in the opinion of a doctor or a teacher, that child may be diagnosed as having ADD.

I was out of elementary school long before 1980, but I'm sure that had psychiatrists been on the ball back then they would have found a gold mine in my second-grade class. By the looks of it, I, along with at least half of the other boys, were top-flight ADD material.

The formalizing of ADD as a mental disorder, and its coupling with the drug Ritalin as the most frequently prescribed treatment, has had huge practical and philosophical consequences in the American educational system. It opened the floodgates for widespread diagnosis of hosts of other previously unknown or rare learning and mental "disorders." A partial list of conditions deemed disorders by the APA includes minimal brain dysfunction, impulse disorder, developmental reading disorder, developmental writing disorder, and developmental arithmetic disorder.

ADD also eventually led to the sanctioned, indeed endorsed, use of powerful psychotropic, potentially addictive drugs in the nation's classrooms. The irony is not pleasant: Problem-solving and reading ability may have declined, but American students can beat the pants off the rest of the world when it comes to drug use. Not surprisingly, the early introduction of drugs to American children is carrying over as a dependency into adulthood. A study published in the *Journal of American College Health* found that 17 percent of men and 11 percent of women used drugs intended for children with ADD.

The total U.S. market for Ritalin and other ADD-controlling drugs is almost $3 billion per year, according to one estimate. In the first quarter of 2005, Pfizer sold $644 million worth of the antidepressant Zoloft in the United States, and less than a third of that amount elsewhere around the globe. In 2002 the FDA approved using Prozac to alleviate depression in children eight years and older. In the 1990s, the number of prescriptions for Ritalin and similar drugs in the United States rose fivefold, to nearly 20 million, according to IMS Health, a national prescription auditing firm. Almost all the Ritalin manufactured in the world is sold in the United States. This suggests that outside the United States either the disorder doesn't exist, or if it does, it is treated by other, less intrusive methods. It also raises questions about the legitimacy of the criteria used by the American Psychiatric Association to establish mental disorders.

From 1952 to 1994 the number of mental disorders listed in the APA's *DSM* rose from 112 to 374, an increase of over 300 percent. But how does a mental disorder make it into the vaunted *DSM*? Years of scientific research, no doubt? According to Renee Garfinkel, a psychologist and representative of the APA who attended *DSM* meetings, the process is slightly less rigorous. Garfinkel told *Time* magazine, "The low level of intellectual effort was shocking. Diagnoses were developed by majority vote on the level we would use to choose a restaurant. You feel like Italian. I feel like Chinese. So let's go to a cafeteria. Then it's typed on a computer."

Not exactly confidence inducing. In her book *And They Call It Help*, Louise Armstrong comments on the "scientific" methods used to establish mental maladies in the *DSM*. "To read about the evolution of the *DSM* is to know this: it is an entirely political document. What it includes, what it does not include, are the result of intensive campaigning, lengthy negotiating, infighting and power plays."

This is exactly what you would expect when there is little or no scientific evidence to support a given view. Armstrong cites the story of the "discovery" of a disorder called "self-defeating personality disorder." The chairman of the *DSM-III-R* committee at the time, Robert Spritzer, thought it up on a fishing trip and, upon his return, persuaded enough of the committee to include it in the *Manual*.

According to Dr. Sydney Walker, many doctors choose psychiatry because, after entering medical school, they discover they don't like medicine. Walker writes in his book *A Dose of Sanity*, "The visceral dislike of medicine among many psychiatrists is a primary reason why *DSM* is so popular (after all, you don't need to touch a patient to administer a *DSM* label) and hands-on diagnoses are not."

At the heart of the ADD epidemic and its treatment with Ritalin lies the debate about whether ADD-like symptoms have a true biological or medical origin, or are brought on by environmental and social factors, such as schooling conditions or lax parenting. Like the process used to decide whether a certain behavior is a disorder, this discussion has largely devolved into political squabbling. Strictly on the basis of logic, however, the claim that ADD is an *abnormal* neurological or genetic condition would appear to be on rather shaky ground.

First, there is no direct physical or chemical way to test for ADD or ADHD. There are no physical tests because, unlike the diagnoses involving illnesses such as flu or heart disease, there are no measurable symptoms. The only method for diagnosing the disorder is by subjective observation of the person. Second, we are talking about an illness without any true clinical, medical symptoms, such as those shown in the genetic diseases sickle cell anemia or cystic fibrosis. ADD is merely a pattern of behavior. Shyness is a pattern of behavior, one that may be socially debilitating for some people, but the American Medical Association has never endorsed that we prescribe powerful drugs en masse to kids in order to treat this epidemic. To the extent that the vast majority of children diagnosed with ADD are boys, then there is most definitely a genetic correlation with fidgeting, running, and climbing. But abnormal?

The fact that the vast majority of children diagnosed with ADD and ADHD are boys naturally raises the suspicion that the trend is part of a larger feminist agenda. In *The War Against Boys*, Christina Hoff Summers argues that women's groups have systematically campaigned for preferential treatment for girls in schools, where boys are viewed as a hostile and aggressive presence. Summers writes, "Leaders in the equity movement take a dim view of errant boys, speaking with straight faces about schoolyard harassers as tomorrow's batterers, rapists and murderers." From this perspective Ritalin, it would appear, is being used to treat nothing more than a "boy" gene, not a true medical condition.

Numerous educational associations, government officials, physicians, and even psychiatrists have questioned the validity of the theory that ADD/ADHD has a biological basis. For instance, in a 1994 letter to Dr. Baughman, Paul Leber of the Food and Drug Administration said, "As yet no distinctive pathophysiology for the disorder has been delineated." Nonetheless, the view that ADD/ADHD is a product of some as-yet-undiscovered biological mechanism is widely supported within the psychiatric establishment.

Yet, even conceding, for argument's sake, that ADD is one, a real, abnormal medical condition, and two, a condition that is mainly caused or exacerbated by biological rather than social factors does not automatically imply that psychotropic drugs should be used to treat it. As Dr. Diller notes in his book, the acceptance of ADD as a biological brain disorder does not logically imply that the treatment must also be biological, that is, medication. Diller points out that for many biological conditions, hypertension or adult-onset diabetes, for example, the initial treatments are changes in lifestyle, more exercise, better diet, and weight loss.

The deeper one digs into the ADD-Ritalin proliferation, the stronger the distinctive aroma of a greenish ink on a crisp paper hinting of an unholy professional-political boondoggle. Many critics of ADD, and the entire learning disability industry as a whole, believe psychiatrists have used drug-based psychotherapy to provide their profession equal footing, both professionally and remuneratively, with traditional medicine. The pharmaceuticals used to treat the growing number of mental and psychological disorders are themselves the basis of a multibillion-dollar industry. Even the schools get a piece of the action, with many school districts collecting extra funds, called "bounties," for each student diagnosed with a specific learning disability.

Far be it from me to sound alarmist, but it seems clear that the explosive growth in the number of students diagnosed with ADD, depression, and other learning disabilities in schools, and their professionally sanctioned treatment with medication, is fundamentally changing the nature of American education, with troubling consequences for both students and critical and creative thinking. Studies have shown that Ritalin, for example, does not substantially *improve* learning and, on the contrary, creates a sedative effect with a reduced sensitivity to reward. Old-fashioned study of human nature tells us motivation and incentive, although not always in response to the expectation of a reward, are keys to tapping the brain's magnificent potential. Even if a particular student responds brilliantly to Ritalin or other medications, the increase in the probability of a drug-dependent life is not an especially healthy antecedent for a life of long-term stability and mental sharpness. Last, the introduction of drugs into the nation's schools radically changes the role of education from that of teaching reading, writing, and problem-solving skills to managing classroom social dynamics and modifying behavior, attitudes, values, and beliefs. Small wonder tests show American students are falling behind the rest of the world in the core learning skills needed for professional and academic success!

YET, ON A MUCH broader scale, the huge, unprecedented boom in various learning disabilities is in keeping with America's transformation from a self-reliant culture to a culture of dependency. In their book *One Nation Under Therapy*, Christina Hoff Summers and Sally Satel attribute this trend to a shift in philosophical values, away from the common acceptance of the view that one's shortcomings are a result of flawed character or lack of initiative and toward the idea of a self in which one's flaws are a product of hardwired maladies and disorders. Thus, people's excesses—food, gambling, shopping—are not problem behavior caused by lack of self-control, but addictions. One common explanation for poor scores on exams is a type of panic syndrome. Failure to capitalize on opportunities and achieve one's full potential can be chalked up to that old pothole, self-defeating personality disorder.

Not all of this, then, can be the concoction of greedy psychiatrists, compliant physicians, and lazy teachers. Americans, in particular baby boomers, are apparently in need of absolution for their own, and their children's, shortcomings and failures. There is a burgeoning demand for reasons to believe we are guiltless. In essence, we have created a huge market for both disabilities and therapy.

In *The Progress Paradox*, Gregg Easterbrook observes that the significant increase in America's quality of life in the past fifty years—more disposable income, less heart disease, less discrimination—has not made people any happier. Easterbrook posits that one underlying cause of this trend is a lack of meaning in people's lives. As meaningful pursuits go, none is more consuming or fulfilling than one's own children.

The tremendous growth of the self-esteem movement is itself a sign that the lives of many adult Americans have a deficit of meaning and that people are seeking it by throwing themselves into the lives of their children. Since 1977, there have been over seventeen thousand professional psychological journal articles and dissertations containing the term "self-esteem" in the title. Self-esteem has become something of an all-around catchphrase for a trait or outlook most deem indispensable to American life. It has also acquired social import arising from the avowed missions of various self-esteem groups, associations, and task forces. The end product of one such task force set up in California in the 1980s, a report titled *The Social Importance of Self-Esteem*, boldly proclaimed that "many, if not most, of the major problems plaguing society have their roots in the low self-esteem of the people who make up society."

While we're at it why don't we use self-esteem to pay off the national debt? Of course, the idea of boosting self-esteem to solve problems has an automatic, Blinklike appeal: Yeah, if people felt better about themselves there's bound to be less crime, less drug abuse, and better performance in the workplace and in schools. Common sense, right? The facts, however, paint quite a different picture.

The only consistent finding of research done on the subject appears to be that people with high self-esteem are happier. One study conducted by a group of University of Iowa researchers on twenty-three thousand high-school students found little correlation between high self-esteem and better academic performance.

Indeed, some educators, psychologists, and parents are beginning to wonder if programs such as No Child Left Behind and other efforts to create a noncompetitive classroom are a formula for lowering academic excellence. In an article, "When Every Child Is Good Enough," John Tierney writes, "Some critics of education believe that boys especially are languishing in schools that emphasize cooperation instead of competition." Tierney quotes Joyce Clark, a planner in the Pittsburgh public school's gifted children program. "In practice No Child Left Behind has meant No Child Gets Ahead. There's no incentive to worry about them [gifted stu-

> "In practice No Child Left Behind has meant No Child Gets Ahead."

dents] because they can pass the tests." In other words, the goal of educators has become to enforce mediocrity, not inspire excellence.

Author Michael Barone, in his book *Hard America, Soft America,* argues that the reason American students lag behind students from Western Europe and Asia is that from the ages of six to eighteen Americans are coddled in the soft, uncompetitive environment of the nation's schools. By contrast, he reports, European and Japanese schools are extremely competitive. This contrasts with the free-market work environment in the United States, which is much more competitive and performance-based than that in Europe.

There seems to be a seamlessness in the end results of both the learning disability industry and the self-esteem movement. If a child is diagnosed with ADD or developmental arithmetic disorder, the self-esteem of the child is retained as teachers use alternative learning strategies to help him with a problem that is not his fault. Likewise, eliminating competition and special recognition, such as honor rolls, creates a nonthreatening environment for underachievers or students with learning disabilities, boosting self-esteem, again. The use of psychotropic medication in the class is the last piece of the puzzle, ensuring a state of pharmacologically induced stability in the classroom, a condition in which everyone is indeed on the same page.

Yet behind this entire cooked-up melange of busybody do-goodness may be nothing more than supreme selfishness: the alleviation of guilt and fault and blame.

Dr. Diller doesn't suggest anything as sinister as selfishness; however, he does say he believes factors such as the changing structure of family life and an overtaxed educational system are strong contributors to rising rates of ADD diagnosis. Two parents, both working, do not have the time, inclination, or stamina to practice proper, consistent discipline with small children. However, if ADD and other learning disorders are biologically caused, no one, neither teacher nor parent, is to blame. Yet, as Diller documents, parental intervention can be just as effective as Ritalin in mitigating ADD-like behavior. He relates the story of a divorced father who stopped giving his five-year-old son Ritalin and took over parenting duties from the mother with "firmness and immediacy." Three weeks after the boy had ceased taking medication, there was no deterioration in his behavior—the hardwired, biologically based ADD disorder had miraculously vanished.

The explosion of the therapy culture, the learning disability industry, and the self-esteem movement can only harm the prospects for improving critical and creative thinking in America. With an educational system chiefly focused on the political aims to maintain the status quo, suppress guilt, modify behavior, and attend to the needs of slow learners, how realistic is it to expect excellent, inspired teaching? If everyone is automatically special, what incentive is there to devote extra time studying to obtain a B instead of a C, or an A rather than a B? Low expectations and mediocrity breed more of the same. If I am labeled as having a learning disorder, it says right there, in black and white, certified, I'M IMPAIRED! THINKING IS A BIG PROBLEM FOR ME.

So perhaps the quickest way out of this mess is to recognize and admit we are all suffering from one learning disorder or another, low self-esteem, or a composite of afflictions. This statement is not intended to be dismissive of the serious effect disorders such as autism, dyslexia, or even ADD-like symptoms can have on learning. Nonetheless, it is true that some of us are better at history than math, or memorizing rather than spatial visualization, or cooking rather than home repair. Only some of these subjects or thought processes may come easy to us, but that doesn't mean that a good cook can't learn to fix things around the house, or vice versa. Even more hopeful and uplifting for those of us suffering minor and major learning disorders or low self-confidence are the stories of great critical and creative thinkers, many of whom were afflicted by gravely debilitating learning or psychological ailments. Einstein, whose name is synonymous with genius, was believed to have been dyslexic at an early age. As portrayed in the movie *A Beautiful Mind*, Princeton mathematician John Nash overcame schizophrenia to win a Nobel Prize.

The human mind's ability to critically reason is the essence of our self-reliance and, ultimately, freedom. Self-reliance and freedom are universally associated with the American way of life. If we continue to feed the feel-good monster it will very happily and contentedly devour that way of life.

CHAPTER 5

The Rise of the Political and Correct, the Fall of the Smart and Quick

I magine being awakened in the middle of the night by a hard knocking on your door. You jump out of bed, stumble down the stairs, and yank open the door. In the bright glare of the porch light you see two men, one in a business suit, and the other in a police-style uniform.

"Sir, please get dressed and come with us," the man in the suit says.

"Why?"

"Your job, career, and personal reputation are in extreme, perhaps mortal danger."

"Why?"

"For taking reasoned stances that are incompatible with the views of society."

I don't think Larry Summers, president of Harvard, ever received a nocturnal knock on his door from two men, but everything else in this depiction is factual.

On January 14, 2004, Summers was addressing a small, private conference on Diversifying the Science and Engineering Workforce, organized by the National Bureau of Economic Research. The conference was convened in response to statistics showing women are not represented in fields such as science and math in proportion to numbers taking advanced graduate training. When the topic turned to the relative scarcity of women in tenured positions in science and engineering faculties at top universities, Mr. Summers speculated that the situation was more directly a result of choices made by women, or gender differences in cognitive skills, rather the upshot of discrimination.

Mr. Summers added in summary:

So my best guess, to provoke you, of what's behind all of this is that the largest phenomenon, by far, is the general clash between people's legitimate family desires and employers' current desire for power and high intensity, that in the special case of science and engineering there are issues of intrinsic aptitude, and particularly of the variability of aptitude, and that those considerations are reinforced by what are in fact lesser factors involving socialization and continuing discrimination.

The furor caused by Mr. Summers's remarks has astounded even those hardened to the nail-scratching, gloves-off stridency of academic gender wars. At this late date pundits have apparently given up on recording the number of public apologies Mr. Summers has tendered. Columnist George Will characterized Mr. Summers's ordeal as a "cringing crawl away from his suggestion of possible gender differences of cognition." Not only has Mr. Summers apologized and apologized, he has been forced to endure, in a fashion reminiscent of the show trials of China's Gang of Four, repeated public dressing-downs from irate alumni, students, and faculty. He has instituted a program to make hiring and promoting women a top priority at Harvard—an objective hardly neglected even before his remarks. He has even been given a style coach.

The abject sight of Mr. Summers being flogged, drawn, and quartered by the very people he is supposed to lead, a torture of his own making, his gleeful critics contend, has won the sympathy of some moderate liberals. Writing in the journal *Commentary*, Ruth R. Wisse, professor of comparative literature at Harvard, argued that Summers was being censored and ostracized even though "there was little in his remarks that others hadn't been saying or speculating about for years," perhaps because of Summers's "being the first president in four decades to challenge, however gingerly, the near hegemony of the liberal and radical Left on campus."

And what of Mr. Summers's "crimes"? In a syndicated column Linda Chavez, president of the Center for Equal Opportunity, observed, "But as uncomfortable as it might make feminists, the evidence points to small but important differences in scientific and mathematical abilities between women and men." Chavez points out that while boys outnumber girls in remedial reading classes by large ratios, boys are even more likely to outnumber girls among the most gifted in science and math. In a study of gifted preadolescent students conducted by Johns Hopkins University, boys outperformed girls among the top-scoring students in math by thirteen-to-one.

The average scores for males taking the College Board's 2004 Advanced Placement Test in the subjects of biology, calculus, and physics were 3.23, 3.09, and 2.84, respectively (out of a maximum score of 5); while the average scores for females in the same subjects were 2.9, 2.82, and 2.37.

In their five-alarm anger with Summers (MIT biology professor Nancy Hopkins told reporters his remarks made her feel like vomiting), are feminists and the left implying this information should be ignored, suppressed, blotted from the records? If so, they are hurting their own cause. The irony, apparently not appreciated, is that Summers's retractions, along with the likelihood that the issue will never be honestly raised in a public- or privately funded forum again, will actually work against the objective of recruiting more women into science fields. How can one begin to address the issue if the ground rules ban free and open examination of the facts?

So what does it mean to say, on the basis of decades of test scores and grades, that women appear to have less "intrinsic aptitude" than men in math and the sciences? It certainly doesn't mean women as a group can't do science, as the presence of many high-profile female scientists across all branches of the natural and physical sciences attest. It could mean that, on average, the female brain is not as adept at performing the types of abstract mental algorithms needed for math and science problems as the average male brain. It could also mean that women, on the whole, are not as naturally motivated and interested in studying math, science, and engineering subjects.

The latter could very well account for much of the gender

difference in science and math performance. A longitudinal study of twelve hundred young women and men conducted by Jacquelynne Eccles, a senior research professor at the University of Michigan's Institute for Social Research, found that young women place higher value on occupations that provide greater opportunities for social interaction, a perk generally not associated with technically oriented science. Two widely publicized studies, the Program for International Student Assessment and the Trends in International Mathematics and Science Study, have indicated that most girls' interest in science and math begins to wane as early as middle school.

There is another reason to suspect that lack of interest and low motivation may be a compelling factor accounting for the smaller ratio of females among the top performers in the math and sciences. In an article exploring the nature of genius in gifted scientists and artists, Dan Falk, writing in the magazine *Walrus*, observed, "Unrelenting drive is seen in nearly every great thinker or creator one can name, seemingly in accord with Edison's famous dictum about genius being 99 percent perspiration." In other words, it's hard to excel at science (or anything) unless you really like it.

Knowing these things, as Summers surely did, why didn't he stand his ground? Why, as Harvard's Wisse put it, did he feel obliged to apologize, "for a mistake that you, I and many others didn't feel he had made in the first place." Wisse concluded it was probably because Summers genuinely felt remorse for having sent women an "unintended signal of discouragement." That may in part explain Summers's actions, but one certainly cannot discount the effect mob rule, and the call for his head, played in making the president of Harvard recant views largely grounded in factual evidence and reason.

IT'S BEEN OVER fifteen years since the illustration of a wall with the lettering "Thought Police" appeared on the cover of *Newsweek*. In the intervening years, political correctness (PC), in all its many social and cultural disguises, has gained, not lost, vigor. The success of PC results from the espousal of views no reasonable person can disagree with. Diversity, inclusion, and tolerance are the key official words of the PC movement. Hosts of educators and corporate executives trumpet the benefits of multiculturalism and diversity. Almost every company and private or public institution and organization has a policy on diversity, and an official plan to promote it, usually in the form of its hiring practices. Proponents of PC view it as a sort of advanced sensitivity training with an entirely legitimate use: to keep at bay the Archie Bunker mentality once prevalent in American life. At its best, say supporters, PC teaches respect and tolerance for the views of others. There is certainly nothing wrong with inclusion and tolerance, and American society has benefited from a heightened civil awareness of individual and cultural differences. If the worst thing the PC movement induced were *Sesame Street*-like, mind-numbing conformity to the concepts of fair play and respect, we could all celebrate by hugging each other and holding parties to honor one another's diversity. However, PC also works to instill a fear and uncertainty in our academic institutions and wider society that acts as a poison to open inquiry and the values of material progress and high-quality critical and creative thinking. By restricting certain outcomes, PC acts to hamper the process of open, critical questioning and reasoning itself.

In reality, however, PC isn't merely about diversity and tolerance and hugging. It's about power and the threat of legal action. Here's the unspoken menace hovering just behind all PC warm-and-fuzzy mantras, as inscribed on the back of a brochure promoting the services of the USDA's Forest Products Laboratory in Madison, Wisconsin:

> *The United States Department of Agriculture (USDA) prohibits discrimination in all its programs and activities on the basis of race, color, national origin, sex, age, disability, political beliefs, sexual orientation, or marital or family status. . . . To file a complaint of discrimination, write USDA, Director, Office of Civil Rights.*

Discrimination is deplorable, but where does discrimination begin and end—a person overlooked for a promotion, an inappropriate phrase, an attitude? The PC police must be ever vigilant. A few years ago, my wife and I took a guided tour of the Henry Ford Estate in Dearborn, Michigan. Our guide, a man in perhaps his early thirties, provided a colorful narration about the life of the industrialist, including details about his work habits, inventions, colleagues, and family. At one point the guide joked about an upper-floor room Mr. Ford used to "hide from the nagging of his wife, Clara." Everyone seemed to laugh. The tour ended and as we walked down the stairs, there was the guide being upbraided by two women (I have to admit, they looked academic), in full public view, for his "unfair and inappropriate" remarks. Understandably, the man appeared petrified.

Glancing at the guide's face, it occurred to me that PC had become the Terror of our time—one never knows when or which way it will strike. Like the Terror during the French Revolution, PC turns the perpetrators into victims, the victims into perpetrators. Like the Terror, PC has acquired a life and will of its own to become an insidiously disruptive and demoralizing force that works to blunt talent, spontaneity, passion, and critical and creative thinking in the name of "higher" ideals. Like the Terror, PC is slowly turning liberation into incarceration, sapping the moral and intellectual energy from America's private and public institutions.

All this would still be endured, I assume, if there were tangible signs PC was helping to create the world it aspires toward. This is a world of equality of condition, rather than equality of opportunity—a world in which no one gets hurt, diminished, or left behind. Yet, by setting ground rules laying out the "right" and "wrong" way to think, by short-circuiting free, open, rational debate, PC is undoing anything it could do before it gets around to doing it. For example, feminists have insisted for thirty years that educators and politicians can approach the issue of gender discrepancies in math and science only on the path marked "lack of self-esteem and self-confidence," not on the trail designated "different intrinsic aptitudes." In a recent article in *Education Week*, "Educators Revisit Girls' Loss of Science and Math Interest," Elizabeth Spelke, a Harvard University psychology professor, trashed the mere suggestion there are any differences between the way boys and girls learn. "We don't have a male brain or a female brain; we have a human brain with a whole lot of human commonality."

Ms. Spelke's remarks would have made a good case study for Harry Frankfurt's best-selling book, *On Bull-*****. I would bet on the certainty that men and women have different brains before I would bet on the certainty that a water molecule has two atoms of hydrogen and one of oxygen. In fact, the one area in which evolutionary psychologists have recognized the significance of differences over commonalities in human evolution is the realm of the sexes. As Steven Johnson reports in his book *Mind Wide Open*, "Viewed with modern imaging technologies, men's and women's brains are nearly as distinct from each other as their bodies are." Not likely, either, that our brains will be reverse-engineered very easily after being shaped by several million years of natural selection. As a generation of feminists-cum-mothers has discovered: "Boys really are different." In his book *Why Gender Matters*, Dr. Leonard Sax argues that gender-blind approaches to teaching could end up discouraging girls in science and math.

Then again, maybe the reason there are relatively fewer women (and African-Americans, Hispanics, and aboriginals) entering the science-related professions is not that they are being discouraged, but that they are choosing to pursue careers more in line with their interests, abilities, likes, and lifestyles. (There is currently, for instance, an over-representation of Asians in engineering, but there is no great outcry to get more Asians into law or medicine.) In *Why Men Earn More: The Startling Truth Behind the Pay Gap*, Dr. Warren Farrell argues that job fulfillment and lifestyle perks, such as fewer hours, are more important to many women when weighing a career choice than prestige and pay. This view is supported by demographics in professions such as law, in which the ratio of women who actually practice law after graduating from law school is far smaller than that for men.

PC is the wholesale replacement of rigorous thought with virtuous ideas and behavior. In order to gain the upper hand on reason and analysis, PC relies on two potent tactical weapons: pretense and dishonesty. If, in a formal or socially professional setting, one's views on human nature, the environment, diversity in the workplace, and so on run counter to the approved version, the jaw-dropping response simply means one has been marked "Neanderthal." In the background, as always, there is the unspoken menace; the chance that one's un-PC views or stance will cause such offense that one becomes marginalized or even dispensable. Understandably, this leads individuals and organizations to suppress information or whitewash, unofficially of course, certain points of view from public discussion. Critical thinking in this environment is a luxury, even a danger. As Larry Summers can attest, open inquiry and discussion are fine as long as they don't begin to refute a set of judgments about the way the world is or should be.

This view runs counter to the position of the radical left, which has long argued it is the right that sets the tone of the national debate. The argument may have some validity in corporate boardrooms, but in wider society there is more evidence that PC predominates today. PC is closely related to egalitarian intelligence and the value it places on the collective consciousness; in this case, the collective "moral" consciousness. PC accounts for the proliferation of platitudes and dull, uninspiring rhetoric spewed by CEOs, politicians, and other public figures. It explains the often insipid, unimaginative, uninformed views of highly educated people. When a person has become overspecialized, cut off from general knowledge about the world, he or she can always ape a certain amount of intelligence by repeating the standard, PC-informed party line. Unoriginal, secondhand thinking is largely PC thinking. It is the voice in the emotional, heart-tugging columns and stories that dominate daily newspapers. It asks, demands, that we put our critical thinking and questioning on hold in favor of preapproved, "safe" stances and opinions.

"The Debate's Over: Globe Is Warming," the front-page headline in USA Today's June 13, 2005, edition pronounced. The story, written without a shred of critical examination, was a promo piece for the theory that the earth is warming as a result of carbon dioxide emissions. The proof, provided by writer Dan Vergano, included an estimate by the U.N. International Panel on Climate Change (IPCC) that the earth's temperature will rise two to ten degrees by the year 2100, a picture of a portion of the West Antarctica ice sheet falling into the ocean, and initiatives by large corporations such as General Electric to cut carbon dioxide emissions.

In fact there is vehement disagreement among climate experts all around the world about many aspects of the global-warming theory, including the very assumption that the global warming is occurring to any great extent or, if it is, that it is being caused by carbon emissions. Many thousands of scientists disagree with the conclusions of the IPCC summary, and especially with its estimate (based on a computer model) of two to ten degrees of warming over the next century. Dr. Claire Parkinson, Oceans and Ice Branch, NASA Goddard Space Flight Center, has found evidence that sea ice is actually thickening in the Antarctic. The entire Antarctic ice sheet is over a mile and a half thick and more than 7 million square miles in area. Yet, apparently in order to keep the angle of the story simple, Vergano did not seek even one second opinion. The story, thus, is remarkable for the information it excluded. It did not mention that the total current warming is less than one degree Celsius, with most of that warming occurring before 1970, before any significant buildup of carbon emissions in the atmosphere. It neglected to mention that water vapor accounts for up to 97 percent of the greenhouse gases, while carbon dioxide makes up less than 2 percent of the total—hard to see how such a small amount is cooking the earth. It omitted pointing out that the earth has been in a cyclic warming and cooling pattern for millions of years—a pattern that allowed the Vikings to once grow crops on Greenland, well before the invention of the automobile. Finally, it failed to report the near-unanimous agreement of all scientists that the Kyoto Agreement, even if fully implemented at a cost of billions of dollars, would do little if anything to slow global warming.

There are two reasons a newspaper, magazine, or TV show deliberately filters and suppresses this type of information. One, it makes for a good pull-them-in story known as "impending disaster." Second, it is PC-approved. Only curmudgeons argue against protecting the environment. If some of the nuance in the debate gets missed, who cares? The only ones it will hurt are the big oil companies. Can you imagine a newspaper omitting second and third opinions in an article on, say, low literacy rates in African-American teenagers?

How powerful a force is PC? I was once asked to speak, along with two other magazine editors, at an internal company workshop on the topic of "writing award-winning editorials." At the time, the company I worked for, a division of Hollinger, Inc., based in Canada, published more than thirty different trade journals for a variety of industries and markets—everything from engineering to health and safety to dentistry. To kick off, the moderator asked each of the guest panelists to give, in his or her view, the single most important factor in writing a standout editorial with the potential to win an award. I and one of the other editors both gave something of a standard response about the writing, research, structure. The third editor, at the time the publisher-editor of a magazine for medical doctors, said before an editorial was even written, the topic had to be certifiably PC-approved. The editor, who had won several awards for editorial writing, said he very deliberately took care to write several editorials arguing left-of-center, PC-approved stances, knowing when it came time to submit for awards he'd have material ready. The formula, while perhaps a bit simplistic, has also seemed to generally apply to awards given in American journalism and the letters over the years.

The automatic, uncritical acceptance of "virtuous" views and opinions does not necessarily lead to a better world. The proposed solution to carbon-induced global warming, a theory that has not been scientifically confirmed by any evidence, is a massive expansion in the power of government to regulate and tax energy. Not only could the money be put to more ef-

The automatic, uncritical acceptance of "virtuous" views and opinions does not necessarily lead to a better world.

fective use in solving more pressing problems—education in this country, AIDS and the lack of clean water in the developing world—studies have shown the burden of these new taxes is likely to be felt more heavily in lower-income households with less disposable income.

The intuitive, Blinklike, virtuous thinking on which PC-inspired views and laws are typically based can often harm the interests, in unanticipated ways, of those it intends to help. Supporters of affirmative action see preferential treatment based on race and sex as a slam dunk, not only for minorities but for a society in which achieving diversity is apparently one of the most pressing official concerns. Racial preferences, they argue, are the only way to effectively reverse the effects of years of "institutionalized" discrimination and provide minorities with upward socioeconomic mobility. However, the requirement that top-flight universities allot a certain percentage of their admissions to minorities is often the beginning of the end of the career aspirations for many people.

A recent study conducted by Richard H. Sander, a law professor at the University of California, Los Angeles, suggests that affirmative action programs may actually lower the number of black lawyers. The study, published in *Stanford Law Review*, found that 19.3 percent of African-Americans fail to finish law school, compared to 8.2 percent of white students who fail to get their diploma. Professor Sander argues that if racial preferences in admission were eliminated, the nongraduation rate for blacks would drop to 13.5 percent. He contends that African-Americans who weren't admitted would go to lower-echelon schools and get better grades.

Advocates of affirmative action fail to see how preferential treatment in university admissions or company promotional practices undermines the credibility of the achievements of minorities, John McWhorter, a professor of linguistics at the University of California, Berkeley, claims in his book *Losing the Race: Self-Sabotage in Black America*. McWhorter, who is African-American, believes holding minorities to a lower standard perpetuates low academic performance, as it instills a sense of entitlement to avoid harsh competition and to produce less than one's best possible work.

McWhorter seems to have a point. Despite nearly thirty years of affirmative action policies implemented across the country in government, universities, and businesses, African-Americans still lag behind the general population in many educational performance measures. The 1999 National Assessment of Educational Progress long-term reading assessment found that only one in one hundred African-American seventeen-year-olds can read and gain information from specialized text, such as the science section of the local newspaper, compared to one in fifty Latino and one in twelve white seventeen-year-olds. By high-school graduation, the average African-American student is about four years behind the typical white or Asian student, and the gap has been growing over the past fifteen years.

Affirmative action seems to play a role in creating a sort of "dependency" mind-set that contributes to educational underperformance. Contrary to the uncritical, PC rationale, as these numbers show, it is definitely not the long-term solution to the problem of raising the performance, and thus the socioeconomic prospects, of minorities.

BECAUSE PC INSTITUTIONALIZES a form of dishonesty by suppressing free, open inquiry and filtering or fudging information, it turns intelligent people into accomplices to institutionalized lying. Over the long term, it creates a morally ambivalent society, a society no longer inclined to distinguish or capable of distinguishing right from wrong in a fully humane way, or ascertaining truth from evidence and reasoning. Under PC dictates, everything indeed does become political, as feminists prophesied, at the expense of both common sense and good judgment. There is probably no better example of this principle at work than the debacle that took place at the *New York Times* under the reign of executive editor Howell Raines from September 5, 2001, to June 3, 2003.

The *New York Times* is widely perceived by most journalists and many readers to be one of the best newspapers in the world, if not *the* best. This lofty reputation is only partly based on myth. Despite its obvious liberal bias (some people reckon the *Times* may have invented PC), the paper simply has more resources at its disposal to cover more stories in a timely and original fashion than any large metropolitan daily aspiring to be its competitor. The newspaper's unmatched prestige is a magnet for the country's most talented and driven journalists, but it's more than just that. Where many newspapers will rely on wire reports and a journalist making phone calls from her desk to cover a breaking story, the *Times* will usually fly a reporter, or several, to the scene to probe and dig and conduct reams of interviews. At least that's the way it is supposed to work at the newspaper.

When publisher Arthur Sulzberger, Jr., tapped Howell Raines to replace retiring executive editor Joe Lelyveld, he was giving his tacit approval for Raines to shake things up at the paper. Raines, a southerner, had acquired a reputation as a demanding and authoritative manager, first as the *Times'* Washington bureau chief, then as the opinion page editor. Raines's campaign for the job, which had begun years before, was built on the premise that the newspaper had become lax, complacent. As detailed in Seth Mnookin's *Hard News–The Scandals at the New York Times and Their Meaning for American Media,* the future editor "had constructed a narrative in which he was needed to rescue the paper from editorial and financial ruin." He told Sulzberger that the paper needed to return to its glory days when it dominated every story and that he would provoke his reporters to "flood the zone" to outmuscle the competition. He vowed to break up the paper's "old-boy network," a promise with many loaded connotations, but one in particular that Sulzberger no doubt approvingly picked up on—diversifying the newspaper's staff.

Sulzberger himself had been haranguing managers and editors for years to hire more minorities at the *Times.* Raines made diversifying the racial makeup of the paper, along with the overarching goal of outdueling every newspaper on the planet for the best stories, the two main pillars of his winning pitch for the executive editor's position. According to a review of Mnookin's book in *The Economist*, "Both objectives converged in the career of Jayson Blair, whose talent as a writer was matched by his dishonesty as a reporter."

Jayson Blair's talents as a writer and reporter were in fact questionable from the beginning. By the time he arrived at the *Times* in 1998, the young African-American intern had already picked up "a reputation for trafficking in nasty gossip, stealing story ideas and cozying up to superiors so he could get credit for work he didn't do," from a stint as an intern at the *Boston Globe*, Mnookin reports. Nonetheless, despite standing questions about his character, and an uneven performance as an intern, Blair was invited back to the *Times* in 1999 and given an entry-level reporting position, a beneficiary of Howell Raines's drive to diversify the newspaper. His reputation as an office gossip, backstabber, and self-promoter ever on the rise, Blair was nevertheless promoted to full-time staff reporter in 2001. When Blair resigned in May 2003, a subsequent internal investigation turned up some three dozen stories the reporter had invented or plagiarized in a six-month period. The tipoff was a story Blair claimed to have researched and written about a Texas woman whose enlisted son was missing in action in Iraq. The editor of the *San Antonio Express-News* was reading the *Times* one day at his weekend cabin when he happened to notice that Blair's story was almost identical to one written earlier by his own reporter, Macarena Hernandez. Blair had never been to Texas. He had stolen almost every word from Hernandez's story.

In a sense it seems Howell Raines and Jayson Blair were destined for each other. Both were instinctively political creatures. The careers of both were advanced by their ability to play up and capitalize on one of the most fundamental PC precepts—diversity. (Blair often referred to anyone who criticized his work as "racist.") The psyches of both men appeared to be built around the notion that truth is a rather abstract, unknowable thing based less on empirical evidence than on a kind of arrogant assertiveness, laid over a thin veil of virtuous, impeccable ideals spun out of the air like moral cotton candy.

Many writers have blamed the Blair fiasco and the devastation it wreaked on the *Times'* reputation on Mr. Raines's all-too-obvious character flaws—his vaulting ambition, his huge ego, and an abrasive, conceited manner that made him aloof to the mollifying ideas and opinions of others. Character does determine behavior, but what many appear to have overlooked is that Raines's biggest character flaw was that of being a demagogue with preconceived ideas about the way the world should work. Even as the *Times'* op-ed editor, Raines had developed a reputation for using the pages as his own personal soapbox. As documented by Mnookin, in his first year as editor of the *Times*, Raines ran well over thirty stories about Augusta National Golf Club's men-only membership policy. As Augusta is a private club, with a right to set its own membership policies, this endless journalistic drumming came off as a brazen attempt to pressure Augusta officials and manipulate public opinion.

One can reasonably argue that this same tendency, the desire to show and demonstrate to the country, rather than report *on* the country, also accounts for Raines's managerial problems at the helm of the *Times*. It is the haughtiness of a doctrinaire, deluded that he is more virtuous and honest than everyone else. As the crisis of Jayson Blair began to spin further and further out of control, Raines didn't miss the signals, he ignored them. At one point metro editor Jon Landman sent newsroom personnel an e-mail: "We have to stop Jayson from writing for the *Times*, Right now." Then, in response to Raines's arrogance, the signals stopped coming. As an internal investigative team dug deeper into the Blair scandal, they found the root cause was Raines himself. Knowing that he would dismiss or bully them, reporters and editors hid concerns about Blair's shoddy work. Is it a coincidence that the two essential tactical weapons of PC, pretense and dishonesty, are the two most appropriate words to describe the Raines's tenure? Raines calculatedly used the politically correct canon to advance his career. As he did, he became less inclined to be objective. Over time it made him functionally PC-dysfunctional. Mr. Raines could no longer form opinions, he could only dictate them. He could no longer react, he could only act.

BECAUSE THEY ARE OFTEN associated with virtuous behavior, PC views and beliefs form one of the most common and reckless types of demagoguery in America (and the world) today. But PC isn't the only type of dogma that can adversely affect our ability to think critically and clearly. Any ideology, if adhered to rigidly, can throw a monkey wrench into our brain's intellectual machinery.

In his book *Intellectual Morons: How Ideology Makes Smart People Fall for Stupid Ideas*, Daniel Flynn posits that people have a strong tendency to think with their ideology, rather than with their brains. In an interview on FrontPageMagazine .com, Flynn said the inspiration for the book came from observing how ideology often acts as a mental straitjacket in otherwise intelligent people, breeding fanaticism and rationalizing dishonesty. Flynn elaborates:

> It doesn't matter how intelligent you are if you don't use your brain. Intelligent people aren't necessarily rigorous thinkers. In fact many of them are mentally lazy. Ideology provides a way for lazy people to respond to issues, ideas, people and events without thinking. For the ideologue, ideology is the Rosetta Stone of everything. Why think when the system provides all the answers?

Flynn argues his point from the right, skewering the errors and absurdities arising when assorted activists, feminists, and academic intellectuals think with political blinders on. For instance, Flynn takes Noam Chomsky to the woodshed for his denial in a 1997 book review of wide-scale genocide in Cambodia under the Khmer Rouge, and his gross overestimate, before the war in Afghanistan, of the number of civilian deaths that would result from the conflict. What's good for the goose, as they say, is good for the gander. Rigidly held views can short-circuit the thinking of those on the right as well. The denial by some on the religious right of the evidence for biological evolution basically implies that science and faith are incompatible—not good promo for the conservative cause. Ideology of a "third kind," whole lists of belief systems rooted in new-age mysticism and paranormal phenomena, also increasingly imperils the thinking of more people. The late Carl Sagan's book *The Demon-Haunted World* is an elegant critique of the growing numbers who willfully choose the paranormal

and fantasy over reality and reason, with troubling consequences for themselves and society.

More and more, large numbers of people substitute PC
views, hard-line political ideology, or cultish balderdash for
hard-won knowledge and flexible, powerful reasoning and
problem-solving skills. Some bias or ideology is inevitable, of
course. Everyone needs beliefs and a working value system not
only to make it through the day, but as a necessary part of the
mental apparatus to form and test thoughts. To paraphrase an
old wisdom, the only way to be completely without prejudice
or bias is to be completely indifferent, or completely ignorant.
The uniqueness of our individual genes and experiences predisposes us to a certain outlook or attitude. Beliefs of children
often mirror those of their parents, whose beliefs were in turn
influenced by their parents.

But it is one thing to have belief, a political ideology, a
management style, a game plan, and another to let it become,
in effect, one's de facto mind. A de facto mind is not a healthy,
vigorous mind. In American society, business, and government, time and time again, we see signs of the same stubborn,
hard-headed approach—stake out a position and by God stand
by it, come hell or high water. Do not waffle or shift, even
when new information demands reevaluation. Change is a
sign of backtracking, which is a sign of weakness. But how
weak or ineffectual is it to change when the very world we live
in changes by the day, the hour, the minute, and the access to
the information recording that change is instantaneous? Strategy can be the same, but in a world of continual flux and recal-
ibration, thinking and tactics need to be fluid, adaptive.

Every organization these days aspires to be fast and fluid,

but few really make it. Could the problem be that the thinking of the individuals in the organizations is not fast, fluid, and adaptive?

Many people, on both the left and the right, have associated the problems in postwar Iraq with poor thinking and inflexible planning. "For starters we don't have enough troops," said Republican senator Chuck Hagel from Nebraska in an interview. Others have accused the Pentagon of having no plan. In General Tommy Franks's book, *American Soldier*, it is clear the military had both detailed plans and a greater degree of flexibility built into the plans than was suspected by the general public. So why has so much gone wrong in the attempt to stabilize the country after the removal of Saddam Hussein? Yossef Bodansky, onetime director of the Congressional Task Force on Terrorism and Unconventional Warfare, conjectures that it was the government's failure to anticipate the important influence of the postwar conditions on the fabric of Iraq society. In *The Secret History of the Iraq War*, Bodansky claims that the most grievous error has been:

> *Washington's abject failure to address and comprehend the profound transformation the Iraqi populace, in its entire ethnic and national tapestry, has undergone since American forces entered Baghdad. The enduring failure of occupation forces to normalize life in Iraq has bolstered the grassroots withdrawal into religious and ethnic social frameworks that are inherently and uncompromisingly anti-American.*

This is no place for the definitive analysis of the postwar occupation of Iraq, what was done, and what could have been done better, which no doubt will occupy the time of many experts in the upcoming years. I will simply note that the success of a "lean" strategy, that is, the use of a limited number of troops, in a Middle Eastern country so long repressed by dictatorship, absolutely depends on securing the goodwill of the populace. If military planners knew this, they did not act as if they knew it. Franks implies political infighting, especially between the Defense and State departments, exacerbated the problems in postwar Iraq. Whatever way you paint it, it is clear that somewhere or somehow, for political or other reasons, what could have been done was not done, and what was done was not enough. Somewhere along the line, we must once again acknowledge the presence of the Great Disconnect, the same type of disconnect that led to journalistic fiasco at the *New York Times* and the disaster in New Orleans, the same disconnect many Americans face every day at work, in schools, and at home.

INPUT, BUT NO OUTPUT: information that is filtered, ignored, or denied. This is not a matter of declining to be swayed by "collective consciousness" or refusing to base decisions on egalitarian intelligence. This is the denial of meaning of verifiable information that stands in direct context of events and our understanding and ability to shape those events. Whatever the cause of the Great Disconnect—virtuous, PC-approved views, ideology of all stripes, political machinations, bureaucratic fixation, my-way-or-the-highway management style—the net effect is like turning on the sprinkler to water the driveway: It doesn't matter how long you leave it on, it's not going to make the asphalt green.

As American society becomes more and more political, it becomes a more divided, rigid society. We seek our own. We stop listening and begin to tune out. We learn the rules and keep our heads down. There really is a reason why, as the common complaint goes, "Nothing seems to get done around here." As more than one philosopher has noted, if we ignore what other people are thinking, or have thought, rational discussion will come to an end. Over time such a society becomes more and more alienated from objectivity and the instinct to seek truth. Change and progress become dreams for businesses, armies, schools, and people on the lower end of the socioeconomic scale.

Politics, which is the just relationship between people and power, cannot be an end in itself. Unless a democratic society has a shared theme, there is no starting point for dialogue and understanding, there is no *demos* in the equation. That theme must be reason based on empirical evidence, an idea that transcends race, gender, sexual orientation, religion, or income. Reason is by its very nature tolerant and inclusive. Reason admits mistakes. Reason takes in new data. Reason builds and learns and adapts. Reason goes by results.

You can't file a discrimination complaint against reason.

CHAPTER 6

It's the Real Thing:
Marketing, the Media,
and Mayhem

Television, like politics, is something we all think we could do better than how it's being done. Lewis Lapham, the patrician editor of *Harper's* magazine, dared to try. Lapham once arranged a meeting with the then president of CBS, Larry Tisch, to propose a new public affairs program that took a big-picture, historical look at current events. As Lapham relates in an interview that appeared in *Wild Duck Review*:

> He [Tisch] listened politely to the pitch and then waved it off by asking whether I ever watched television, or whether anyone I knew ever watched television. Not often, I said, not when I could avoid it. Neither do I, said Tisch; neither does anybody else with anything better to do. Television, he said, was for people who were too poor, lazy or depressed to do anything else.

It's refreshing to finally hear a TV kahuna put the depth of his admiration for his audience into words. Tisch obviously meant to impress on Lapham the hard facts of life about television: It is what it is. The interesting thing is that in doing so he appears to have missed the rich irony of his logic: In the most economically secure, culturally influential, politically powerful country on the planet, how is it that the best means of mass communication ever invented can only be an outlet for the crude, stupid, mindless, and meaningless? The barbarians aren't at our gates, they're dining with us. Their names are J.Lo, Ja Rule, and Paris Hilton. Through the magic of network television, the scientific prediction of multiple universes and multiple realities has been made to materialize on our home entertainment systems. Which reality will you tune in to? *Temptation Island? Extreme Makeover? Fear Factor?* Ah, too many realities, too little time.

> The barbarians aren't at our gates, they're dining with us. Their names are J.Lo, Ja Rule, and Paris Hilton.

But trashing the trash culture churned out by television is too easy. Not only has it been done, but the standard lathering rant is ineffectual. Ranting lets us quickly wash our hands of the whole sordid spectacle modern television has become. It short-circuits any critical examination of both the limitations and the possibilities of television. Why is television the way it is? How did it get this way? Why is television seemingly tracking backward on the evolutionary time scale? Why is it confounding any hope that it might, in part, be used as a medium for enlightened democratic debate or a probe for citizens to extend their worlds, and thereby their critical- and creative-thinking capabilities? Has television created trash culture, or has trash culture created television? What came first, the idiot, or the idiot box?

This is a classic chicken-or-egg puzzle. A TV executive such as Tisch would say the audience is getting the type of programming it wants. Television watchdog groups and critics say the television programming, in striving for ever new lows of sleaze, violence, sex, and da-da, is dragging its audience down with it.

The truth is probably grayer. Television is moronic, but television alone is not turning people into morons—at least not directly. Neither are we getting moronic programming because we are demanding it. As Tisch in his unmitigated honesty implies, in the commercial, hermetically sealed world in which television exists, what TV is, or what it is not, is essentially beyond debate. It is what it is: a product created to flow into and swim around a mind put in neutral. It's not that resistance is futile—we accept the rules before we flop into the La-Z-Boy and reach for the remote. Here, the remote takes on new meaning: the remote chance we'll find anything that stimulates impulses in the brain's neurons. (Discovery and History channels, not received by everyone, are still mutant orphans in TV land.) Every time we turn on the TV, we mentally sign off on the following waiver: I hereby understand that I am about to spend the next x amount of hours in a near-fungal state, and I personally accept responsibility for any and all risks to my mental and physical well-being posed by such activity. Is it a coincidence that television predisposes a listless psychic condition "pretuned" to be receptive to the buying messages advertisers are about to send into it? Could the

Tisches of the world be sandbagging us? It's not that *we* want shows and programs created for stupid, lazy, depressed people; it's that the advertisers want such shows.

This is one old, favorite saw pulled out now and then to dissect television—it's the unseen, insidious hand of advertisers that is making TV shows increasingly moronic.

In a way, this sounds right. If TV is an affront to our intelligence, it's because it is run by corrupt people for corrupt reasons. There is something big and conspiratorial and emotionally appealing to the idea that advertisers and big corporations are pulling all the strings in TV land. Unarguably, television strives to create programs that reach the "mass audience" desired by advertisers. But to claim TV is solely out to meet or exceed advertisers' standards for dumbness is antiempirical. Many successful shows on TV—*The West Wing, The Simpsons, Seinfeld*—are clever and intelligent, even if they still meet the criterion of serving a mass audience. In the case of really horrifically stupid shows that lots of people watch, the public has to accept some responsibility for the product they're consuming. No one is forcing people to watch these programs.

Conspiracy theory and the TV/media seem to go hand-in-hand. A cadre of social critics and academics have professed to seeing signs of various unholy alliances between the media and corporate and governmental power for over a century. The key element to all these conspiracy yarns is some sort of media-corporate alliance (which includes advertisers) that is controlling information, and thus the way we think, or if we even think at all.

MIT professor of linguistics Noam Chomsky, along with Edward Herman, professor of Finance, Wharton School of the University of Pennsylvania, proposed the granddaddy of all media-political-corporate conspiracy theories in their book, *Manufacturing Consent*. The title is taken from a phrase coined by the American journalist Walter Lippmann. Lippmann felt the same propaganda techniques used by the British and American governments to rally a reluctant population around the cause of war could be used by educated, responsible people to "manufacture consent" on issues in the common interest of the public. Lippmann thought a bit of propaganda was a small pill that would spur individuals in democratic societies to put aside their differences and act for the common good. Lippmann's notion would eventually give us a new species of professional, the flak—the public-relations-field Dostoyevsky-equivalent of a lawyer, a conscience for hire. Yet Chomsky and Herman leap from the observation that types of promotion, persuasion, and propaganda exist in society to the conclusion that everything we read and hear is a bald-faced lie. The media is the mere lapdog of those in power, according to this grand unified theory of paranoia:

> We have spelled out and applied a propaganda model that . . . suggests that the "societal purpose" of the media is to inculcate and defend the economic, social and political agenda of privileged groups that dominate the domestic society and state.

In another book, *Corporate Media and the Threat to Democracy*, Robert McChesney sketches a similar take on the media industry:

The preponderance of U.S. mass communication is controlled by less than two dozen enormous profit-maximizing corporations, which receive much of their income from advertising placed largely by other huge corporations. But the extent of this media ownership and control goes generally unremarked in the media and intellectual culture, and there appears to be little sense of concern about its dimensions among the citizenry as a whole.

If, in reading these excerpts, you have a vague feeling of being in college again, it is because this type of breathless, "penetrating" analysis is one of the favorite indulgences of undergraduates everywhere who have discovered there is power in the world and that relationships of power strongly influence what can and cannot be accomplished. Power is one aspect of the objective world. But to propose, for example, that uncritical coverage (whatever that means) of the war in Iraq is a proof that the media are in the keep of the U.S. government is to malign the integrity of tens of thousands of broadcasters, journalists, and editors. Another problem with the view that the media are beholden to corporate and political interests, a problem general to all conspiracy theories, is that it rests on the assumption of intricate, improbable collusion between parties with greatly diverse vested interests. If the purpose of the media is to "defend the economic, social and political agenda of privileged groups," that's a lot of groups, and a lot of agendas. And even if the media in its entirety were coerced to do just this, it is impossible to imagine a way in which they could carry out their mission while hoodwinking an entire country. As the letters-to-the-editor section of any newspaper reveals, the American public is acutely sensitive to the slightest hint of bias, in any political or social respect, and prone to protest bitterly about it. Sure, biases find their way into the media, but they are almost always the result of the idiosyncrasies of owners, ignorance (of many types) of journalists and producers, or the desire to capture attention and audience, not institutionalized conspiracy.

While it may disappoint antibranding purists, the most conspiratorial thing you can say about the influence of advertising in television is that it subsidizes shows with good ratings and lets shows with poor ratings die. Advertising isn't creating trash culture per se; it's the commercial mission of television/media to win audiences *for* advertisers that's sparked the race between the dumb and dumber. If *Masterpiece Theater* had a 40 percent audience share in prime time with the eighteen-to-thirty-five-year-old segment, Budweiser would advertise on it.

"Advertising is a very conservative industry," says Alan Middleton, assistant professor of marketing and executive director at the Schulich Executive Education Centre. "Advertising doesn't set trends it follows them." This doesn't mean, as we'll see, that advertising's influence on the content of television, or the media in general, is necessarily impartial. As Middleton allows, advertising is not out to change things. It's not trying to raise literacy rates or improve our knowledge of history or increase appreciation for Shakespeare. Following the trend could simply mean reinforcing it, as Curtis White argues in *Middle Mind*. White observes how television's *Antiques Road Show* has turned arts and antiques into "crude commodity fetishism." When it comes to soaps and so-called dramas, the "trend" has long been settled on story lines built around greed, sex, and violence.

This is what has many parents and educators up in arms. In an article that appeared in *USA Today*, Sam Brownback writes:

> *Some people in the [TV] industry assert, "We don't make the culture, we just reflect it. Television is a mirror of society." However, today's programming is less a mirror image than a mirage. The world of television characters is far more violent, conflicted and perverse than the typical American life.*

Brownback has a point, but neither were the violent depictions in ancient Greek dramas an accurate representation of Greek society. Brownback's complaint is one of degree. He cites a study by the Parents Television Council that shows violence, vulgarity, and profanity during the networks' traditional "family hour" have more than tripled since 1990. He points to thousands of medical and psychological research studies that have found repeated and prolonged exposure to violence on TV can have a negative effect on youngsters' behavior and, inevitably, performance in school. Perhaps many of those in Brownback's corner would happily accept programming content that was simply tending toward neutral on the high-low culture scale. Instead, it appears that networks are rushing to hit bottom before their competition does. The unnerving thing is, the bottom is hypothetical. "The logical outcome of reality shows is snuff movies," says Middleton.

But if advertisers, or a yet-uncovered grand conspiracy, are not directly responsible for sending television programming to cultural hell in a hand basket, what or who is? The answer appears to be a combination of declining television market share for major networks, cutthroat competition, lifestyle changes, the medium of television itself, and us, the viewers.

NETWORK TELEVISION RATINGS have been in steady decline for more than two decades; in 2002–03 cable networks overtook broadcast media in total share of TV audience, with 53 percent of aggregate viewers. With declining cash flow, TV executives have been charged with the improbable mission of reducing costs and also creating new programs to attract large numbers of viewers. In 2000, the possibility of achieving these seemingly contradictory objectives dropped into their laps in the form of a novel type of show, CBS's *Survivor*. When it debuted, many television analysts considered it a one-off that would die a deserved death in a few seasons. Neither drama nor sitcom, quiz game show nor sport, talk show nor news, the only precedent for the show's premise, manipulated nonfiction, seemed to be the disreputable amateur talent show, a type of program that had vaporized in low ratings many years before. Today, hundreds of reality television shows are produced around the world.

"Many people, including myself, have completely underestimated the appeal of reality shows to program producers and networks," says Middleton. "They are dirt cheap to produce and create enormous profit."

Reality shows have helped the networks stem the bleeding brought on by declining market share of viewers—in 2004–05 the networks took in a record $9.3 billion in up-front ad dollars. In that season, *American Idol* commanded the highest price for a thirty-second commercial ($658,000), and five of the top ten shows with the highest thirty-second ad price were reality shows. Some TV journalists attribute the success of reality shows to a generational change—the Gen-Xers and Millennials, who have been weaned on cable, the Internet, and channel surfing, are impatient with the plot lines and the sentimentality of soaps and dramas. This is just another instance of television adapting to contemporary circumstances and doing what it has to do to stir up a new audience for advertisers. Others say the trend is emblematic of a medium that never has been and never will be able to communicate complex ideas or nuanced thought and argument.

The organic substance of television is not the world around us or our ideas but the camera. The camera takes in the world, society, and events and reshapes them. It is a dictator. It sets the agenda. It makes people act in certain ways. Marshall McLuhan, in *Understanding Media*, was the first to recognize that the discontinuity of impressions and images captured by the camera was a totally different means of communication that had ipso facto created new modes of meaning and thought. Television, we now know, is about emotion and fantasy, not reasoned argument and science. *Harper's* Lapham tells about working on a television series on American foreign policy in which he was required to explain the origins of World War II in seventy-two seconds using a little more than forty words. Lapham reports that writing for television requires "simple declarative sentences . . . no irony, none of the rhetorical devices that shape a nuanced, inflected prose," and argues that the medium "doesn't like ideas, doesn't have the patience for ideas." No great hope for educational television in this assessment.

Lapham, here, seems to be concurring with the executive: Television is what it is. In the 1979 movie *Being There*, Peter Sellers plays the character of a gardener (Chauncey Gardner) who has no knowledge of the outside world, except what he's seen on TV. A patron of Gardner's walks him into Washington's inner political-social circle, where he is received like a savant. At one meeting he is quizzed by the president:

> *President:* Mr. Gardner, do you agree with Ben or do you
> think that we can stimulate growth through temporary in-
> centives? [Long pause]
> *Gardner:* As long as the roots are not severed, all is well. And
> all will be well in the garden.
> *President:* In the garden.
> *Gardner:* Yes. In the garden, growth has its seasons. First
> come spring and summer, then we have fall and winter.

Gardner has watched so much TV that his sentences mimic the infantile vocabulary and vapid cadence of those heard in a documentary. Every event that impinges on Gardner in the real world is a comedic hassle that requires him to pause, recalibrate, and mentally search his archive of clichés and simplifications for a glancing connection. "Being there" is what happens to people whose knowledge and view of the world have been primarily shaped by a tool that slavishly glorifies "being here," in thrall to a kaleidoscope of images that conjure fleeting emotions and push away all context and qualification. It is a state of general cluelessness. Unfortunately, the millions of Chauncey Gardners in real life are generally not feted by the rich and powerful.

In the 1960s, George Gerbner studied the behavior of heavy television watchers and found that the more TV a person watches, the more restricted and homogenized his opinions, beliefs, and thinking become. Gerbner's theory about this phenomenon, called Cultivation Theory, ultimately implies that TV makes us less and less adaptive to the shifting complexity of real life. Individuality, spontaneity, and creativity diminish. As a result, at least partly because of increased television watching, more people today seem to have self-described "narrow comfort zones" for hosts of activities and tasks. While the definitive study has yet to be done, I would wager on the basis of what I have witnessed in my own working life that "narrow comfort zones" play a strong part in careers' languishing, thrown off the rails, or hanging by a thread.

As a medium of images and emotion, television intersects with a number of the themes proposed by this book to account for the decline of critical and creative thinking in American society. Television, for example, has been an important factor in the spread of egalitarian intelligence—the view that all ideas and opinions are of equal value and that all knowledge and reasoning tend toward the same conclusions. In a society that spends five times more time watching television than it does reading, the views and thoughts of more of the public will inevitably begin to form around clichés—politically correct, ideological, or dogmatic. Television doesn't nurture new ideas or creative and critical thinking, it encourages uniformity and conformity. Television has also evolved into one of the two technological touch points for a lifestyle dedicated to the pursuit of is-ness—a retreat away from the life of the mind and striving, toward a more or less static contemplation of the pure sensation of being. This sensation is fed by a never-ending stream of passive entertainments, frequently supplied by electronic and digital media.

Aldous Huxley anticipated some of the unexpected ways television and the mass media would affect society in *Brave New World Revisited*, published in 1958. Writing at the height of the Cold War, Huxley laid out a dark vision of the media as an instrument of coercion and propaganda. Even at that time, however, Huxley saw that this was a far too simplistic view of the future of the mass media. While media critics and intellectuals fixated on the power of the media to influence public opinion, Huxley realized that "they failed to take into account man's almost infinite appetite for distraction." As it developed and became more sophisticated, he said, mass communication would be less concerned with the true or false, and more preoccupied with the irrelevant and inane.

"The Cold War made people think the Orwellian vision of dictatorship would eventually come to pass," says Roy Clark, senior scholar at the Poynter Institute. "After the Cold War ended, it surprised people that what actually materialized was more in line with Huxley's view—a society that needs to be constantly entertained."

There is nothing inherently amoral about a life of is-ness. Americans work longer hours than citizens of any other country. Is-ness, as reflected by the common practice of watching three hours of television each evening, is simply a side effect of fatigue and stress, some people say. To the extent that elite groups of thinkers and inventors are able to pick up the slack, is-ness may not induce any serious near-term decline in the country's creativity, productivity, or standard of living—although this may be little more than wishful thinking in a knowledge-based, global economy. But the pursuit of is-ness as an end in itself, as opposed to the pursuit of happiness, is also having an adverse effect on the health of Americans.

Between 1987 and 2002, private spending on obesity-related medical problems ballooned to $36.5 billion, or 11.6 percent of all health spending, from $3.6 billion, or 2 percent of spending, according to a study published in the journal *Health Affairs*. One out of three Americans is obese, which is double the number three decades ago. Americans spend more on health care per person than any other country in the industrialized world. According to a report issued by the Centers for Medicare and Medicaid, by 2014 we will be spending $11,045 annually for each man, woman, and child, which will account for almost 20 percent of the country's entire economy! Americans' obesity, and its associated health problems, is often attributed to lack of exercise and a poor, fat-rich diet. Certainly these are the direct causes. However, I believe the underlying and primary cause of obesity (other than a genetic or medical condition) is quite possibly the increasingly barren intellectual life led by many people.

Americans expend nine times as many minutes watching television as they do on sports or any other leisure-time physical activity, according to a group of University of California researchers. The results on face value imply that watching TV is displacing exercise, which is making people fat. But watching TV is also displacing reading, conversation, and other pursuits needed for the growth of good critical- and creative-thinking skills. Studies show that people with more education have less tendency to be overweight. It appears that an appetite for knowledge, as opposed to food, is the best belly-burner. Knowledge begets curiosity, interest, and involvement. Knowledge makes it difficult to sit in your chair. Knowledge *produces* activity.

Flopping in front of the television and putting our minds in neutral for a short spell each day can recharge us; putting our minds in neutral indefinitely can (literally) do us in.

CONTRARY TO THE POPULAR BELIEF, the computer/electronic/digital age did not begin with the computer. It began with music. Before about 1980, few people had any firsthand experience with a computer. The personal computer with its graphic, user-friendly software had yet to be invented. But everyone had heard the amplified crescendos of Jimmy Hendrix's guitar, the haunting, alien sounds of electronic, synthesized music, and the driving thump and laser lights of a disco. Electronically produced music and an increasingly sophisticated armada of stereo symphonic hardware to reproduce it in the comfort of one's living space were the first certifiable geek toys enjoyed by a mass market. Guys boasted about their watts-per-channel and subwoofers with a passion once reserved for hemicharged engines and Mag wheels. Amped music pumped through the sound "systems" of the day were the harbingers of everything electronic and "iPod" cool. New-age gurus such as Timothy Leary and Alvin Toffler tapped into the subconscious of this electronically induced euphoria to imagine new types of decentralized, wired utopias, "global villages" in which power rested with the individual people, not corporations and governments. No matter that computers were still large, clunky things that sat Ozlike out of view in temperature-controlled rooms. To a generation accustomed to having their souls stirred and their dreams enlivened simply by flipping a switch on their stereos, these visions of a society living better and smarter through electronic gadgetry had a wide audience. When personal computers did arrive on desks, an electronics-loving public were eager adepts, ready, willing, and able to learn how computers could help them on their jobs or in school. It was a public with a will to endure eons-long startups and plodding, obtuse word-processing and spreadsheet programs in order to generate a memo or small report and claim the token of being an official member of the computer age. It was a public avidly predisposed to believe in the premise that a computer, like a nifty sound system, could extend the realm of human consciousness.

Today, one cannot imagine life without computers. One can easily imagine, however, a life without the music—the music being produced by many contemporary groups and "musicians." That's because some time between the introduction of the personal computer in the 1980s and this, the early part of the twenty-first century, something completely unforeseen and more than a little tragic has happened—young people aspiring to make music stopped learning how to play music. One caveat to my everything-in-the-past-was-better curmudgeon label: The assessment is not just mine. (Trumpeter Wynton Marsalis has called rap a modern-day minstrel show, saying it has less to do with musical expression than with making money by pandering to racial stereotypes.) Where are candidates of the current generation with the technical musicianship and creative savoir faire, not to replace, but to succeed Bob Dylan, Miles Davis, Eddie Van Halen, Joni Mitchell, Bob Marley, Frank Zappa, Mark Murphy, Elvis Costello, Bono, or Philip Glass? This is not a style issue. This is about evidence of the absence of the essential skills needed to create new music—singing, writing lyrics and music, and playing instruments. We have people who know how to download music, people who know how to mix music, people who know how to produce a turgid version of funk or an execrable Eagles imitation on a synthesizer or "dream machine." But we evidently have fewer and fewer young people who have learned their scales.

When Walter Carlos released *Switched-On Bach* in 1968, it inspired a host of young musicians to incorporate the Moog synthesizer into their music. Songs such as Emerson, Lake, and Palmer's "From the Beginning" and "Trilogy" showed the startling new musical tones and harmonics it was possible to make with the Moog. For a moment it seemed a total immersion of electronics with music might lead to entirely new dimensions of musical exploration. Then, electronic music quickly fizzled out. In a 1994 article in *Sound on Sound* magazine, journalist Jonathan Miller suggests the decline might be a result of an emphasis on the technology, and a neglect of the music. In a 1997 interview in the online magazine *Perfect Sound Forever*, the Moog's inventor, Robert Moog, said he never expected the synthesizer to replace the musician. "First of all, you have to be a musician in order to make music with a synthesizer."

The correlation of the growth of computers and sound-producing technology with an apparent decline in the quality of music could be simply the result of kids' preferring to play video games rather than spend weeks mucking around in a van playing one-night stands. On the other hand, the correlation could be coincidental. There could be other factors contributing to decay in musical creativity, for example, fewer venues for young musicians to play gigs. At the least, however, the trend is a cautionary tale about the potential pitfalls of the computer. A hundred years from now a computer scientist might be rephrasing Moog's words as: "We never expected the computer to replace thought."

More and more people are recognizing that the computer has the very real potential to displace hands-on experience and cognitive skills needed for critical and creative thinking. There have been numerous books and articles published on the topic in recent years, almost all written with a religious-like fervor, expressing shock and dismay that while Johnny spent most of his teenage years in front of a computer, he actually appears to know very little. The argument has largely been made on anecdotal evidence, but a recent study has found hard data to support it. Researchers at the University of Munich surveyed 175,000 fifteen-year-olds from thirty-one countries, discovering that math and reading scores were significantly lower in households with two or more computers, compared to those with one or no computers.

"It seems if you overuse computers and trade them for

other [types of] teaching, it actually harms the student," said lead researcher Ludger Woessmann, in an interview appearing in the *Christian Science Monitor.*

For some reason, this revelation does not bowl me over. E-mail is a form of nearly automatic "verbal" writing, video games may help kids think on their virtual feet, but not their real-world feet, and surfing is surfing, catching a cyberwave and riding it out to wherever it takes you. Computer skills are little more than "vocational skills, as important, and as intellectually shallow, as driving a car," according to Karl Forsyth, writing on a website of the Waldorf schools, an association of 350 schools in which students do not begin to use computers until eleventh grade. Forsyth also argues that software features such as text editing encourage mental laziness, and that "computers also induce a mentality of doing everything fast and efficiently, which serves to cheat the slower and finer thought processes." I agree in principle with most of these points, although I do think that laying out an Excel spreadsheet or using computer-aided design (CAD) software to do solid modeling is a bit more intellectually challenging than driving a car. I also feel there's no more reason to hector intelligent, self-aware people about spending too much time on the computer than there is to harangue people about watching too much television or drinking too much. It's common sense, really. A little parental (and self-) vigilance and the budding problem(s) vanish immediately. But for many people—teenagers and harried, overbooked adults—this may be more easily said than done. I am as easily distracted to start walking down that cyber highway as anyone. But perhaps I'm fortunate to also have a built-in alarm system, an instinct to seek the yin when I've had too much yang. I do not know why I have this particular alarm system, and it is far from perfect in bringing perfection into my life, as I frequently invoke free will to flatly ignore it. I do know when I've been logged on too long, however. I know when I have to talk to people. Sometimes I have an overriding desire to grab a monkey wrench and breathe in the aroma of grease on hard metal. Or I'll need to run, watch ants working in the grass, or study the sky.

I definitely do not even want to think about a world without computers. For all the maddening change they have foisted upon the world, computers are one of humanity's most marvelous inventions, surpassed only by the creation of written language. The problem is not making people aware of the adverse consequences that an obsessively virtual lifestyle will have on critical thinking. It is getting people to act on the awareness. It's making them realize, again, the crucial importance of the "other," the reality outside their computer screens, and why this is vitally important to the quality of their thinking, their work, and their self-interest.

William Gibson, whose futuristic novels such as *Neuromancer* are predicated on a society enmeshed with an advanced virtual reality, cautions that while electronic communication now provides "a sensory expansion for the species," virtual reality can only augment physical reality, never replace it. Gibson has lauded the importance of "skin," shorthand for contact with humans. For a futurist, he's soundly rooted in the present: Researchers have found that communication conducted strictly through e-mail, for example, is inadequate for building lasting personal or professional relationships. Conversational nuances such as dialogue, facial expression, and tone of voice convey a rich bevy of emotional and practical information needed for intellectual understanding and trust.

Both educators and parents have observed how the computer is increasingly a substitute for outdoor activities, imagination games, and quiet reading and tinkering time. Still, stripped of its video games and chat rooms, many people believe the computer is a potentially unrivalled educational tool. Clifford Stoll, author of *Silicon Snake Oil*, disagrees: "Seems to me that most learning grows out of childhood curiosity, for which there is no readily installed software package. Curiosity usually begins with our physical world."

In his book, *What Just Happened: A Chronicle from the Information Frontier*, James Gleick says that with the dawn of computing, "Human invention crossed a threshold into a world different from everything that came before." But Gleick implies that the computing world in and of itself is not the *stuff* of invention. The real world is.

UNLIKE COMPUTERS, but like network television, newspapers are gradually losing their audience. Newspaper circulation has been declining by 0.5 percent to 1.0 percent per year since the late 1980s. In a six-month period ending March 31, 2005, the newspaper industry suffered a 1.9 percent drop in daily circulation, the largest circulation loss in a decade, according to Audit Bureau of Circulation figures. Today, only about 50 percent of American households buy a daily newspaper, compared to 67 percent in 1990, and over 100 percent in 1950 when many households subscribed to more than one newspaper.

"I don't see any bright spots and I don't see any reasonable expectation this is going to change any time soon," John Morton, a newspaper industry analyst, told the *New York Times*.

Newspapers make about 80 percent of their revenues from advertising. Thus the newspaper industry is facing the same essential challenge as television—how to create and keep a large enough audience for its product to be attractive to advertisers. Its approach to accomplishing this, however, has been slightly different from that of the television industry. In the face of growing competition from the Internet, and more ferocious catfighting for a piece of the shrinking ad pie, newspapers' survival strategies seem to be less about dumbing down and more about mucking around, with a little sucking up thrown in for good measure.

Sensationalistic journalism has been around for over a hundred years. Rival New York newspaper owners William Randolph Hearst and Joseph Pulitzer are reputed to have started the practice of using blatant exaggeration and hyperbole to sell newspapers in a media war during the 1890s. Hearst, some historians claim, even played a role in helping to instigate the Spanish-American War by running a story that blamed the Cuban government, without evidence, for the sinking of the battleship *Maine* in Havana Harbor in 1898. The style came to be known as "yellow journalism" after a comic strip whose artist Hearst had coerced away from a rival newspaper.

Today, no one on the masthead of any credible newspaper would admit or even want to remotely appear to be engaging in the low, vulgar, voodoo craft of yellow journalism. Nonetheless, there is no shortage of sensationalism, hyperbole, "celebretease," junk science, and heart-tugging melo-drama used to sell newspapers.

The stock list of impending catastrophe, contagious out-break, natural disaster, stalking, unforeseen accident, technol-ogy and science run amok, and other scare stories, commonly placed on the front page, runs in the dozens. Some of the more popular story lines on this grim register in recent years include shark attacks, mobile phone perils, killer asteroids, mad-cow disease, domestic violence, schoolyard bullying, genetically modified food, snipers, overhead power lines, pol-lution, heatstroke, a coming oil shortage, and secondhand smoke. These scare stories are fundamentally different from genuine bad news, such as an "insurgent" attack in Iraq or death and damage resulting from a hurricane—although some argue prominent coverage given these stories is not justified by their overall newsworthiness. Scare stories are stories in which nothing has really happened, or stories in which the signifi-cance of what has happened is deliberately dramatized or ex-aggerated. The gold standard of scare stories right now is, of course, global warming, with every sticky summer heat bout or period of mild winter weather initiating a new round of earth-as-sauna articles and op-eds, quickly erasing the memory of the previous "summer that never was" or this spring's snow-storms and ice dams. As handy as global warming is on a slow news day, it's a career day in the newsroom when a paper gets to break a fresh, unfolding catastrophe. And there's always a new one sooner or later: Legionnaire's disease, the Bhopal chemical spill, Toxic Shock Syndrome, SARs, a missing child. Last summer in my neighborhood the scare of the moment was West Nile Virus, a pathogen transmitted by mosquitoes that can cause flulike symptoms or more serious illness in about one in 150 people who are infected. The previous summer there had been an "outbreak" of West Nile with a handful of cases reported. Now in early May of the following year, local newspapers began running reports on the symptoms of the infection, how it was spread, and "how to minimize the risk of catching it." Public health officials urged people to drain their pools early and eliminate all standing water from their property. One person I know canceled her summer vacation at the cottage, where mosquitoes were more abundant. Either as a result of luck or heightened public vigilance, the great mosquito-borne pandemic never developed. A total of ten confirmed cases of WNV infection were reported in 2004 in a region of hundreds of thousands of square miles.

It's no mystery why newspapers report on scary stuff—to sell papers. Almost all the best sensational scare stories have in some way the hand of death hovering over them. Many, if not most, of these stories have some factual basis. Often, however, the tone of the headline or the mere positioning of the story on the front page inflates its importance or danger. Sometimes a reporter simply neglects to clearly state the low risk associated with an event or disease. This is the case with West Nile Virus—a disease that, measured by mortality rates, is more than one thousand times less dangerous than the common flu. Hyperbole may help newspapers sell a few more issues on a given day; however, over time it begins to breed cynicism toward print news in general. Perhaps part of the decline in newspaper readership can be explained by the growing feeling that much of the content of a typical issue is hype, untrue, or biased.

Sometimes scary stories are an outcome of new technologies that give humans the ability to measure and investigate the world in ever-greater detail. This seems to account for the proliferation of killer asteroid stories in recent years. New satellites with the latest instrumentation positioned near the asteroid belt have allowed scientists to probe, name, and calculate the orbits of individual asteroids. Newspapers have used this development to fixate on the possibility that an asteroid or comet could collide with the earth, causing millions of deaths and catastrophic damage to the environment. In one six-month period between July and December 2000, NASA's Near Earth Object Program website listed eighteen news stories or press releases about Earth-bound asteroids that had "just missed" the planet or could hit it in the future. Some of the stories picked up by newspapers, websites, and television around the country were "Estimate of Killer Asteroids Zooms" (*Albuquerque Journal*), "A Close Encounter with a Space Rock" (*NASA Science News*), and "Canada's Asteroid Protection Plan" (space.com). Asteroid mania has certainly made us more aware of the dangers posed by near-Earth objects. However, it glosses over the only firm conclusion scientists can give us—there will be no Earth-asteroid collisions in this century, which is about as far in the future as scientists can predict asteroid trajectories with any accuracy.

Sensationalism or subtle deception in newspaper stories is sometimes the product of laziness, ignorance, or the deliberate massaging of facts by reporters or editors. In an article appearing in *Skeptical Inquirer*, "Ringing False Alarms—Skepticism and Media Scares," Benjamin Radford reports that very often the reports or statistics generated by organizations or people intent on publicizing themselves are flawed. For instance, a Department of Justice report that estimated that 440,000 children were lost or missing every year included children missing for any amount of time ranging from a few minutes to overnight. An analysis of the figures found that 73 percent of the "lost" children were home within twenty-four hours. Articles built around such data patched wholesale into a story can have misleading "hooks" or reach erroneous conclusions. Radford cites a 2001 study conducted by University of Pennsylvania professor Richard Estes, which vastly overestimated the number of children who are victims of sexual exploitation. The study seemed to contradict the findings of earlier research, such as that done by professor David Finkelhor ten years before. Nonetheless, Estes's results were reported in USA Today as "the most comprehensive study yet." After the article was published, Finkelhor discovered that Estes's data were flawed and without much scientific basis. He blamed the hype created by the report on the media: "The biggest failure was the journalists' failure to question findings," said Finkelhor. The lesson, according to Radford, is that reporters need to dig deeper for a story than skimming a press release.

In today's lean-running newspaper environment, getting to learn such a lesson may be wishful thinking. Many newspapers are cutting, not adding staff. This directly and indirectly affects the types of coverage most metropolitan dailies are able to provide their readers. Section editors have to make decisions about how to allocate resources, and this often means that work-intensive but valuable investigative reporting, in-depth features, and analysis get short-changed. Whether they want to or not, editors must often fill space with news stories taken verbatim from wire services. The wire services themselves are often reiterating story lines supplied by news releases from universities, science publications, or environmental groups. This means many newspapers are acting more like a clipping service than a news organization. It accounts for the similarity of the content of many newspapers. It also implies, in a sense, that newspapers are as much pawns in the global fear trade as they are purveyors.

In a recent column for the British newspaper *The Guardian*, Guy Browning writes, "Most of what you read in newspapers is exaggeration. In fact, it's surprising there isn't a paper called The Exaggerator." Harmless merrymaking? Browning doesn't think so: "Exaggeration is a lot like inflation, in that it erodes the value and credibility of what you had in the first place." When someone tells us every day that the sky is falling we begin to tune out. Tuning out, it is proposed in this book, is one of the key reasons we have a crisis in critical and creative thinking in this country.

One excellent case study on the inflation effect of exaggeration in the news is the recession mongering that went on during the economic expansion of the later 1990s. The recession watch began in 1997 with the meltdown of many Asian countries' currencies. The fear, speculated about in the business pages of newspapers across the country, was that the Asian crises would spread like a pathogen to Western economies, setting off a global recession. At a business conference I attended in late 1998, economist Derek Holt of the Royal Bank did not mince words—continued personal wealth deterioration would lead the global economy into a recession. Throughout all

1999, recession panic was relentlessly played up in newspapers. Journalists pounced on Federal Reserve Board Chairman Alan Greenspan's assessment of the "irrational exuberance" of the stock market and sent it echoing into the nation's collective subconscious in a thousand articles and opinion columns. When equity prices, led by high-tech stocks, continued to climb through the year, fear of a stock market crash was absorbed into a more all-encompassing fear, the Y2K mother-of-all-crashes. Dawn broke uneventfully on January 1, 2000, and, after kissing the ground, pundits immediately began scanning the economic horizon, soon discerning that historically high prices for oil and gas were the tip of the iceberg called recession. When investors dumped significant chunks of underperforming stocks, newspapers gleefully reported the carnage: "Billions Lost in a Day," the stories ran, neglecting to mention that these same investors were now in tow of large amounts of cash with which to reinvest. As 2000 chugged along, recession sitters crossed their fingers and tallied the results—the U.S. economy had grown at a robust 4.7 percent! What irrational exuberance! Undeterred, the newspapers kicked off 2001 by rolling out their stockpile of recession stories anyhow. Canada's *Globe and Mail* ran a feature article titled "Have a Nice Recession," arguing that as the U.S. economy dived, so would Canada's. The media had to wait until 9/11 for the recession they had been predicting for four years, but then there were more important things to write about.

In his novel *State of Fear*, Michael Crichton takes a dig at today's super fear that global warming will lead to catastrophic climate change. Crichton's bigger theme is how fear is manufactured in a passive, media-saturated society, and how diverse groups have an interest in cultivating fears. When the data do not seem to be supporting the "certainty" that the earth is warming, environmental extremists concoct high-tech ploys to manufacture catastrophes—flash floods, the breakup of ice in the Antarctic—they can attribute to global warming.

Crichton's novel is part fantasy, part reality. In real life, the life blood of the global fear trade is the media, which either actively publicize fearful notions or do so inadvertently by their unwillingness or inability to question, fact-check, and qualify. Recession panic, Y2K, global warming, the fears themselves acquire the status of conventional wisdom or self-propagating ideas, which, according to communication theory, are called "memes." According to this view, a meme (rhymes with theme) copies itself in culture in much the same way a gene duplicates itself in nature. A successful meme, like a successful gene, is one that is useful in some way for an individual host or segment of the population. In the case of a fear-inducing meme, that host or group of people could be a special interest or interests.

"In a sense the whole political economy of the mass media, in which people tend to make money by gaining audience share, is a demonstration of the memetic thesis," says Jack Balkin, author of the book *Cultural Software: A Theory of Ideology.* "If there is a struggle for space in the human memory, you have to find a way to get through all the competing din and arrest the attention of people."

With declining circulation and greater competition from the Internet, many newspapers are out to arrest attention first, worry about details later. Whether in the form of memes, panic beliefs, or scary stories, the global fear trade, and the media's complicity in it, have become a poison to critical thinking in modern America. One reaction, already mentioned, has been to indiscriminately tune out information. Another response, equally damaging to reasoning and thinking skills, has been to draw the blinds and avoid risk taking altogether.

Frank Furedi examines the power of media-induced fear to modify people's behavior in the book *Culture of Fear*.

> *Scare stories about new dangers do not simply make people more anxious or fearful. The stories reinforce already existing apprehensions and help to shape and even alter the way that people conduct their lives.*

Furedi observes how a single report of a terrorist incident involving U.S. citizens in Greece led to a major decline in the numbers planning to travel to Europe, despite the fact that more Americans drown in their bathtubs than are killed by terrorists in an average year. Furedi affixes a large part of the blame for society's increasing aversion to all forms of risk on the media, but also allows that other factors are at work:

> *There exists a disposition towards the expectation of adverse outcomes, which is then engaged by the mass media. The result of this engagement is media which are continually warning of some danger. But the media's preoccupation with risk is a symptom of the problem and not its cause. It is unlikely that an otherwise placid and content public is influenced into a permanent state of panic through media manipulation.*

But what, then, is the ultimate source of this unrest or anxiety that leads us to dwell on obscure threats and harmful but unlikely outcomes? Could it be our surrender of a life informed by reason and critical thinking for an existence based on Blinklike judgments, intuition, and emotion? Could it be that, with the help of the media, we are changing our outlook and growing alienated from the very capacity that fuels our sense of security, well-being, and sanity, namely, a firm belief in an objective reality and our ability to rationally make our way through it by observing, reflecting, and reasoning?

IN HIS SPOOF of the newspaper business, *Scoop*, Evelyn Waugh describes the heretical work habits of an imbibing, world-weary journalist, as follows:

> *Why, once Jakes went out to cover a revolution in one of the Balkan capitals. He overslept, woke up at the wrong station, didn't know any different, got out, went straight to a hotel, and cabled off a thousand-word story about barricades in the streets, flaming churches, machine guns answering the rattle of his typewriter as he wrote.*

A native gift for hyperbole, it seems, was the key to creating a believable fictional journalist even seventy years ago, when Waugh wrote the book. But newspapers and journalists today face challenges that mere exaggeration and sensationalism won't solve. Foremost is to regain the public's trust. A 2004 survey conducted by the Pew Research Center found that the credibility ratings for newspapers have reached an all-time low. The percentage of those saying they can believe most of what they read in the newspaper has dropped to 54 percent, from 84 percent in 1985. This compares to 64 percent who say they can believe most of what they hear on network television news. For those in charge of running newspapers, the conclusion is sobering: Where once newspapers were viewed as the foundation of open debate, objectivity, and critical reasoning in a democratic society, today half the people in America don't read a newspaper, and half of those who do don't trust what they read.

The challenge for newspapers will be formidable, not only because pressures to reduce costs ultimately diminish resources for reporting. Newspapers are also up against declining literacy rates and stiff, growing competition from the Internet.

It is perhaps as much in the public's interest as it is in the interest of the newspaper industry that America's newspapers discover a business model that will reverse the circulation slide and regain the readers' trust. As yet, neither the Internet nor TV news can elucidate today's fast-changing social, political, and economic landscape with the scope and interpretive detail of a newspaper. Ultimately, however, the onus is on the American public, not the corporate publishing entities, to decide the type of newspaper it wants to read, or whether it wants to read one at all. As the American public has more power to choose alternatives to dumbed-down programming on television, so it has more power to choose print and electronic alternatives to newspapers. The stakes are high. Sensationalism and scare-mongering are not only providing diminishing returns to newspapers, they are providing lower returns to Americans.

If we continue to tune out or seek to live in only the narrowest of risk-free comfort zones, it will be us, not the media, that ultimately lose.

CHAPTER 7

I'm Too Busy:
The Myth of "Stress"
and "Information Overload"

The truth is cruel, but it can be loved,

And it makes free those who have loved it.

—GEORGE SANTAYANA

In the world of mountaineering, David Breashears is a legend. He has made it to the top of some of the tallest, most treacherous peaks, including four ascents of Everest, at 29,028 feet the world's highest mountain. He has won Emmy awards for his documentaries and films; in 1996 he codirected and photographed the first large-format film of an Everest ascent. It was the same year eight people died when a violent storm ripped across the mountain, trapping several groups of climbers in its uppermost reaches. Breashears and his team helped evacuate some of the survivors of the climbing disaster off the mountain.

While Breashears's feats in film and in the high mountains of the Himalayas have won him awards and renown, his acclaim among fellow climbers largely rests on his early exploits in free-climbing (without aid of ropes) the sheer vertical sandstone towers of Colorado's Eldorado Canyon. The smooth faces of these geological paroxysms offer the climber little more than finger-width cracks and pea-size surface blemishes to make upward progress. In his 1999 book, *High Exposure*, Breashears writes: "Imagine standing on the edge of a nickel and looking down 500 feet between your legs." It is an activity that demands the marriage of technical skill, clear-headed, critical thinking, and the utmost acceptance of responsibility for one's actions. Take away one of these and the whole enterprise, not to mention your life, is jeopardized.

Fortunately, most of us do not have to stand on the edge of a nickel a few hundred feet above hard rock, but we all have our daily mountain to climb—a difficult coworker or boss, multiple demands on our time, or money or marital problems. The rise of "stress," or rather the symptoms of stress, in contemporary society is a sign not only that more people are in difficult situations, but tellingly, that they are unable to respond to or think their way out of these situations. It is a sign, ultimately, that more people are having trouble taking charge of their lives. Today, stress and its co-conspirator, so-called information overload, are two major factors in the weakening of mental energy needed to do creative, technical work and solve everyday problems. It is why so many people say they are in perpetual "crisis mode" and have the feeling that their lives are "out of control." It is why some are falling off the side of their mountain.

But how real is stress? There are obviously traumatic events that can introduce severe stress into people's lives. But the meaning of stress, a word once applied to extreme, relatively rare situations, has been inflated to apply to just about everything that happens. Indeed, stress, say some experts, is largely a matter of perception and attitude. The word "stress," it turns out, generally has no more medical meaning than the phrase "life is not perfect." It is a word meant to convey a highly subjective psychological condition, which in turn is meant to lift the burden of responsibility for the quality of our thinking and decisions from our shoulders. Comedian Flip Wilson used to get a laugh with the line, "The devil made me do it." Today, "Stress made me do it" would be the modern drop-in for the line, signifying consignment of a person's mood and behavior to mysterious forces beyond his or her control. The modern version of the line is just as far-fetched as Wilson's, although less comedic. We associate stress with a frazzled, unhappy person, or a person in a rage, or someone wound up tight as a drum. Not very funny.

In *Who's in Charge? Attacking the Stress Myth*, Dr. Scott Shepherd argues that stress is the most overused and misused word in the English language, suggesting a physical condition, a situation, even a way of living, as in "she lives a stressful lifestyle."

The word stress now seems to stand for all kinds of things. Stress has gone from a physiological process, during which certain hormones are released into the body, to some vague, malevolent force running rampant in life. In fact, stress now means so many different things, I don't think it means anything at all. And yet we blame stress for most of our problems.

Despite its dubious meaning, or perhaps because of it, "stress" gets prolific coverage in the media. My search engine retrieved 80 million hits on stress in less than two-tenths of a second. Madonna, by comparison, netted 20 million hits, marijuana only 11 million. Stress, and the promise of relief from it, has become a topic of such familiarity in American newspapers and checkout-aisle magazines that nearly everyone can name a favorite "stress-buster" or provide a friend or coworker with a tip on "coping skills." Stress and anger management courses are common employee-training fare at many companies. Theories for dealing with stress can range from the mundane "stress is an unfortunate part of modern daily life" to the esoteric "rational emotive behavior therapy." Stress can apparently manifest itself in specific disorders such as chronic anxiety, chronic fatigue syndrome, and depression. If breathing, self-hypnosis, meditation, autogenics, or neck and shoulder exercises fail to ease stress, a person can compose and consult a checklist for "getting and staying organized" or book an appointment with a "certified relaxation practitioner" or study "two-thousand-year-old secrets to find peace, fulfillment, and wisdom." One can discover if one has a high-stress job, or find stress management programs for specific occupations. A person can join a stress support group, sign up for a stress-management newsletter, or become a stress blogger.

Here's an entry aptly titled "Stress" from a blogger by the name of Minnams in Newton, Pennsylvania, dated October 2004:

> *When I come home, here are two ways you should be able to tell I've had a shitty day: I begin reading a children's book.*

*They are like aspirin to me—they let me return to a happier
time, before thoughts of death and taxes. . . . I bring home an
Us magazine from the grocery store.*

More musings on stress are contained in this anonymous
posting found on a site called secraterri.com:

*Mornings used to be an absolute minefield of "potential stres-
sors" for me. Oversleep by fifteen minutes? Run out of Folgers?
Discover a missing button on the only clean blouse on my
closet floor? Any glitch in the routine was enough to send me
spiraling off into a toxic funk for the rest of the day.*

Not only can just about any event or circumstance induce
stress, unrelieved stress has been fingered as the cause of up to
50 percent of all diseases! It has appropriated the stress-
inducing pseudonym the "silent killer." The American Institute of Stress calls stress America's number-one health
problem. According to the institute, stress has been linked to
cardiovascular disease, neurological disorders such as Alz-
heimer's, migraines, and memory loss, psychiatric problems
such as anxiety and panic, gastrointestinal disorders such as co-
litis, hemorrhoids, and irritable bowel syndrome, and the der-
matological maladies of baldness, hives, and rashes. Yet, while
it may be under the institute's radar screen, stress is also having
a debilitating effect on Americans' critical thinking, creativity,
and work performance. When a missing shirt button sends a
person into a "toxic funk," he or she is hooked in to an emotional roller coaster likely to lead anywhere, anytime.

While stress is a relatively new phenomenon, it doesn't appear to be a passing fad. For millions of Americans, the symptoms of stress are neither trivial nor easily managed, but seemingly an everyday fact of life. A 1983 *Time* magazine cover story called stress "the epidemic of the eighties," citing a survey in which 55 percent of the people surveyed said they were under great stress at least one day a week. By 1996, nearly 75 percent said they were under great stress on a weekly basis, according to a survey in *Prevention* magazine. Today, as indicated in a National Institute of Occupational Safety and Health (NIOSH) report, *Stress at Work,* 40 percent of American workers report their jobs are very or extremely stressful, and 75 percent of employees believe workers have more on-the-job stress than the previous generation. The National Institute of Mental Health estimates that more than 19 million Americans between the ages of eighteen and fifty-four suffer from anxiety disorders, and millions of others from conditions ranging from post-traumatic stress disorder to depressive ills.

Yet before 1950, stress as we know it today essentially didn't exist. Hans Selye, a Hungarian-born scientist who spent most of his life in Canada, institutionalized the concept, both in the medical profession and in the public's imagination, with the publication of his monumental tome *Stress.* Selye, who eventually became the director of the Institute of Medicine at the University of Montreal, had degrees in both organic chemistry and medicine. As a medical student, Selye noticed that patients suffering from different diseases often exhibited the same symptoms. He proposed that "stress" was the underlying cause of various illnesses and disorders and put forward a mechanism, called the general adaptation syndrome (GAS), to account for the way it worked to undermine human health. Scientists had some understanding about this biological process before Selye anointed it GAS. Like the similar "fight or flight" response, GAS and the chemical imbalances it produces are a biochemical fail-safe plan hardwired into our bodies by natural selection to help us survive. Thinking she might get put outside in cold weather, our cat displays the fight or flight response anytime I get within ten feet of her. In response to a threat, the nervous system commands endocrine glands to pump hormones such as adrenaline into the bloodstream. These hormones cause the heart to beat faster, the lungs to breathe harder, the muscles to tense, and the eyes to dilate. Selye found that if the cause of the stress is not removed, the response goes to a second stage, called resistance. The body secretes more hormones in order to raise blood sugar levels and blood pressure needed to sustain energy. If the stress source is still not removed, the response can suppress the immune system, cause exhaustion, and trigger a collapse of the body's health.

There are two problems with Selye's theory. The first is the word "stress" itself, which, as one early critic noted, "in addition to being itself, was also the cause of itself, and the result of itself." Selye had to create a new word, "stressor," to distinguish between the thing or event causing the stress and the physical and chemical responses of the body to it.

The second problem with the theory is that the biological mechanism Selye proposes to explain stress is an automatic response acquired by humans through evolution to help us survive immediate physical threats to our life. The stressor in this case could be a bear or mugger. In these situations we don't have time to think, and pausing to analyze might spell a permanent, quick end to the person's analytical skills. Today, however, stress is almost exclusively associated with a response produced by perceived psychological threats or unpleasant social or professional circumstances—overwork, perceived personal shortcomings, family dynamics. Small wonder there is an "epidemic" of stress. The perception is that stress is a gut-level reaction; that there is little we can do about it other than "managing" it or, worse, running from it or shutting ourselves up within four walls. Stress, in this sense, has hardly anything to do with a strong physiological reaction of the body and is more comparable to a highly subjective state of mind, as encapsulated by this definition of work-related stress from the U.S. National Institute of Occupational Safety and Health: "Job stress can be defined as the harmful physical and emotional responses that occur when the requirements of the job do not match the capabilities, resources or needs of the worker."

Not a mention of a hormone here.

"Many people equate the so-called stress response to the flight-fight response, and do it in a way that makes stress seem natural, as if there's not much you can do about it," says Dr. Sheperd, the author of seven books and a professional consultant/counselor to people who have experienced traumatic events. "I don't think the comparison holds." Sheperd says a person's biological reaction to a snarling, charging dog is much more automatic and programmed than the emotional or psychological response that has come to be commonly associated with everyday stress.

Stress has become a self-propagating idea or "meme," a concept mentioned in the previous chapter to explain the spread of fear stories in the media. Regardless, the stress epidemic is having a profound effect on the ability of people to think and reason. "Critical thinking has dropped totally off the map for many people," Sheperd says. Stress seems to work in a twofold way to short-circuit thinking. First, the overuse of the catchall term "stress" prevents people from employing precise language to assess their situations. Instead of saying, "The boss is asking me to babysit her clients," and adopting a constructive action plan to deal with it, a person will say, "The boss stressed me out today." The word and concept of stress inclines people to wash over and rant, rather than analyze and pinpoint the problem. Second, the widespread acceptance of the notion that there is a massive amount of stress in society creates a feeling of melancholic or angry resignation toward life. The goal becomes to "manage stress," which reinforces the belief that the power in life lies in events, not people, Sheperd claims.

> We have a society where many, if not most people do not accept responsibility for their own lives. I am not just speaking of those who want to blame their parents or society because they turned to a life of crime. I am referring to those who blame everyone and everything for the way they feel and behave in life.

As shown by the NIOSH *Stress at Work* report, many people single out work as the main stressor in their lives. In one passage, the report carries us into the lives of two hypothetical workers, David and Theresa, presumably to impart some flesh-and-blood context to stress. Increasingly tired and irritable, David has booked an appointment for a complete medical checkup. He is waiting in his doctor's office when he runs into Theresa, a friend who had left David's company three years ago to take a job as a customer service representative.

"You got out just in time," he told her. "Since the reorganization, nobody feels safe. It used to be that as long as you did your work, you had a job. That's not for sure anymore. They expect the same production rates even though two guys are doing the work of three. We're so backed up I'm working twelve-hour shifts six days a week. I swear I can hear those machines humming in my sleep."

"Well I miss you guys," she said. "I'm afraid I jumped from the frying pan and into the fire. In my new job, the computer routes the calls and they never stop. I even have to schedule my bathroom breaks. All I hear the whole day are complaints from unhappy customers. I try to be helpful and sympathetic, but I can't promise anything without getting my boss's approval. . . . The other reps are so uptight and tense they don't even talk to one another. We all go into our own little cubicles and stay there until quitting time."

David works in a manufacturing or an "old economy" job, and Theresa works in a service or "new economy" occupation, and each is living with pressures people of previous generations apparently did not have to endure. For David there are longer hours and less security. For Theresa there are productivity enforced by technology and the hassles of dealing with unsatisfied customers.

Certainly longer workdays are frequently cited as a prime

source of stress. According to a study by the International Labor Organization, the average American worked 1,978 hours in 2000, or thirty-six more total hours than he or she did in 1990. Americans not only lead the world in labor productivity, but work more hours on average than workers from any industrialized nation, working about one hundred hours per year more than the average Canadian or Japanese worker. Against this backdrop fewer Americans have company pensions, relying instead on their own savings for retirement. More two-parent working families also mean work continues after work.

There is no doubt that unalleviated psychological stress—a term, as Dr. Sheperd suggests, that can be applied to just about anything that happens in life—can cause people problems. It has been shown that long-term stress, or rather the failure to address or improve undesirable circumstances, can cloud a person's judgment and thinking. One study of the performance of surgeons found that sleep-deprived doctors with elevated heart rates (a sign of stress) were indecisive and used poorly planned operating procedures. Other research has found that prolonged high levels of hormones called glucocorticoids, produced by stressful events or certain medical conditions, can cause shrinkage of the hippocampus region of the brain. This region is responsible for declarative memory, such as the ability to recall a name, address, or other fact.

"I'm not saying there is no stress if we define stress as certain physiological reactions within the body," says Sheperd. "The problem is, now stress is everything. In reality there really isn't stress, there are only good situations and bad situations. People that think in certain ways get through the bad situations better." In an article published in the *Economist,* Howard Goldman of the University of Maryland School of Medicine expresses even less sympathy, suggesting much of stress is perception: "Every generation thinks it's more stressed out and souped up than the rest."

The common belief is that stress is a thoroughly contemporary disease, brought on by more demanding workloads, a changing economy, and other social factors. Yet, simply measured by hours spent on the job, workers may have had more stress one hundred or two hundred years ago. Passed in England in 1833, the Mills and Factories Act limited children nine and older to forty-eight hours of work a week and teenagers to sixty-nine hours. Adults generally worked even more hours, and desired to. Indeed the relationship between stress and workload appears somewhat fuzzy. Most people find not working much more stressful than working long hours. Many truckers put in working weeks of eighty or more hours. Growing up, I knew many people who worked in car factories who routinely volunteered to work a double, sixteen-hour shift, and many did it three or four times a week. While most admitted to fatigue, I never recall anyone saying they were stressed. The shop-floor joke was that old-timers hated overtime, but they hated the thought of losing it even more. Nor are Americans alone in their workaholic tendencies. In Hong Kong, 70 percent of the workforce works more than fifty hours a week. One survey found that the majority of people in most Asian countries rank work more important than leisure. As Dr. Sydney Walker observes in his book *A Dose of Sanity,* in a chapter titled The Stress Myth, "A reasonable amount of stress is *good* for you. In fact, lack of stress may be more harmful to physical and mental health than high stress levels."

So if workload or work conditions are not directly causing on-the-job stress, what is? One answer could be the very medical model, proposed by Selye, on which the theory of stress is based. It's the same basic model that has led to the proliferating use of Ritalin and other drugs to treat student behavioral problems. Indeed, the entire concept of stress is now enshrined as a "disorder" in the psychiatry profession's bible, DSM-IV, and some doctors are now prescribing a potentially addictive drug, Xanax, as a "stress pill."

But the medical model neglects to take into account human free will. In an interview with Dr. Jeffery Mishlove, American psychologist and philosopher Rollo May states his belief that anxiety and stress should not be treated as symptoms to be removed, but embraced as a necessary stimulus for all productive work. May elaborates:

> I think anxiety is associated with creativity. When you're in a situation of anxiety, you can of course run away from it, and that's certainly not very constructive. . . . What anxiety means is it's as though the world is knocking at your door, and you need to create, you need to make something, you need to do something.

Many people, of course, like their jobs and find them fulfilling, or at least tolerable. But what of the person who is "stressed out" by his or her job for any number of reasons—perhaps not because the job is demanding, but because it is demeaning and boring? According to May's viewpoint, this would be a totally natural and understandable response. The source of anxiety or stress in this case is the person's resistance to the signal of stress and what it is telling him or her—to assume responsibility and change his or her behavior, thinking, or life. As Sheperd writes in *Who's in Charge?* "If you see yourself as *having* to do what you are doing, you will find no answers to make it better because you won't even look for them. You will be living like a victim."

Stress need not have a totally rational explanation. It could be the product of seemingly surreal or circular forces. Perhaps the affluence and freedom of American society is itself a source of stress. Working in a free-market economy is more stressful than a job in a government-run shop, but maybe boredom is stressful also. The expectation that the country's standard of living should insulate people from any anxiety or stress, when it doesn't, becomes stress. Maybe some people not only seek stress for "good" reasons, they create it for any number of perverse reasons—to attempt to make others as miserable as they are, for instance. Maybe there is an unreckoned pharmacological or addictive component to stress. Author Steven Johnson describes the unexpected results of a biofeedback (lie detector) test he took in his book *Mind Wide Open*. The machine measures changes in his adrenaline levels, the fight-or-flight hormone identified by Selye as the precursor of stress. Johnson lets us know he has a compulsion to wisecrack in unexpected social situations. Each time he regales the tester with his humor, the machine registers a sharp spike. The test, he realizes, has given him a chemical insight to his personality: "Suddenly, [the jokes] seemed less like casual attempts at humor and more like a drug addict's hungering for a new fix."

You can bet on "stress," that is, problems, difficult situations. It is one of life's certainties. But we've somehow let our egos become too fragile and sensitive. The attitude that lets the smallest, most trivial incidents induce anger, frustration, or bitterness is a form of psychic surrender that is sapping the intellectual and creative vigor from the lives of many people. The challenge is to liberate ourselves from this mass hypnosis and reclaim our curiosity, our thirst for knowledge, as opposed to pure emotion, and the full powers of our critical thinking—the best stress-buster there is.

NEXT TO WEATHER, information glut is one of the most popular topics of conversation and sources of complaint. The subject has been widely covered, both in book form and by the mass media. My purpose here, as with the topic of stress, is not to reinvent the wheel and serve the reader another exhaustive analysis of the causes or prescriptive cures for info-overload. Rather, I intend to briefly summarize how the trend detracts from objectivity, the search for some kind of truth, and critical reasoning. I'll also try to build into these few pages a compact philosophical and practical info-overload ventilator.

The tension created by information proliferation seems to arise from a basic conflict: our need for more, better information in our jobs and life on the one hand, versus our need to do our job, have a life, and get on with things. It is a tension, illustrated by the following no doubt familiar scenario:

After 10 days of travel a colleague of mine returned to his office. He collected his paper mail from the mail room, went to his office, found on his chair another stack of paper mail far too large to fit in his mailbox, discovered 290 email messages in his inbox, and listened to 14 telephone messages on his answering machine. After scanning the topics of his email, he checked 21 in detail and quickly answered 6, he returned to his phone messages, answered four that were still timely, and then he sat on the carpeted floor, pulled over his garbage can and began tackling his paper mail. As he worked he started building piles on the floor. Journals and magazines for his lab went "there," requests for article reprints he put over "here," [and] he began filling a large manila envelope with letters and receipts he was going to take home. Newly arrived software went beside the journals for the lab, and so on. Halfway through, he stopped to read 30% of a newsletter before trashing it. When he was largely finished he had nine untidy piles in different parts of the room—mostly on the floor, and then he left, carrying the pile designated for his lab.

This person, described in cognitive scientist David Kirsh's article, "A Few Thoughts on Cognitive Overload," has been in his office for perhaps half the day and done little or no productive work. What's especially distressing or demoralizing for people who live through this situation in various degrees every day is that, one, the knowledge economy is making information more, not less, crucial, and, two, there is a corresponding need to generate this knowledge faster, lest a competitor beat them to the punch. And this is real. Unlike generic "stress" arising from mostly subjective demands of everyday life or work, information overload is concrete and measurable and so, it would appear, is the stress arising from it.

There are as many as 700 billion documents on the Internet, according to one estimate, and the Internet is growing at a rate of at least 7.3 million pages per day. The world is now churning out information at a rate of two billion gigabytes a year, a pace that has allowed human beings to produce more new information in the last thirty years than in the previous five thousand years. There are over eleven thousand newspapers in print, another eleven thousand periodicals in circulation, and some 60 billion pieces of junk mail produced every year. According to a study conducted by the Institute for the Future, employees at Fortune 1000 companies now send and receive an average of 178 e-mail messages a day. Two-thirds of managers report tension with work colleagues and loss of satisfaction because of stress associated with information overload. Forty-three percent of managers think important decisions are delayed as a result of having too much information.

This information explosion has unleashed a number of unique forces, says Kevin Miller in *Surviving Information Overload*. One with the most alarming implications for knowledge and thinking is that more information is badly presented or incomprehensible. Anyone who has spent even half an hour searching the Internet for useful, specific information knows the truth of Miller's observation. To find the few precious nuggets of gold one must wade through a mountain of garbage. Often, the information on a given topic is sketchy, outdated, or simply not available. Kirsh has been able to quantify the watering down of quality in our information fortune: While the amount of information has been rising in a steep, exponential fashion, the amount of usable or quality information has been rising only marginally, at a plodding linear rate. Kirsh writes, "The increase in low-cost information now readily available with the web has massively outpaced the increase in quality information available. This drives up the individual cost of search for quality information. Where before we turned to trusted information sources, such as refereed journals or quality magazines, we now do more information hunting ourselves."

The unspoken critique in Kirsh's analysis is that many people are trying to use the Internet to get a free lunch. The Internet and its attendant information explosion have created the expectation of being able to retrieve valuable information instantaneously, on demand, without having to locate and wade through a "trusted information source," such as a peer-reviewed journal or quality magazine. Yet very often this is exactly where the golden nugget resides. In this sense at least, information overload *is* a myth. People are not after just information but good information, and this remains as elusive as ever, tucked away in a library, a filing cabinet, or an expert's head. As the editor of a business-trade magazine for nine years, I can testify that our best information, the information that distinguished us from our competition, was always won the old-fashioned way—by conducting interviews, visiting businesses, and asking questions.

Another insidious effect of information overload, closely related to quality dilution, is informational confusion. As outlined in David Shenk's book *Data Smog*, people now have at their fingertips an oversupply of statistics, expert opinions, and widely circulated but simplified stories with which to interpret the world. Nothing is muffled and context is vaporized. As Shenk relates:

> The proliferation of expert opinion has ushered in a virtual anarchy of expertise. To follow the news today is to have the surreal understanding that the earth is melting and the earth is cooling; that nuclear power is safe and nuclear power is not safe; that affirmative action works—or wait, no it doesn't.

Or a bit later in *Data Smog*:

> Since nearly any argument imaginable can now be supported with an impressive data set, the big winner is . . . argumentation itself. Journalist Michael Kinsley calls this "stats wars." Factionalism gets a big boost from volleys of data, while dialogue and consensus—the marrow of democracy—run thinner and thinner.

Perhaps this is the best point to lob in Einstein's aphorism, "Information is not knowledge." The point to extrapolate from Shenk's analysis is that the information explosion is not leading to better critical and creative thinking; it is largely being used to spout off, preach, or confirm existing biases and flawed thinking. As *Washington Post* writer Norman Chad observes, "The Internet is the Wild, Wild West on a mouse pad. In chat rooms around the clock, you can say anything you

> The information explosion is not leading to better critical and creative thinking; it is largely being used to spout off, preach, or confirm existing biases and flawed thinking.

want about anybody you like, without accountability." The Internet, and information it contains, is growing into the electronic linchpin of an emotional, intuitive, debate- and dialogue-free society.

A third way information overload adversely affects critical thinking is by acting to create shorter and shorter attention spans and to short-circuit thinking before it can get started. Maybe the problem is not information overload, it's information euphoria. And who, other than a Luddite (which this thinker is definitely not), cannot love the Internet, an American invention that has changed the world? What else can give you so much—an update on the ballgame, weather, hotel or flight reservations, a means for instant communication with family and friends, or the means to rescue your relationship with an order of flowers—and ask so little. The magic of the Internet is captured by J. C. Herz in her book *Surfing on the Internet*:

> When I look up, it's four-thirty in the morning. "No Way." I look from the clock to my watch. Way. I've been in front of this screen for six hours, and it seems like no time at all. I'm not even remotely tired. . . . In fact, I'm euphoric. . . . I start thinking about this thing that buzzes around the entire world, through the phone lines, all day and night. It's right under our noses and it's invisible. It's like Narnia, or Magritte, or Star Trek, an entire goddamned world. Except it doesn't physically exist. It's just the collective consciousness of however many people are on it.

Yet this worldwide consciousness places new demands on us that even the most ardent Internet-phile can find grating.

Through the ever-mounting variety and amount of information, "The world attacks us with a constant assault of stimulation and distraction, assigns us more tasks than a regiment of wizards could ever finish, and forces us to multitask," says Melinda Davis in *The New Culture of Desire*. Small wonder, notes Davis, that *Wired* magazine has crowned ADD the "official brain syndrome of the Information Age." Technology has altered people's very perception of time, as James Gleick documents in *Faster*. What was once fast is now slow, and what was or is slow (such as rational or creative thought processes) is now virtually intolerable. Gleick shows how even the preferred length of a sound bite for presidential candidates has shrunk from forty seconds in 1968 to less than ten seconds in 1988. In an article on contextmag.com, Larry Rosen and Michelle Weil, authors of *TechnoStress*, observe, "The more we juggle (multitask), the less efficient we become at performing any one task. And the longer we go before returning to an interrupted task, the harder it is to remember where we left off." In their books, Shenk, Miller, Rosen, and Weil offer reams of advice on managing infoglut, most of it common sense, which doesn't necessarily mean it gets practiced.

But perhaps the most pernicious side effect of information overload is a sanctioning of the attitude that "ignorance is bliss." Massive filtering, or in some cases completely shutting down information inflow, is considered either a coping skill or a liberating, personal statement. People talk about the anxiety of receiving a book over two hundred pages long, even as most watch nearly three hours of television every night. Yet, in reality, once a person begins practicing the fine art of extreme filtering, there is no anxiety or stress. The world is not knocking. There is only the serenity of the self seeking the self.

THE MYTH is not that there is too much information—there is. The myth is that there is too much *good* information; that information, good or not, has somehow become hazardous to one's health. Good information is still a rarity, and rarer still is the intellect that can polish it and turn it into knowledge. Nonetheless, in response to infoglut, people are now talking about information pollution in the same way they talked about air pollution thirty years ago or noise pollution more recently. Information is on the activists' radar screen and this can't be seen as a positive development. In the book *Code and Other Laws of Cyberspace*, Lawrence Lessig argues that it is a misconception that the Internet cannot be regulated. "But how cyberspace *is* is not how cyberspace has to be. . . . With some architectures, behavior on the Net cannot be easily controlled; with others it can." Lessig is not just talking about popups and porn. He is talking about the way information is presented, how we interact with it, how we use it. And make no mistake, as Lessig argues, the way the cyberspace is configured can be changed, controlled. It's all in the code, which humans write. Information contains data, reports, words of experts, but also ideas, values, beliefs. A certain code can, conceivably, "cook" the information we see on the Internet. Whatever sort of benefits a coded, top-down regulation of electronically borne information might provide, its potential abuses are to be far more feared.

Perhaps one answer for easing information overload and

related stress is more information. In *Brain Dancing*, Patrick Magee writes, "The most powerful information is MetaInformation—information that improves the process we use to interact with information." Before you break your pencil in two, consider the implications of what Magee is saying. Perhaps there is information overload because we are still at a primitive stage in our ability to handle and process information. As information expands exponentially, we lag behind but eventually adapt to our new cognitive circumstances. Two thousand years from now, humans may reminisce about simpler times when people only had to deal with a few terabytes (the equivalent of a million pages of text) of new information each day.

But at least part of the solution to reducing the tension created by information and modern life lies with accepting personal responsibility for one's actions and decisions. One of the main unifying themes of Western philosophy over the last two thousand years has been man's free will; his ability to use reason to understand his world and shape his destiny. In his *Meditations*, the Roman emperor Marcus Aurelius writes, "In the morning when thou risest unwillingly, let this thought be present—I am rising to the work of a human being. Why then am I dissatisfied if I am going to do the things for which I exist and for which I was brought into the world?"

Information and "stress" are not going to diminish. So the question becomes, Do we let stress and information shape our response to the world, or do we use free will and critical thinking to make good decisions in response to inevitable stress and the influx of new information? The mountaineer and filmmaker Breashears chose the latter course: "I believed I was in the process of creating myself. Like Gatsby, I thought that I alone heard the drums of my destiny, that I could become the product of my own imagination."

Breashears, in fact, was drawn to rock climbing as an escape from the anguish and stress created by an angry, bullying father. He writes: "My father was full of bravado, but I never saw him once reckoning with the consequences of his actions." Reflecting on his own anger after a close relationship fell apart, he observes: "My father had been a violently angry person and it had gotten him nowhere in life. . . . With time I began to see that anger is soul destroying. Nothing can be gained from it."

Anger, frustration, stress, and anxiety are themselves a form of information. They are the emotional precedent for critical and creative thinking. One of the main problems in contemporary society is that many people mistake the emotion for the thought. Difficulties, sensation, emotion, information—they're the beginning of the heroic journey of the life of the mind, not its end.

It's a journey that can and should lead to the top of a mountain of our choosing.

PART TWO

INSPIRATION

CHAPTER 8

Great Thinkers

W hy should we uphold reason as the most essential, common attribute of a fulfilling, productive life and a well-functioning society? As detailed in preceding chapters, empirical, reason-powered critical and creative thinking and rational discussion are the very basis of democracy. Effectively used, they ultimately call out the poseur, the potential tyrant, and assorted misguided fools and miscreants. They ask for accountability and evidence. Yet just as important to a society founded on the notions of liberty and free enterprise, reason is the only proven method humans have of ordering their lives to solve everyday problems, improve the quality of their work, generate important inventions, and create works of art. This brief selection of profiles is an attempt to shed light on the thought processes of some of history's greatest thinkers: their desire for knowledge; their high tolerance for risk, failure, and rejection; their perseverance and work ethic; and their tenacious unwillingness to accept the commonsense, best-guess, almost-true, half-baked lie.

HERACLITUS AND THE GREEKS:
LEARNING TO ASK THE RIGHT QUESTIONS

Heraclitus appears to have anticipated, twenty-five hundred years before Sartre and Camus, the philosophy of existentialism, with its emphasis on individual responsibility in an indifferent universe.

Heraclitus is best known, however, for his view that the universe is in constant change and that there is an underlying order or reason (Logos) to this change. As quoted by Hippolytus in *Refutations*, Heraclitus states, "Listening to the Logos rather than to me, it is wise to agree that all things are in reality one thing and one thing only." This idea seems to be the first explicit expression of a view that forms the basis of Western, rational scientific inquiry till this day—namely, that there is an underlying causality to the physical events of the universe and, further, that the multiplicity of causes are themselves a consequence of a single source or cause. Because of this, "Heraclitus's philosophy is perhaps even more fundamental in the formation of the European mind than any other thinker in human history, including Socrates, Plato and Aristotle," according to Washington State University's *World Civilization* primer on philosophy.

In other fragments of thought attributed to Heraclitus, we can see a basic grasp of the cycles of matter and energy (hydrological, carbon) that power the earth's biosphere, as well as a rudimentary formulation of the first law of thermodynamics, the principle of the conservation of energy defined in exact mathematical terms over two centuries later. But arguably the most important contribution of Heraclitus is to the invention and refinement of the method of critical reasoning itself. His ideas were not conceived in isolation, but in response to the views of other Greek philosophers, particularly those of Thales, Anaximander, and Pythagoras.

Of these men, Pythagoras is most recognized today, immortalized (again) every school year in a formula spelling out the relationship of the various sides of a right triangle. The Pythagorean Theorem, however, may have been used by the Egyptians and mathematicians in India before Pythagoras wrote it down. Pythagoras's enduring fame rests on his pioneering insight into the relationship between the notes of the musical scale and numerical ratios, the basis of modern music theory. He was also a mystic, believing the celestial spheres of the planets produced a sweet harmony, the so-called music of the spheres, and that the souls of people ventured into other life forms after death. Heraclitus directly stated the concept of unity hazily implied in the music of the spheres and rejected Pythagoras's belief in reincarnation. Heraclitus also applied simplifying logic to the ideas of Anaximander.

The passage of time cannot, or at least should not, dim our admiration of the achievements of Greek civilization. The Greeks singlehandedly invented geometry, musical theory, modern drama, logic, and the method of rational, scientific inquiry, the classical order of art and architecture embodied in proportion and balance, biological taxonomy, physics, and democratic government. The essence of this civilization was the practice of critical inquiry and dialogue that reached its height during the time of Socrates and Plato. The Greeks weren't superhuman. In fact they understood better than most the fallibility of human reasoning. Under an often not-so-gentle goading, the objective was to clear the mind of false assumptions, bias, superstition, and ideology. Today, we stand in wonder at the results.

ALBERT EINSTEIN: THE MIND THAT DREW A MAP OF THE UNIVERSE

In 1905, at the age of twenty-six, while most bright, young scientists his age were already working in laboratories under the tutelage of established professors in their chosen field, Albert Einstein was holding down a job at the patent office in Bern, Switzerland. Not for long. By the end of the year Einstein had published four papers proposing solutions to problems that had bedeviled the most renowned scientists of his day.

But it is his third paper, "On the Electrodynamics of Moving Bodies" (now referred to as the special theory of relativity) that blew the proverbial doors off our commonsense, intuitive view of the universe. In formulating the special theory of relativity, Einstein takes as his starting point the findings of other scientists; in this case an experiment conducted by A. A. Michelson and E. W. Morley in 1881. Ever since it was found that light acted like a wave, scientists had speculated that a substance dubbed "aether" must permeate the universe. The rationale for the existence of aether was that, just as water is needed to propagate waves of energy through the ocean, a substance was also needed to propagate waves of light through space. Shining a beam of light into this aether, Michelson and Morley supposed, would create some interference or drag on the light, which could then be detected by measuring the difference in the beam's speed. But the two scientists found no such interference.

Enter the precocious patent clerk, Mr. Einstein. In *Einstein: A Relative History*, Dr. Donald Goldsmith notes how, in his paper, Einstein dealt quickly with the question of aether: It didn't exist. While he was at it, Einstein also did away with absolute motion, absolute time, and absolute space, relatively useful but increasingly quaint concepts that had been around since the time of Newton. Now, as a result, Goldsmith observes, "When you said 'I am at rest,' you had to answer the question, 'Yeah, but at rest with respect to what other system?'" But it is the idea of relative time that often gives most people a problem. The notion can be grasped (sort of) by looking at the stars in the night sky. The twinkling light of a nearby star, say Arcturus, that we see "now" left the surface of the star about thirty-eight years ago. For all we know, Arcturus may no longer exist. All in all, special relativity leaves one gasping in its counterintuitive implications. At speeds close to the speed at which light travels:

- Time slows as measured relative to a stationary clock.
- Moving objects shrink in the direction of motion.
- An object, such as a spacecraft, will become more massive and therefore more difficult to accelerate.
- As well, nothing can travel faster than the speed of light, 186,000 miles per second.

In his fourth and final paper written in 1905, Einstein derived, almost as an afterthought, a mathematical relationship showing that energy and matter are different versions of the same thing. This discovery is summarized by the famous equation $E = mc^2$ often seen on T-shirts and posters around the world. The c^2 or "squared" term has especially significant implications, as it means that pulverizing even a small amount of matter, by splitting up some of its atoms, will release an enormous amount of energy—a prediction that was confirmed forty years after Einstein wrote down the formula with the explosion of the first atomic bomb in the New Mexico desert.

Einstein could have retired a Nobel laureate on any one of these 1905 papers. Yet he had an encore up his sleeve. Eleven years later he published the general theory of relativity. Just as special relativity led to unification of matter and energy, general relativity proposed that time and space were intricately interwoven across the unimaginably vast distances of the universe, and that this time/space continuity was bent by the force of gravity. This bent space in turn determines the motion of objects. A few years later, during a solar eclipse, scientists experimentally measured the bending of a star's light as it passed by the sun, once again confirming Einstein's predictions.

Despite arriving at these previously inconceivable insights about the workings of the universe, Einstein wasn't perfect.

> Einstein has provided us with the most remarkable examples of how critical reasoning is used to confirm or refute our intuitive snap judgments of the world.

He made a number of gaffes, including his self-confessed "greatest blunder," the invention of a cosmological constant that would allow the universe to remain static. He also spent the last forty years of his career in a futile effort to disprove the notion that "God played dice," an implication of quantum theory. Yet, through his hard-headedness, self-discipline, solid educational grounding, and, yes, genius, Einstein has provided us with the most remarkable examples of how critical reasoning is used to confirm or refute our intuitive snap judgments of the world.

NICOLAUS COPERNICUS: THE MAN WHO DARED TO UTTER THE DANGEROUS TRUTH

In the Middle Ages people had a pretty good hunch about the design of the solar system. The earth, home to God's creatures, was in the center, and the sun, moon, planets, and stars revolved around our comely orb in a system of nested, celestial spheres.

To fifteenth-century European society, the best thing about this model was that it was in accord with passages in the Bible describing the sun moving in relation to a motionless earth. Not surprisingly, problems with a geocentric model of the universe soon became apparent. The Babylonians, for instance, were puzzled that the sun did not seem to travel at a constant speed in its yearly orbit around the earth. This and a few other wrinkles were irritants under the skin of scholars, one being the Polish monk Nicolaus Copernicus.

Copernicus had studied medicine in Padua, but apparently never taken a degree. At the time, one of the main diagnostic tools of medicine was astrology. It was this aspect of his studies, no doubt, that spurred him to think about a sun-centered solar system. Copernicus eventually took a position as a canon at the Lidzbark castle as the bishop's personal physician. It was a job made for stargazing, and Copernicus's room in a tower of the castle gave him an ideal vantage point for the pastime. It was here that Copernicus produced his masterwork, *De Revolutionibus*, a four-hundred-page document composed of six separate books that clearly, in scientific principle at least, refuted the idea of the Ptolemaic, earth-centered universe. Copernicus argues that "since the Planets are seen at varying distances from the earth, the center of the earth is surely not the center of their circles." He accurately fixes the order of the planets outward from the sun, and includes several chapters on plane and spherical geometry that he uses to support his argument.

Coming when it did, Copernicus's work launched the scientific renaissance that would lead mankind out of the dark ages and, through Newton, into the Enlightenment and the Age of Reason. Because he feared punishment from Church authorities, Copernicus hid his work for nearly thirteen years, publishing it only just before his death. His model of a sun-centered solar system is the first modern application of Occam's razor, a principle that states that the simplest of two competing theories is preferable. Seventy years after Copernicus's death, the German astronomer Johannes Kepler would replace circular orbits with elliptical ones, giving humans the first accurate inkling of something they had been gazing at in mystified wonder for tens of thousands of years.

SHAKESPEARE: SHAKING THE HUMAN OUT OF HIS PEN

As Copernicus rekindled society's will to explore the mysteries of the universe and world around us, Shakespeare stirred the imagination to consider the secrets of the human heart. What Greek dramatists began, Shakespeare brought to full fruition. One's reaction to the art of this enigma is of course intimate and personal. Unlike, say, the discoveries of Newton or Einstein, Shakespeare's finely slivered poetic perception can get plowed under by modern life's avalanche of monosyllabic trash culture. A person can live his or her entire life in diligent flight from the challenges presented by the Bard's music. The choice, however, will mean a significantly diminished critical appreciation of life's human dimension.

In critically exploring the contours of the human condition and laying out a sequence of controlled action, Shakespeare makes us evaluate and understand our own situations more clearly. For instance, in portraying the complexities of love and jealousy in his comedies, Shakespeare provides us with insight into our own relationships, a perspective that could cause us to reflect about how we might change or improve them. These "lessons" can have immensely practical applications. As John O. Whitney and Tina Packer observe in their book, *Shakespeare's Lessons in Leadership and Management*, King Henry in *Henry IV* teaches the newly hired or promoted person to be alert to people who do not trust you right away because they view you as an outsider. True, you can pick up some of this from movies or television shows, but Shakespeare's characters are able to find and express infinitely more degrees of nuance in their circumstances, which makes them both less lifelike in a "real" sense and more lifelike in an artistic sense, as representatives of the human condition. The key is his language, which tells us not only what the character is feeling, but how he is feeling. The words illustrate it. Shakespeare conveys meaning through metaphor, something a television show wouldn't touch with a ten-foot pole. "Lear himself, as the king of this world, is a metaphor for what has gone wrong with nature and a microcosm of the world itself," says Bruce Meyer in *The Golden Thread, A Reader's Journey Through Great Books.* Shakespeare has consciously constructed Lear's temperament to reflect imbalances, such as those found in the wider natural or social-political world, that lead to strife and disorder. Cognitive scientists have found that the human mind can effectively interpret and use metaphor as a tool for mapping and understanding abstract concepts.

Assessing Shakespeare as a thinker, the central question is simply, how did he do it? It's a contentious issue, because scholars are not really sure who "he" was. We simply don't know much about how the personal circumstances of his life groomed him to become a "literary genius of universal acclaim."

Shakespeare's eminence is not simply due to the plots of his plays—the basic stories of *Romeo and Juliet, Othello,* and *King Lear,* as well as most of the histories were in wide circulation in Elizabethan England in folklore or literary works. Rather it is the universality of Shakespeare's characters that makes Shakespeare different. Still, we must ask, how did he do it? One explanation seems to be by having a master plan but being willing to alter it as good ideas welled up from his imagination. As Robert Brustein reports in an article, "Character and Personality in Shakespeare," the playwright originally envisioned the character of Falstaff as a bad guy, "a Vice figure in a medieval morality play about the moral education of a True Prince." But Shakespeare was a poet first and the play "got away from him and Falstaff escaped" to become one of the most charismatic characters ever invented.

One of the hallmarks of a good critical thinker is the ability to adjust and add in new information. Shakespeare was so good that today, as Oscar Wilde once noted, art doesn't imitate life, life attempts to imitate Shakespeare.

THOMAS EDISON: TURNING BIG IDEAS INTO THINGS THAT WORK

When he died at the age of eighty-four in 1931, Thomas Edison had patents on 1,093 inventions. As historian Thomas Hughes writes, "Only Leonardo da Vinci evokes the inventive spirit as impressively, but unlike Edison, Leonardo actually constructed only a few of his brilliant conceptions."

Many of his inventions were simply improvements on things that were already operational, but cumbersome or impractical. He scored his first success in 1869 with an improvement on the standard stock telegraph tape printer. Western Union paid him thirty thousand dollars (a few million in today's currency) to produce twelve hundred of the devices.

But it was with his invention of the first practical incandescent lightbulb that Edison proved his tenacity and prowess as an inventor. Arc lights using two carbon electrodes to create a spark of light had been around for ten years but were much too powerful for use in a home. It was a demonstration of a small dynamo at a foundry that inspired Edison's creative flurry to build a workable lightbulb. The dynamo was not his invention, but he realized it could be used to carry current into all the offices and apartments in Manhattan.

First, however, there were some huge technical hurdles to overcome. Edison experimented for months with different types of filaments, which were all very fragile, of low resistance, and usually flamed out within a few seconds after applying current. A second problem was evacuating the glass bulb of all oxygen so that the filament wouldn't oxidize. His first demonstration of one trial bulb to investors failed when the bulb exploded. Step by step Edison solved the problems, at last producing a bulb with a thin carbon filament that stayed lit for forty-five hours. The year was 1878.

There was still much work to be done. As Edison once noted, "There is a wide difference between completing an invention and putting the manufactured article on the market." He had to basically conceive, invent, and manufacture the entire power-generating industry—commercially workable dynamos, insulated wiring, safety devices, meters to measure electrical consumption. When at last 106 lamps were turned on in Lower Manhattan on September 3, 1882, it was a world-changing event, brought to fruition by the energy and clear thinking of a single man.

In a sense, Edison may have been the world's first knowledge worker. He took new, untested technology and through trial and error and applied critical and creative thinking invented not only new products, but new markets. He was a risk-taker and a frenetic, diligent worker, to be sure. But he was also wordly and intelligent. Every job applicant to his lab was required to take a test consisting of 150 questions, such as, "What is the first line of the *Aeneid*?" A colleague described seeing him plow through a five-foot-high pile of journals in his spare moments. If Edison suffered from information overload he appears to have made the best of it.

ISAAC NEWTON:
MANKIND'S SCIENTIFIC MESSIAH

No all-star lineup of thinkers would be complete without the man whose intellectual brilliance and discoveries launched modern science and, say some, the modern Western European model of culture and society, Isaac Newton. Newtonian "mechanics"—his three laws of motion plus his law of universal gravitation—is not only the first completely coherent scientific theory, it is easily the most magnificent. Relativity and quantum theory may be sexier and more philosophically appealing, but Newton's laws explain 99 percent of what human beings see and experience as we move in, around, and through our surroundings. The laws allow us to fly airplanes, build cars, houses, and skyscrapers, design bridges, predict tides and eclipses, and put satellites in orbit.

In the summer of 1665, officials in London discovered the bodies of two French sailors infected with the plague. In the fourteenth century the plague had killed more than a quarter of Europe's population, and it had made periodic reappearances since. Cambridge University closed its doors and Newton retired to an English country manor house in Wollsthorpe. Over the next sixteen months, the twenty-three-year-old Newton lost himself in a state of fervent, frenzied study that is commonly acknowledged as yielding an *annus miralibis*, year of miracles. In this relatively short span of time, Newton found a new way of approximating a series of numbers, the bionomial theorem, invented a new type of math, calculus, and discovered the theory of optics, positing that white light was a mixture of distinct colors, the spectrum.

In typical fashion, Newton published none of this. It was only when he was threatened with having the feather of discovering calculus plucked away by another mathematician, Gottfried Leibniz, that Newton made his work public. It is now generally agreed that Newton and Leibniz, working independently, had codiscovered calculus, using slightly divergent methods and terminology, at about the same time. Calculus was needed to put science on strenuous, modern footing. To understand its importance, consider how easy it is to find the area of, say, a rectangle, or for that matter, any shape with straight sides. You just multiply the sides or divide the shape up into areas you can calculate and add them together. Now try to use the same method to find an area under a curve. Before calculus, scientists and mathematicians could only guess at areas under curves. Needless to say, in real life there are more curves than there are straight lines. Calculus gave scientists a completely reliable method of finding areas and calculating things such as instantaneous rates of change of objects in motion, the mathematical socket wrench set Newton would use to take apart the universe and reassemble it.

Newton was spurred into writing his scientific treatise *Principia*, the work that laid out the laws of motion and gravitation, by a question posed by a fellow Royal Society member, astronomer Edmund Halley, in 1684. Halley asked Newton, who by then held the Lucasian Chair in mathematics at Cambridge, if the shape of a planet's orbit could be predicted assuming the force of attraction to the sun varied by the inverse square of its distance. Newton replied he had already worked it out—it would be an ellipse. Newton had worked it out only hazily, so he now proceeded to throw himself into a creative frenzy that recalled his days at Wollsthorpe. As David Berlinski relates in *Newton's Gift*:

> The two years Newton spent writing his masterpiece were by all accounts years in which he was intellectually consumed. The raw massive energies that he had discharged in alchemy or Biblical studies or inconclusive mathematical tracts now came together and fused. He hardly ate; he slept irregularly; his life was lived in a circle that passed from his study to the Cambridge dining rooms and back again by means of a garden walkway. He rose early and retired late. His friend and associate, Humphrey Newton . . . looked uneasily on the actions of a man who had allowed everything in his life to be subordinated to an uncontrollable intellectual urge.

What can we conclude about Newton's intellectual passion and the psychology of his thought process? Clearly he was a mathematical prodigy. But this fact lends itself to a number of gross parodies about both the man and his work. His *system of the world* is often characterized as a clock, a set of mechanical cogs and gears moving the planets, man, and the universe on a preordained course through absolute space and absolute time. Order is everywhere. It has often been said that we need know only the exact parameters of this machine at a given moment and we can faithfully predict the future historical course and whereabouts of everything into eternity. This absolute depiction is absolute bunk, and Newton himself never made such a claim. In this universe, on this planet, man moves with absolute free will. Newton's equations cannot predict the rise of Adolf Hitler to power, the invention of the computer chip, the making of *Star Wars*, or the direction of the stock market.

Because Newton used supremely honed methods of abstract reasoning to arrive at his universal laws, and perhaps because of his penchant for solitude, there is also a tendency to see him as an abstraction of a man, someone or something far removed from the human realm. He was decried even in his own time as the father of scientific reductionism, and with the inflated political importance this type of criticism has assumed since then, one can imagine he would probably be demonized on the typical campus of today as the icon of white male oppression, the progenitor of corporate technocracy and mass production. In fact, Newton was first and foremost a craftsman. He had an innate mechanical gift that allowed him to construct ingenious working models of windmills, the solar system, and other devices. He built by hand the world's first reflecting telescope. It was beautifully crafted and a vast improvement over the refracting telescope, eliminating problems with color distortion. He was also, as his stubborn fascination with alchemy and biblical studies suggests, a bit of a mystic. Yet even in these shadowy and spiritual pursuits, Newton's approach was exhaustively, if naively, rational. He *was* human. But the other side of this "mysticism" was a neo-Platonic belief, passed down by Galileo, that the language of the universe is written in numbers. This puts him, as we shall see, in company of the vast majority of physicists working today.

CHARLES DARWIN: THE MAN WHO FIGURED OUT HOW LIFE WORKS BY ACCIDENT

When, in 1831, the twenty-two-year-old Charles Darwin accepted an invitation to take a spin around the globe on HMS *Beagle*, he was engaging in the grand English tradition of the young gentleman setting out to explore the world. This, however, was no romp across the continent and Darwin was no dandy. The *Beagle*'s scientific mission was to gather plant and animal specimens, and the journey was to last five years, with stops in the Galápagos Islands, Tahiti, and Australia. Darwin was already a budding naturalist, having taken several natural science courses as a student at Cambridge.

The isolated Galápagos Islands, off the South American coast, were a natural laboratory for observing how the process of evolution had resulted in small alterations between different species. Darwin returned from the voyage with dozens of notebooks crammed with drawings and specific details about animals' anatomy, behavior, habitats, and populations. For instance, Darwin identified thirteen different species of finches with slightly modified beaks. Still, nearly two years after the journey, he had yet to come up with a general explanation or theory that would tie all his observations together. According to Jim Glenn in *Scientific Genius*, Darwin's insights may have begun to take shape after he read the *Essay on Population* by Thomas Malthus. Notes Glenn, "The Malthusian thesis, that population and food supply grow at disastrously different rates impressed on Darwin the struggle of competition for scarce resources." The idea provided Darwin with a rule for rating the needs or success of a species and a rationale for the direction of evolutionary change. "Now it was clear to him that species existed precisely because specific adaptations conferred a survival advantage." Any new feature that helps, say, a frog stay out of the jaws of a predator (better camouflage, faster reproduction) means that over the long haul the new frog (because the mortality rate of the old frog is higher) will come to predominate in the frog population. Today we know these new features are produced by random changes in an organism's DNA. Darwin knew nothing about DNA, but he understood the process. He called it natural selection.

This is a classic example of lateral thinking, and Darwin urgently sat down to work out the implications of his serendipitous moment. In the case of the finches, each random change produced in the shape of a bird's beak gave the bird a specific advantage for a special type of feeding habit—narrower beaks for probing crannies for insects, and broader beaks for crushing seeds and chewing plants. All of these species were "descended" from a common ancestor. The generalizations of Darwin's theory, like a run of cards in solitaire, then began to fall out automatically: Species appear one at a time, not suddenly in large batches; some species last much longer than most do; extinction is forever; the later species in a group are often more specialized in structure and function than earlier species.

Darwin spent the better part of the 1840s writing and rewriting the *Origin of Species*. Steve Jones, professor of genetics, University College London, calls *Origin* "the book of the millennium," and argues that Darwin's wide-ranging intellect is the force behind the powerful logic of his "long argument."

The Origin *is the high point of the literature of fact. Darwin wrote well because he read well. In a single summer, his diary records, he enjoyed* Hamlet, Othello, Mansfield Park . . . The Arabian Nights *and* Robinson Crusoe. *His prose read like a Victorian country house. It radiates confidence from whatever direction it is viewed.*

Could his lateral thinking have been enhanced by his reading of *Hamlet?* In the end, the beauty of Darwin's theory of natural selection, like that of a sun-centered solar system, lay in its simplicity. Life's diversity is explained by organisms' knack for acquiring and transmitting inherited differences in the ability to reproduce. As Darwin's contemporary peer and biologist T. H. Huxley remarked after reading the *Origin,* "How extremely stupid not to have thought of that!"

LYNN MARGULIS: CONTINUING TO ASK THE RIGHT QUESTIONS

Science almost always advances by focusing on the exception rather than the rule. A really good theory must explain *all* of the relevant facts, not just some of them. Scientists who insist on reminding their colleagues of this are often regarded as either true keepers of the scientific flame or irritants. Lynn Margulis, an evolutionist, teacher, and researcher at the University of Massachusetts, is widely viewed as both, but seems to especially relish her role as scientific hell-raiser.

Margulis, an authority on micro-organisms, has been instrumental in the advancement and growing acceptance of the "symbiotic" theory of cell evolution, which posits that the essential membrane-enclosed components of cells with nuclei (including animal cells like those in our body) were once free-living bacteria that became incorporated as the cell formed. The theory has potentially huge ramifications for what has become biologists' standard interpretation of the way life evolved on Earth. Her work has won her formal acclaim and in 1983 she was elected to the National Academy of Sciences. In 1999 she received both the National Medal of Science and the Sigma Xi Procter Prize for Scientific Achievement.

In an article published in the *Smithsonian*, writer Jeanne McDermott described Margulis as "one of the few living scientists who has shifted a paradigm." In the same article, Peter Raven, director of the Missouri Botanical Gardens, says, "Her mind keeps shooting off sparks. . . . To me she's one of the most exciting, original thinkers in the whole field of biology."

Margulis's thinking appears to have been influenced by her early education and in particular by her exposure to the Great Books curriculum while an undergraduate at the University of Chicago—when she enrolled at the age of fourteen. The curriculum emphasized the reading of original works to trace and understand how an idea developed, rather than the use of half-truths of textbooks or the language of specialized academic disciplines. This approach she uses and still advocates today.

The biosphere is filled with countless examples of symbiosis or behavior that comes from two different kinds of organisms that live together. The desert termite, for example, has several different types of micro-organisms living in its hindgut that digest wood. Margulis's breakthrough contribution has been in recognizing the importance such microbial symbionts might play in the evolution of nucleated cells, and thus in the evolution of animals such as people. For instance, some mitochondria, the cell organelles that generate energy, were probably once invasive, oxygen-breathing bacteria that arrived on the scene about 1400 million years ago. Most of the time they killed the other bacteria they invaded, but in a few instances the prey cell survived and the oxygen-breathing bacteria were incorporated into its cellular metabolism.

Many scientists now accept the theory that microbial symbionts played a role in the evolution in the nucleated cell, although there is less agreement with Margulis's contention that the symbiosis is also a major source of inherited variation in animals and plants, and thus a strong driving force of the evolutionary history of Earth's biosphere. Some scientists have ridiculed the hypothesis as lacking any firm evidence. However, in *Acquiring Genomes*, co-written with her son Dorion Sagan, Margulis points to genetic evidence that seems to contradict the classic neo-Darwinian view that species evolved gradually, over a long period of time. Rather, whole new sets of genomes have been incorporated geologically (suddenly) from free-living microbes.

Anyone can be a rebel. Margulis is a rebel *with* a cause, and reasons to back up the cause.

ED WITTEN: GLIMPSING THE UNITY BEYOND THE DOORS OF PERCEPTION

Hardly a household name, Princeton's Ed Witten is nevertheless the only living scientist often mentioned in the same breath as Newton and Einstein. Like Newton and Einstein before him, Witten works in an area of abstract mathematical physics that for the most part lies beyond (some say way beyond) the edge of his contemporary public's comprehension. In a sense his work is also an extension of the grandest, most ambitious public musing project begun by the Greeks, a search for an explanation of the unity underlying the diversity of the universe. In the parlance of the day, this explanation is called a theory of everything, or often a grand unified theory (GUT). But where the Greeks were groping in the dark, Witten and his fellow theoretical physicists are hot on the trail. This is the bold and controversial contention of scientists in Witten's camp, at any rate. The claim is not based, as yet, on experimental evidence. It is based on a theory that is so recondite, so counterintuitive, yet at the same time so mathematically elegant, it is assumed by many physicists it simply has to be true. It is called superstring theory.

Superstring theory, first developed fully during the 1970s, is a consequence of physicists' dogged pursuit of a unified theory of everything. At the heart of the present-day search for such a theory is the premise, undoubted by most scientists, that the four fundamental forces of nature (electromagnetism, strong and weak nuclear forces, and gravity) are different aspects of the same essence. Newton's and Einstein's discoveries, while magnificent mathematical elucidations of the laws of nature, were not directly focused on finding a theory of everything. Newton found that terrestrial-produced forces and gravity were aspects of the properties of matter, and Einstein's theories of relativity mostly explained unifying aspects of the *structure* of the universe. Einstein did show that energy and matter are the same ($E = mc^2$). But all energy (movement, work, heat) is a result of forces. Think of anything you can that moves, that is, has energy: someone running, a firecracker exploding, a kid falling out of a tree. All these movements are a consequence of the action of one of the fundamental forces—an electrical potential in the muscle of the runner, a violent chemical reaction in the firecracker, and gravity in the case of the falling kid.

Equations uniting electricity and magnetism were discovered by James Clerk Maxwell in the nineteenth century. Then, in the 1960s, with the development of powerful atom smashers, scientists began to find evidence of hundreds of different subatomic particles no one had suspected existed. Protons and neutrons, the particles that make up the nucleus of an atom, were not fundamental after all but made up of still tinier particles scientists termed quarks. In turn, somewhat demonically, quarks come in various types—three "colors" and six "flavors." There are also antiquarks. The strong nuclear force holds the whole ball of wax together. Another class of particles, called leptons, make up the electron and a few other subatomic particles. These are governed by the weak nuclear force. In the 1960s, a number of physicists managed to unite the electromagnetic, strong, and weak forces in a single theoretical framework. That framework is called the Standard Model and, as its supporters truthfully claim, it fits all known experimental data. There's one problem however—the theory doesn't account for gravity.

Enter superstring theory and Ed Witten. Superstring theory was conceived in the 1970s and scientists have been tweaking it since. Whereas a subatomic world composed of particles, like tiny billiard balls, is intuitively grasped by the mind, superstring theory describes a universe quite alien to the human imagination. Superstrings are a hundred billion billion times smaller than an atom's nucleus and require ten dimensions (that's right, ten) to exist. The vibrations of the strings in ten-dimensional space, say string theorists, correspond to the multiplicity of particles found in the Standard Model and all the fundamental forces, including gravity.

"Superstring theory is really the only game in town when it comes to a grand unified theory of everything," says Michio Kaku, a professor of theoretical physics at City College, City University of New York. In his book *Hyperspace*, Professor Kaku has criticized the Standard Model as too "unwieldy and awkward" to be a good candidate for a theory of everything. "The goal is to have an equation an inch long that would allow us to read the mind of God," he says.

Witten's mathematical prowess has played a key role in the development of superstring theory. Using breakthrough mathematical techniques, Witten helped pare down the number of competing superstring theories from a messy five to an elegant one. British mathematician Michael Atiyah has written that Witten's ability "to interpret physical ideas in mathematical form is quite unique." Witten has received the prestigious MacArthur "genius" Fellowship and has also been awarded the Fields medal, often called the mathematician's equivalent of a Nobel Prize. In a column written for the Mathematical Association of America, Keith Devlin compares Witten to Newton: "Just as questions in physics led Newton to develop some far-reaching new mathematics that found many applications well outside of physics, so too Witten's mathematics has been of a depth and originality (and incidentally of a difficulty equaled by few mathematicians) that will surely find other applications."

Witten himself has called string theory twenty-first-century physics that fell accidentally into the twentieth century. But it is the extra dimensions required by string theory that give people, and many scientists, fits. The extra dimensions, beyond the three spatial dimensions and one of time we experience every day, are thought to be "compactified" inside observable space. Speaking in an interview that appeared on the Public Broadcasting System's *Nova*, Witten said the benefit provided by the extra dimensions is the ability "to describe all the elementary particles and their forces along with gravity." For physicists, that's a huge gain, but is it real? Witten says he takes the theory literally to mean the extra dimensions actually exist. He also takes issue with the charge leveled by supporters of the Standard Model that superstring theory is not testable. Witten claims that one feature of string theory, supersymmetry, is "definitely testable."

As bizarre, abstract, and counterintuitive as superstring theory seems, there is a well-established precedent for the mathematical elegance it embodies pointing the way to truths about the physical universe. Einstein simply used mathematics, especially in general relativity, to deduce profound insights about the nature of the physical universe. Many of the predictions of relativity were confirmed only years later. Likewise, using mathematical and critical reasoning, physicists first formulated quantum mechanics and later found evidence to support many of its bizarre implications, such as the uncertainty principle. These and other surprise discoveries seem to verify Newton's faith that the language of the physical universe is written in numbers. In the absence of confirming evidence, Witten allows that string theory may be wrong, but if it is wrong, he says, "It would seem like a cosmic conspiracy."

BECAUSE WE LIVE in the age of digitally encoded information, because we can hop on a jet and be anywhere in the world in a few hours, because we can open a man's chest and repair his heart's damaged arteries, it is natural to assume that we contemporaries, as a rule, have superseded the critical- and creative-thinking skills of all civilizations and ages that came before us. As a brief consideration of great thinkers of the past demonstrates, this view is at best naive, at worst deluded. Today, in wide swaths of the public, even among the so-called educated, people have put their minds on hold. One-sided emotion and Blinklike intuition dominate the so-called life of the mind. More and more people rely on politically correct or ideologically tainted received knowledge, which is nothing more than refined propaganda. I certainly cannot approach the profound technical or artistic wizardry of the critical and creative thinking employed by Newton, Shakespeare, or Witten. But I can throw away all assorted dogma and begin to think as well as I can. The distinguishing element of the great thinking analyzed here is not necessarily brilliance—there are many highly intelligent people in every age but not everyone becomes a Mozart or Frank Lloyd Wright. What is unique about these people is an unquenchable desire for knowledge and the vigorous self-discipline and drive to effectively put that knowledge to some good use.

Motivated thinkers are good thinkers.

PART THREE

FIXES

CHAPTER 9

If You Don't Ask,
You Don't Get: A Return to
Discipline and Standards

"I put a picture of the Playboy *Playmate Stephanie on my wall because I think she's hot. The Barbie Twins are pretty good looking, also. My mom got the pictures for me actually. She knows I like that. When we moved in, my room was pretty dull. She wanted me to decorate it."* (Ari, age 13, Encino, CA)

"A lot of the parents of the kids in my grade don't care about their kids. They just let their kids roam free in the city— left with nannies or drivers. I feel sorry for them, because I don't think they will ever really have a relationship with their parents. I think all of the kids from my school are like that, basically, because their parents work a lot of the time. They don't get attention from their parents, so they don't know what is

right and what is wrong." (Alison, age 13, Santa Monica, CA, who gets by with a personal trainer, driver, counselor and nutritionist)

The above passages are taken from Lauren Greenfield's book *Fast Forward, Growing Up in the Shadow of Hollywood.* Greenfield's book is a fascinating and unsettling photographic essay documenting the emulation of wealth, image, and celebrity among the youth of Southern California. In the preface, Greenfield says she set out to tell a story about her hometown of Los Angeles, but realized the story of the early loss of innocence in a media-saturated society was one that went beyond L.A. She writes:

Kids from suburban and urban areas, big cities and small towns alike, share a cultural (and often architectural) landscape of malls, chain stores, music, television and Internet information and chat that shapes their values and world view. Thanks to programs like Sex and the City *and their widespread popularity among teenagers, one doesn't have to grow up in Beverly Hills to know and desire Prada and Jimmy Choo.*

The adolescents and teens captured in Greenfield's gifted lens are appendages to adult values and lifestyles. One boy observes how his friends look older than their parents did as kids. Most of the children's parents are "getting divorced, been divorced, going through a divorce." Their kids are showered with gifts, clothes, jewelry, lavish ceremonies, and love, all at a distance. Tellingly, although they all emulate the adult image culture, none of these children say they want to be like their parents. This, perhaps, is the most uplifting and hopeful sign in a book that is otherwise an abject lesson in America's increasingly fixated worship of the superficial. The irony, of course, is that it is the redeeming good sense of our youth, not our adults, into which we must put our faith to lead the country out of its impending intellectual crisis.

Permissive parenting has flourished mainly as a result of the spread of the liberal "child-centered" model of child-rearing promoted by hosts of child psychologists such as Dr. Benjamin Spock following World War II. In her book, *Raising America: Experts, Parents and a Century of Advice about Children*, Ann Hulbert claims, "Post-War permissiveness stands out as a rare, brief moment when the 'soft' side reigned all but uncontested." Rare? Hulbert offers no real data to back her claim, and a host of anecdotal and statistical evidence lends support to the conclusion that the soft approach to child-rearing is still reigning supreme. Today, the soft approach has no political connotation, because it is used by parents who identify with both the left and right.

It is difficult to get a completely accurate handle on the extent of the abdication of traditional parenting duties in American society. There are gray areas, and many American parents do at least as much mentoring, with a very high set of expectations for their children, as generations of previous parents. Yet, obviously, the decline in problem-solving abilities, reading skills, and math performance among American students previously noted is anecdotal evidence that the roost, for the most part, is being left unattended. Teenage boys now play video games about thirteen hours a week and watch television for another twenty-five hours a week! Presumably, in order to get their homework done, they are becoming as proficient at multitasking as their parents. A 2001 *Time* magazine/CNN poll found that 80 percent of Americans believed their children were more spoiled than children ten to fifteen years ago. Thirty-five percent of parents said they were more permissive with their children than their parents had been, while 75 percent said children had fewer chores to do than kids did ten to fifteen years ago. Forty-eight percent of those polled said children have too much of a role in everyday family decisions.

As illustrated by the vignettes above, one palpable source of spoiling is the wealth of American society. America should have comfortable, guilt-free feelings about its affluence. As Abraham Lincoln once said, "I hold that the value of life is to improve one's condition." (There is at least one study that has found monetary reward improves critical thinking in a business.) Prosperity is good, but the values that produced it are better. Here, I'm not necessarily talking about extreme wealth, but the comfortable, three-car, five-bedroom affluence of middle, professional America. But the connection of the comfort and wealth of American society to academic standards, work, and expectations has, in the past, been impressed on children by parents, teachers, and other adults. Today the thread of that connection is seriously frayed. Moreover, it is clearly the adults, particularly the generation of baby-boomer parents, who have promoted, through either indifference or active encouragement, the shallow, image-obsessed, materialistic, anti-intellectual values and behavior widespread in society. Just as clearly, it will fall largely on the shoulders of parents and teachers to reinstitute standards and discipline upon which clear thinking skills, and America's standard of living, depends. Adults need to impress upon children the tenuous nature of the "good life." Children will indulge in fantasy if allowed to. Yet many kids seem to understand better than adults that the market for divas, supermodels, and pop stars is actually quite small.

It is widely recognized that children not only need standards and rules for healthy social, ethical, and intellectual development, they desire them. The relevance of standards and rules to the development of good critical-thinking skills lies in the role they play in teaching good work and study habits, nurturing an outlook that aspires toward excellence, and acquiring a wide, eclectic base of knowledge. Any standard is overlaid with a method of evaluation that confers or withholds approval, praise, reward. As a baby boomer, I came of age in an era where the paddle at home or the ruler at school was frequently used as a form of punishment. No, I am not advocating a return to corporal punishment. But in retrospect, fear of serious consequences for our actions did not eternally wound our psyches. I grew up in a typical working-class neighborhood in Flint, Michigan, on a street with an average of three to four kids per house. My dad was strict: Chores had to be done correctly, proper dress was required for visiting and other occasions, Bs and As were expected on report cards. I never wanted to quit a sport or activity I had joined of my own free will, but if I had I know there would have been some questions. It's not that my parents would have necessarily made me stay with it if I was miserable. But they would have wanted to know at a minimum, "Why?" Kids' interest in things is very often short-lived, and sometimes simply knowing their parents are curious encourages them to take risks and not give up at the first setback. All this may seem clichéd and terribly old-fashioned, but look at it this way: your kids, like you, dream. Have you achieved everything you wanted to? In some ways I wish my parents had been stricter. I think it's a very valuable, realistic lesson to teach your kids at a young age that nothing is easy or automatic (even though it looks like it is), and that to be good at even one thing is going to take them way more work and struggle than they ever imagined.

My dad's motto was the universal (there's a reason it's parodied) "If you're going to do something, do it right." I was not given the paddle when I screwed up (incurring one of my dad's lectures was scary enough), but many of my friends were. Curiously, I can never recall hearing any of my friends who were paddled speaking disrespectfully of their parents. The only person I remember consistently berating and mocking his parents was a friend whose dad tried to be his pal. His dad would tease him and call him a dummy, and he often referred to his dad as "fat Ed."

I make no claim to be a child psychologist, but it seems clear that in setting out to be mainly the child's friend or self-esteem coach a parent is surrendering his or her most important role in shaping a child's values and character—that of mentor, guide, and authority. In a traditional movie the hero always encounters a wise mentor who imparts special knowledge before he embarks on his journey—think of Obi-Wan Kenobi and Luke Skywalker in *Star Wars: A New Hope*. Writers have long realized that the psychological underpinnings of this storytelling device lie in the essential importance that the knowledge and experience of an older generation has for a younger one. Without wisdom and foreknowledge of the rules, the young apprentice is troubled by doubt, unable to act with confidence, liable to make bad decisions and be misled.

In acknowledging a decline in the standards and discipline children need for healthy development, perhaps, then, one of the first problems to confront is the unwillingness of many adults and parents to grow up. I'm not being flippant. What else is an unwillingness to use the natural power one has been given, for a good cause, other than a sign of immaturity?

I once went to hear Ralph Nader speak when I was in college. I don't remember much about the speech except his remark about college life being a period of "prolonged adolescence." The comment received loud applause and cheering, more in appreciation of this benefit of college than in agreement with his implied criticism. Nader's remark may have been prescient. Baby boomers are the first generation in mankind's history to be officially relieved of the onerous chore of growing old. We are going to burn out before we rust, baby, and more power to us, but we (and the Gen Xers on our heels) also need to take care of some business. Setting standards, being a role model, and being a demanding mentor can be rewarding, but it is also frequently burdensome. Kids may sulk and be visibly unhappy. Parents can feel their pain but know it's not going to kill them. By putting their wisdom to open, effective use, parents, in turn, may appear to others as stodgy and uptight and old as they really are. Understandably, this is not pleasant, but it is an experience our parents and a few thousand generations of humans have lived through and apparently found not entirely unfulfilling. The solace, I suppose, is the knowledge that one is doing the right thing *and* is still able to beat one's son in a game of one-on-one.

The fear of growing up, or fear of loss of a child's love and respect, or maybe just the path of least resistance, has led many parents to choose to be their child's friend rather than their guide and mentor. As is demonstrated by the mother who bought her thirteen-year-old son a Playmate poster for his room, the overwhelming concern of these parents is to make their children happy and build their "self-esteem." Naturally, such an approach focuses on providing kids with material pleasures and comforts rather than demanding that they meet high expectations and do the work required to do so. The net result is a generation of adults who have transformed the traditional meaning of the child-parent relationship by adopting the most lax and permissive parenting practices in the history of modern child-rearing.

In a CNN *Talkback Live* episode broadcast shortly after the 2001 *Time*/CNN poll was published, a number of participants rode to the defense of today's parenting methods and the children being fashioned by them. Some of the responses were enlightening. For instance, Wendy Coles, a Chicago correspondent who reported on the poll for *Time* magazine, when asked about parents' tendency to "consult" with their children rather than command, replied: "Yes, kids are not being told 'no' as often. But they're—the fact that they are listened to better and that there's a kind of emotional intelligence that this generation may be developing may mean this is not an entirely bad thing going on."

Thank you, Wendy. In other words, as long as parents promote emotional intelligence, socialization skills, and learning associated with sitting on one's butt and connecting with your feelings, don't worry, be happy. It is gratifying at least to hear someone make a direct connection between the predominant parenting methods of today and the type of intelligence, as it were, being nurtured. I'm sure the knowledge workers in Asia, India, and elsewhere around the globe will someday be happy to supply the critical and creative thinking for us, while our children handle the "emotional" side of business, government, and education, whatever that could be.

Another guest on the show, Shepherd Smith, with the Institute for Youth Development, attributed the alarmism over the poll to the "old days were always better" point of view. Says Smith, "I think you need to put this in perspective. Every generation thinks that the newer generation has more than they do or is spoiled. If you go back to the thirties and look at what was written about young adolescents then, they didn't have a work ethic, they were concerned about material things, and yet a few years later they came and saved the world from oppression and World War II."

If only things were as black and white today. Globalism has created a new social-political landscape in which no one is a clear enemy but everyone is in competition. The primary, the only, skill demanded in this competition is knowledge. What none of the CNN panelists apparently wished to pursue was the *measurable*, not merely perceived, differences, in the knowledge, aptitudes, and values between the present generation of young people and previous generations. As noted, problem-solving skills, reading comprehension, and math and writing skills have all declined relative to other industrialized countries. Furthermore, some college educators have noted a shift in the attitude of "Millennials" (people born after 1980) toward education and work, with the central expectations being assistance and the view that everything is negotiable. ("I'm on MSN, Mom, can I stay up twenty more minutes?") Claire Raines, who writes about generational differences, maintains that Millennials were raised by parents who "interceded on their behalf, challenged grades, negotiated with soccer coaches and visited college campuses with their charges." Leo Hoke, professor at the University of Tampa and author of the article "Teaching the Millennials: Do We Need a Paradigm Shift?" observes that when these students arrive on campuses they expect that the adults will bail them out when they make poor decisions.

> Dare to try to let your kids fail. Dare to say no. Dare to use punishment when your child misbehaves.

Whatever happened to the edict "Learn by doing"? A few years ago a widely aired commercial showed Michael Jordan shooting a basketball by himself in a gym. In a voice-over narrated by Jordan the viewer learns of all the thousands of shots he's *missed* and all the hundreds of games he's *lost*. The commercial, whose main purpose was to sell shoes, concluded with a punch line similar to "dare to try." Maybe the motto should apply to today's parents: Dare to try to let your kids fail. Dare to say no. Dare to use punishment when your child misbehaves. Dare to turn off the television. Dare to make them do chores. Dare to kick them off the computer and outside on a cold winter's day.

Dare to turn their world upside down and set the agenda. Author Robert Keegan supplies some superb gravitas for the strategy in his book *In Over Our Heads*.

> What . . . is missing is a child's need for parents who can exercise power on behalf of convictions, exert control, be righteously indignant, even express moral outrage (a virtue lauded by the Greeks and in woefully short supply at every level of American life). Power, authority, control are words that make most people uncomfortable, especially in a context such as parenting, which is first and foremost about love. But perhaps effective parental loving of a ten-year-old must include competent executive functioning, a child's sure sense that someone is in charge who believes in something and will stand up for those beliefs.

Giving kids boundless reassurance that they are good in order to boost their self-esteem is not an act of love—it is an act of sabotage. Sooner or later they will learn that, relative to the rest of the world, they are slower on their feet or not very musically talented or that their writing is abysmal. A parent shouldn't be discouraging of course, just realistic. A poor grade should be cause for analysis, not a sob story. Has the child done his or her homework? What exactly isn't he or she getting? A child is not always seeking encouragement and, if that is all he or she hears, soon begins to suspect the praise is hollow, as it is. Neither is letting a child set the agenda for use of time a modern incisive means of empowering a child and creating a sense of responsibility, as some parents seem to think. It is an act of indifference.

One of the biggest differences between the way children are raised today compared to boomers or even Gen Xers is that kids today spend significantly less time engaged in free play while growing up. The frequently overheard grumble "Kids don't play outside anymore" is not a flawed perception, it's a fact. According to one poll, 80 percent of parents think children spend less time playing outside than they did when they were young. One study cited in an article written by Joan Alman for the Waldorf Early Childhood Association of North America found that unstructured children's activities have declined by 50 percent in the last twenty years. A great deal of research over the years has found strong connections between creative play and the development of language and cognitive and adaptive reasoning skills. In an article titled "Play's the Thing" in *New Scientist,* evolutionary biologist Robert Barton of the University of Durham suggests that the stimulus of play is essential to the proper development of a large human brain: "I suspect it's to do with learning, and probably specifically with the importance of environmental input to the neo-cortex and cerebellum during development." If that's the case, why are children playing less? The most frequently cited culprits are computers, too much time devoted to structured activities, lack of play space, and (believe it or not) danger. There is in fact only one culprit: the disappearing or permissive parent.

Depending on when and where you grew up, you may recall a childhood filled with free play, and children playing with other children. In my neighborhood, kids congregated in the streets after dinner for pickup baseball games, kick-the-can, wheelie contests, rope skipping, skateboarding. We "camped out" in our backyards, dug for worms, and took long meandering bike rides to nowhere and back. We were better kids, right? No, we weren't. Our parents not only encouraged us to play, they threatened us with expulsion if we didn't. Houses were smaller then and kids got on parents' nerves. I remember my mother's emphatic words of encouragement, "I want you out of the house," and still see her running at me (don't worry, playfully) with a broom. In today's roomier houses parents are less likely to get bonked in the head by a wayward paraglider or trip over Barbie. Parents and children can conveniently ignore one another.

Play doesn't have to be outdoors, of course. Architect Frank Lloyd Wright has paid homage to "building blocks" and other hands-on arts and crafts he was exposed to in his youth as stimulating his interest in the design of solid shapes. Board games and activity sets to exercise the brain, the eyes, and the hands abound—we are living at the high point in civilization for the invention and design of ingenious new toys. But it seems to me today's children are most in danger of becoming detached from the "physicalness" of the outside world. Renowned Harvard biologist E. O. Wilson traces his desire to pursue a career as a scientist to his observation of ants as a child and his discovery of the insects' fascinating social order. The outdoors is a breathing space for the mind, a repository of the unknown and adventure. To me the outdoors is synonymous with expanded thought, lateral thinking, and the finding of hidden connections in life's innumerable puzzles. It is, in my view, essential to a healthy mind. Yet the typical American lifestyle is so constricted to indoors that even the sight of someone walking is a rarity. Kids are becoming shut-ins and recluses, living in a space defined by their rooms, the car, and shopping malls.

This not an accident. Parents have relinquished their right to intervene, not on behalf of their children to complain about cruel treatment at the hands of teachers, coaches, and others, but to demand things *of* their children. In the inner city, of course, many children have bigger problems than finding enough kids for a pickup baseball game. Recently, some African-American leaders have engaged in an unprecedented version of the "I dare you" challenge. They have dared to challenge the African-American community over the consequences arising from a lack of parental mentoring, discipline, and standards. Actor and comedian Bill Cosby pounced with pent-up rage on the topic in a speech to the NAACP convention in 2004.

> *I am talking about these people who cry when they see their son is standing there in an orange suit. Where were you when he was 2? Where were you when he was 12? Where were you when he was 18 and how come you didn't know that he had a pistol? And where is the father? . . . The church is only open on Sunday and you can't keep asking Jesus to do things for you. You can't keep saying that God will find a way. God is tired of you. . . . People with their hats on backwards, pants down around their crack, isn't that a sign of something or are you waiting for Jesus to pull his pants up. . . . Basketball players—multimillionaires, can't read a paragraph. Brown versus Board of Education: Where are we today? They paved the way, but what did we do with it? That white man, he's laugh-*

ing. He's got to be laughing: 50 percent drop out, the rest of them in prison.

I'm not laughing. In national media that practically print verbatim every word Jesse Jackson utters, I only wish Cosby's speech had received wider coverage; perhaps stirred a much-needed national debate. I have a personal perspective on Cosby's message. I once taught remedial math for a few hours a day in a prison in Miami. Ninety percent of the inmates were black. The government-run program was largely a game for them, a way to earn a little money and get out of their cell blocks a few extra hours each day. I soon realized that these were young men who had never had a father; who had literally been cast out into the street to fend for themselves at a very young age.

Fifty-odd years after Rosa Parks rode in the front of the bus, forty years after anti-discrimination laws, thirty years after the first affirmative action programs, the United States is still dealing with an epidemic of crime and poverty in African-American neighborhoods that is primarily a consequence of little or no parental guidance and poor education. As David Brooks observed in an article appearing in the *New York Times Magazine,* "People without skills really *do* have limited prospects." There is still no doubt about some of the institutional causes for this disparity, but as more educators, sociologists, and African-Americans themselves are coming to realize, the root of the problem is cultural. Improving the socioeconomic status of African-Americans rests on the shoulders of African-Americans themselves. A stable family unit is the primary way *all* children learn values, good work and study habits, and advanced moral reasoning and thinking skills.

Strong parenting is the essential ingredient in a child's success at school. The benefits provided by parents who are involved in their children's lives go beyond merely ensuring their kids do the homework. Caroline Hoxby of Harvard, for instance, has found compelling evidence that it is the role of the parents and their ability to influence who they associate with that is one of the most powerful factors in children's academic success. Children with friends who value academic success also tend to enjoy success in school.

Because of the key role parenting plays in academic success and the evolution of refined thinking skills, parents cannot continue with a business-as-usual approach if the country is to have any prospect of maintaining its current standard of living until the next century. Certainly, many parents may buy into the notion that they need to become better mentors to their children, but they aren't sure how to do it. Obviously, we live in a society in which authoritarian parenting has fallen out of favor. Authoritarian parenting, in which there is little or no discussion about decisions reached, has probably never been the "best" way to mentor a child. Highly effective mentoring, however, still requires a parent who is an authority; who acts authoritatively. The difference is subtle but important.

One study, conducted by Patrick Leman and Tanja Kragh-Muller at the University of London, suggests it may be a matter of style. When asked by a child for the reason he or she is being told "no," an authoritarian parent will respond, "Because I said so." An authoritative parent, on the other hand, will emphasize the equality of the moral universe: "You wouldn't like it if I did it to you." A permissive parent will focus on the consequences for others: "It will hurt her." The authoritarian parent gives no reason, so the child has no moral compass, other than his or her parent, to guide future behavior. The reasoning of the permissive parent involves taking the perspective of someone else, a feat usually lost on a five-year-old. Researchers found that permissive parenting does not promote moral development. The aspect of equality of right and wrong for everyone stressed in the reasoning of the authoritative parent is logical, even to a child. The researchers found that the techniques used by authoritative parents are associated with more advanced moral reasoning abilities in children.

Because it is the most logical method, emphasizing equal applications of all rules, authoritative parenting may get the best response from children, but it is also the most complicated. Using this approach, how can you demand your child watch less television if you are watching at least as much as he or she is? It sure wouldn't hurt adults to watch fewer hours of television. Yet, in a moral sense, adults have more "right" to indulge in certain activities not appropriate for their children. The adult is earning their and their children's keep, after all. The rules don't always apply equally. In this case the better fallback, in most cases, is an authoritarian stance.

The ends can sometimes justify the means. If, as parents often say, the measure of parenting success is a bright, intelligent, creative child who is ethically and morally responsible, then being mildly authoritarian may yield better results than being extravagantly permissive. The bottom line is to become a better mentor to your child, not a better friend. Parents cannot let children simply set their own agendas. Parents need to become reacquainted with the method of aggressive intervention. Here's a simple plan: Tell your kid things are going to change. And here's the first action item—taking control of the television and computer. If you, the adult, also watch too much television and can't assume the moral high ground, use the authoritarian approach with this logic: "If I had to start over, I'd change a lot of things. I want you to be better than me."

Your kids, as my mother used to say, will someday thank you.

MOST OF US have a recollection of a favorite teacher or two. The personalities and the styles of these educators differ but the one thing they all appear to have in common is a commitment to excellence. Some, like Robin Williams's character in the movie *Dead Poets Society*, can be inspirational. I was fortunate to have had such a teacher in sixth grade at St. John's elementary school in Fenton, Michigan—Mr. Smith. He was young, probably still in his twenties, and had come to teach at our little school after traveling around the world. His worldliness came through, not in an arrogant way, but in his sharp wit and easy, confident manner. I recall he had something of an edge. He was approachable, funny, even chummy, but if you crossed a certain line of respect he would cut you quickly down to size. He was dubious of all braggadocio, something quite common among sixth-grade boys. To earn even grudging praise you had to prove yourself. Still, whether we incurred his criticism or wrath we knew he was fair, smart, and cared about us. He would write out a weekly vocabulary list on the blackboard containing words such as "obfuscate" and "laconic," English we weren't aware existed. Under his tutelage we became reading fiends, competing with one another, tearing through a book or more a week. This was before Harry Potter, of course, when school libraries and children's book clubs did not carry many books written especially for, or about, the young. Our reading lists included H. G. Wells, Mark Twain, Robert Louis Stevenson, Hart Crane, Jules Verne, J. D. Salinger, and Ernest Hemingway. The days when we'd give oral book reports were like theater. Mr. Smith, pointer in hand at the back of the room, would toss out praise or criticism or an observation about life drawn from the book under discussion. He invited us to analyze and question. It was undoubtedly our first encounter with critical thinking, and how it can be used to tease out meaning and solve problems. He also encouraged us to seek knowledge for knowledge's sake. He would talk about Zen or Shakespeare, which would somehow lead into a lively discussion about the best pizza or a monologue on the night life of Chicago. We lived in a small town, but Mr. Smith taught us that learning could expand our world by an infinite number of degrees. He motivated us to be curious, to take risks, to open our eyes and stretch our minds beyond our commonsense, immediate perceptions. He taught us to study more than our own feelings.

Mr. Smith is a rarity and should probably not be used as a standard by which to judge good teachers. Many of my best teachers simply knew their subject, came to class prepared, and had a clear method of communicating and teaching the subject. I remember my junior-high algebra instructor building each lesson around the method for solving a particular type of equation. The method led us gradually into more difficult types of problems and taught us to recognize equations, and their possible solutions, by category, almost like using anatomy to identify animals. My high-school trigonometry and chemistry teachers used similar techniques. These are not easy subjects, but an organized, structured approach to teaching made them vastly more learnable and interesting.

Students (or for that matter, people) need structure to learn effectively and succeed. The human mind appears to need structure and organization in order to make sense of new information and ideas. Material has to be presented systematically, concepts defined, examples demonstrated and explained. All teachers know this, but fewer, it seems, are able to execute it. I once sat in on my daughter's French class. The teacher mentioned a few new words, wrote out a couple of haphazard sentences with the words, attempted some conversation with the class, went back to the board to illustrate the conjugation of a verb, and digressed into a story about her recent trip to France and a misunderstanding arising during a conversation with a waiter. No structure, no lesson plan, just sheer improvisation.

The predominance of the "seat-of-the-pants" method of teaching didn't happen overnight. It has been to a great extent institutionalized by the emphasis on "access" and egalitarian intelligence over excellence, by political and social forces, and by a decline in the percentage of teachers with a command of the topic they are teaching—a situation that may be mitigated by No-Child-Left-Behind requirements mandating that teachers of core academic classes be "highly qualified."

It would be unfair to vilify the entire contemporary teaching profession. Bad teachers existed thirty years ago, and there are many good teachers, from grades K through twelve, honestly earning their salaries in schools from coast to coast. Yet general disgruntlement about primary education in America has reached a new, shriller pitch. Declining math performance seems to be an especially sensitive indicator of the growth of socialized, nonrigorous teaching. Students taking the 2005 SAT exam scored slightly higher on math than students in previous years, but SAT scores over the past thirty years have shown a wide variation apparently linked to cohort changes. This, changes in the test content, and the select demographics of the testing group make the test an unreliable indicator of overall student performance. Instead, there is a growing consensus among businesspeople and educators that specific proficiencies in reading, writing, general knowledge, and math are in decline. "A number of us have come to believe that the biggest problem America has is the state of our schools," said Ed Broad, an entrepreneur and founder of the Broad Education Foundation, in an article appearing in the *New York Times*.

Teachers are not solely to blame. The nonstructured approach to teaching is reflected in today's textbooks. "Are you doing analytical geometry this year?" I asked my daughter in eleventh grade. "What's that?" It turns out she was, she just didn't know it. It wasn't her fault—there is no clear terminology identifying subject areas in her math textbook. Educators have apparently phased out many of these terms as too intimidating. The best way to describe the book, as well as most of her other science-related textbooks, is "viewer friendly" or "easy on the eyes." There is lots of color, a lot of pictures and graphs, and a lot of text boxes, but very little coherency in the presentation of material. Definitions, which should logically be given at the start of the chapter, are often skipped, or referred to in an appendix. The omission makes later discussion and development of trickier, technical concepts hazy, or outright nonsensical.

To know anything about how textbooks are created, published, and purchased by school boards is to know one thing: It is a process permeated by politics. Generally, the production of a textbook is overseen by a committee of professional educators. Every educator has his or her hobby horse but the overall trend had been to emphasize full, egalitarian access to the subject matter of all students of all aptitudes, genders, races. To obfuscate the process even further, many teachers or educators involved in the production of a textbook, or in deciding which textbook to use, are not professional mathematicians or biologists or linguists—they're educators. I encourage parents to get involved with their parent-teacher associations and local school boards and investigate how decisions are made regarding which textbooks are used in their schools, and why.

One of the most common and disturbing revelations for parents today, one that adults frequently find themselves consoling one another over, is how little their kids actually know. Several friends of mine were shocked to find out, by probing, that their otherwise bright daughters who would soon be entering high school did not know multiplication tables or long division. Calculators, the reasoning goes, have apparently become the student's mind for carrying out these computations. (Many parents apparently find it difficult to argue against the logic of the calculator, not understanding, perhaps, that these basic math skills provide students with a mental "feel" for doing arithmetic, sort of in the same way practicing musical scales creates strength and touch on an instrument.) A plausible root cause of the "know-nothing" phenomenon is not dumber kids, but a gradual, continual dilution of course content in order to "level the playing field" and appease pleas for egalitarian education. One website posting titled "Why Johnny Can't Add" tells of a high-school science teacher who gave his ninth-grade class a math test taken by third graders in 1932. Only 25 percent of his class answered all ten questions correctly. Math isn't the only curriculum receiving cosmetic surgery in our schools. The grammar folder of many English teachers has either been dropped into the recycle bin or is taught so hastily as to be effectively useless. The vast majority of high-school students wouldn't know the difference between an active and a passive sentence, or a regular and an irregular verb, if it popped out of a Gucci handbag. For proof, make a mental note every time you hear a teenager utter the usage "If we had *went* to the concert." College professors and employers can only shudder at the prospect of reviewing the reports and memos this grammar-challenged generation will soon be writing.

Writing in *Forbes*, Ben Stein provides a derisive summary of knowledge dilution and its adverse effect on American competitiveness, the gist being, says Stein, that we are already headed this way:

> *Do not expect students to know the basics of mathematics, chemistry and physics. Working closely with the teachers'*

*unions, make sure that you dumb down standards so that chil-
dren who make the most minimal effort still get by with flying
colors. Destroy the knowledge base on which all of mankind's
scientific progress has been built by guaranteeing that such
learning is confined to only a few and spread ignorance and
complacency among the many. Watch America lose its scientific and competitive edge to other nations that make comprehensive knowledge base a rule of society.*

Stein's rant is not all ultraconservative bluster. Just as a
family's wealth and prosperity can vanish within a generation,
history has shown that a nation's affluence and power can
erode quite quickly, certainly in less time than it takes to re-
educate an entire generation. But how do we go about making
a comprehensive knowledge base a foundation of American
society?

There is no lack of ideas and grand schemes for enhancing
America's K–12 educational system. In 2003, private dona-
tions and grants to elementary and secondary schools totaling
$1.23 billion exceeded the $1.1 billion granted to higher education, a significant turnaround. One of the largest founda-
tions, the Bill and Melinda Gates Foundation, is investing
hundreds of millions of dollars in K–12 education each year,
with one special focus on converting large high schools into a
multiplicity of smaller schools. The Michael and Susan Dell
Foundation, with assets of more than $1 billion, has donated
large amounts of money to Teach for America, which places
recent college graduates as teachers in classrooms at urban
and rural schools. The No Child Left Behind law, signed in

2002, expands standardized testing and disciplines schools when lower-performing students fail to make sufficient progress. (Some have suggested the law be called No Child Gets Ahead, as it could work to hold back bright and gifted students.) Other ideas include the use of vouchers to enhance the competitiveness and thus the performance of public schools, as is done in Florida's A+ Program; longer school years and days; and merit pay for teachers.

Many of these initiatives are well intentioned, and some, Florida's A+ Program, for instance, appear to be producing tangible improvements in educational performance. But the one idea with the potential to really shake things up and deliver the best results over the long term is not so much practical as it is philosophical: re-establishing excellence as the primary goal of our educational institutions. This is not just a mission statement or a simplistic, meaningless platitude. It basically requires a generational shift in the attitudes and policies in education and child development that have come to predominate in American society. These are permissiveness, a persistent diluting of standards and content, and the embrace of egalitarian education, rather than excellence, as the foundation and informing philosophy of schooling. Making the pursuit of excellence the norm will require grass-roots buy-in from teachers, government, and parents.

If the country is to reach this consensus about the philosophical aims of education, we first need to debunk the myth that striving for excellence means leaving kids behind or limiting access. Carolyn Reid-Wallace, a member of the Boyer Commission on Undergraduate Learning, writes:

The sort of defeatism that makes some people reluctant to en-
force high academic standards is premised on a false di-
chotomy between access and excellence. Specifically, many
assume that achieving excellence requires limiting access for
low income and minority children, and that providing access
requires compromising excellence. These people are wrong. Ac-
cess and excellence are in no way antithetical—they represent
two noble goals that are both worthy of our best efforts.

In the book *Habits of Mind*, William B. Allen, a professor of political science at Michigan State University, along with Carol Allen, a researcher, suggest that the forces of political correctness and the advocates of multiculturalism have had their way for so long that society's first instinct is to accommodate rather than challenge or provoke. In the authors' view, it will ultimately be up to individuals, specifically teachers and parents, to change these long-entrenched attitudes and wean ourselves from the permissive easy button: "Have we bothered to ask our children to do more? To rise to the greatest challenges?" The authors say experience shows that the young almost invariably respond to direct requests to perform at high levels. "One must rather, and quite literally, put before them the large ambition, if one wants the joy of seeing their souls expand."

The mission isn't encompassed by the comforting adage, "Do the best you can." There are new demands and a new accountability in this arrangement. The approach was illustrated in an episode of the nineties sitcom *The Cosby Show* in which Cosby's character, Cliff Huxtable, confronts his son over poor grades. The son pleads for his dad to accept him for who he is, but Huxtable will have none of it: "That's the dumbest thing I've heard and it's no wonder you get Ds in everything. Here's what's going to happen: You're going to study, work your hardest, and you're going to do that because I say so." (Evidently an authoritarian, rather than an authoritative, stance is better suited for the time constraints placed on sitcom dialogue.) Once parents begin to assert their right to high expectations, rather than defer to the lowest common denominator set by their child's peers or self-image, an immediate fresh order is established. There is an outside, immovable force introduced into the equation. Everything is not negotiable. It's true that people generally react positively to the laying out of clear ground rules and directly stated expectations not open to appeal. This may be because, despite three decades of listening to assorted gurus sing the praises of the empowerment movement, humans innately prefer structure over chaos. As Chris Argyris observes in the article "Empowerment: The Emperor's New Clothes," published in the *Harvard Business Review*, "Both research and practice indicate that the best results of reengineering (a change management program embodying empowerment) occur when jobs are rigorously specified and not when individuals are left to define them."

This new order also places demands on parents. As documented in a *Time* magazine cover story, "Parents Behaving Badly," more parents are boorishly acting out Blitzkrieg-type fantasies to counteract any perceived threat to their child's self-esteem. The article reveals that today's teachers must spend a great deal of their time consulting with intrusive parents who aim to influence the social dynamics of the classroom. There is, for instance, the elementary-school teacher in

Tennessee who must contend with parents who insist, in writing, that their children never be reprimanded or corrected:

> When she started teaching 31 years ago, she says, "I could make objective observations about kids without parents getting offended. But now we handle parents a lot more delicately. We handle children a lot more delicately. They feel good about themselves for no reason. We've given them this cotton-candy sense of self with no basis in reality. We don't emphasize what's best for the greater good of society or even the classroom."

This is in keeping with observations made earlier in this book that political maneuvering and egalitarian intelligence have displaced commonly held standards and empirical results as the primary "values" of American society. There's a common suspicion that no one is accountable, everyone cheats, and all success is the result of privilege, favoritism, or luck. The ultimate expression of this contempt for success and a denial of variation in experience is the common rejoinder, "Been there, done that." Been where and done what? Has anyone come close to ticking off all the boxes of this mythic universal checklist? Self-fulfillment and self-esteem have to be based on tangible results. Parents need to desist from acting only in the short-term interest of their children. In order to build real, lasting self-esteem in a kid, parents must allow a child a chance to fail.

Authority in the classroom must be taken out of the hands of parents or the government and returned to the teacher. In turn, there needs to be new emphasis on subject content, as well as clear structure and organization in teaching methods. In order to accommodate different learning abilities and promote excellence, schools should re-establish student "streaming" in earlier grades. Kids in my fourth-grade class were grouped into three different reading levels, and, as far as I know, no one developed a disability later in life as a result.

Finally, parents must understand that education only *begins* in school. Even the best of teachers has only a few hours a day with your child. As well, the naked truth is that much learning and knowledge in life is obtained outside school, through experience and self-study. The home must become an environment for continual, lifelong learning. This is inevitably a personal choice, of course. There are many ways to influence the growth of your children and enhance their (and your) knowledge, powers of reasoning, and critical-thinking skills. Each child has different strengths and weaknesses, a different personality. There is no master plan that would work for everyone. It is clear, however, that no child can benefit from watching five hours of television every evening or playing video games all day. Indeed, polls have found that Americans of all political stripes are concerned about the amount of time their children spend on TV and computer games. Yet books such as Steven Johnson's *Everything Bad Is Good For You* and Richard Keller Simon's *Trash Culture* have become sacred texts to those people, young and old, who suspect an age-old disapproval of any new cultural trend, not anything truly harmful, lies behind this finger-wagging. Johnson's book, for instance, argues that densely plotted TV comedies and intricate and complex video games stimulate and enrich our minds. The implication is that kids raised in this virtual environment will be no less educated or prepared to lead a fulfilling life than previous generations. The logic is faulty and easily refuted. Television comedies are certainly better written than they once were, but are still nothing more than character studies. They may, as *The Cosby Show* illustrates, provide us with a few "lessons on life," but they tell us little about the *nature* of love or jealousy, and have nothing to say about the effects of wider society—religion, science, politics, economics—on individuals. They are passive entertainments and do nothing to enhance our creativity or improve our reasoning, the two central features of our humanity. Video games may indeed test a person's ability to memorize and even think laterally, yet ultimately the only thing a video game teaches a child is to play video games.

THIS ARGUMENT and the other suggestions offered in this chapter may be taken as possible fixes in themselves, or as starting points in a debate leading to some changes and adjustments in the way people live. For it has to be honestly admitted that in order to have any hope of preparing our children to thrive in a global, knowledge economy there must be change. The point is hammered home by the observations of an Australian-born professor at a midwestern university. "My impression of American students is not that they lack the skills of critical thinking but that they often aren't exposed to a wide enough variety of intellectual challenges to hone their skills. This is less a problem at an Ivy League school . . . but when I visit local high schools I really feel as if the kids know nothing except a very small world of real experience and an increasingly inane world of TV experience." Knowledge is the only means people have to expand their horizons beyond the boundaries of the media-marketing culture and their own experience. The effort must start at home. Yet too often we are hamstrung from changing not only by habit, but by idiocy masquerading as enlightened views. Not everything old is better. Some things, such as learning to read, play a musical instrument, write, or do math, have no old way or new way, only a right way.

This is more than a hunch.

CHAPTER 10

Stretching the Horizon:
Embracing Risk and Reward

It seems like only yesterday, I gazed through the glass
At ramblers, wild gamblers, that's all in the past.

—STEELY DAN, "DEACON BLUES"

Two women were chatting over coffee and cake one afternoon, when a bubbling thirteen-year-old, the daughter of the host, walked into the room. The visiting woman inquired about her friends, interests, activities. The young girl perked up: "This year," she said, "I want to take a kickboxing course." The visitor looked alarmed. "I don't think that's a good idea," she said. She had heard of a kid who had been seriously injured while kickboxing. Not only that, but she had been told by a person in sports medicine that young girls in kickboxing are susceptible to leg-joint injuries— something to do with the ligaments and tendons. The girl's bubble deflated noticeably. After a moment, she excused herself and went quietly to her room.

Sometimes it seems we know too much. Fortunately, with reassurance from her parents (whom I know intimately) and pluck of her own, the girl has pursued her kickboxing career, wherever it will take her. Yet the story illustrates a pattern well known to everyone. We live in the age of worry, doubt, and high anxiety. Growing numbers of people spend more sleepless nights fretting about every perceived and imagined threat conceivable. September 11 often gets blamed, but the sophistication of public anxiety surpassed terrorist attacks and stock market doodles a long time ago. A recent article in the *New York Times* reports that owners of multimillion-dollar houses in a rural area near San Francisco are "terrified," trapped inside their homes, and paralyzed with apprehension over a few sightings of mountain lions in their area. I know of parents who canceled horse-riding lessons for their son after reading about a serious accident on the other side of the country. The billion-dollar bottled-water industry is a direct beneficiary of irrational fear that public drinking water is not safe.

Got a fear? Are there things you haven't thought of that you should be fearing? A single Web search will provide a person with more fears, and even the peer-reviewed research, to bolster their repertoire: fear of Iraq, fear of derivatives, fear of globalization, fear of China, fear of freedom, fear of oversight, fear of first strike, fear of India, fear of commitment, fear of outsourcing, fear of forgiving, fear of exclusion. This list of fears, and countless others, can be summarized with a twist on that hangdog law of Murphy's—anything that might be feared, will be feared.

If all this worry were merely creating more people with cautious and paranoid outlooks, maybe we could just learn to live with hosts of silly beliefs and superstitions. Unfortunately, it is also making people stupid. It is making people more emotional, less empirical. It is making people more susceptible to feelings of stress and information overload. It is making people more addicted to television and movies for their views and ideas. It is an overweening anxiety that is turning otherwise intelligent people into pawns of marketers and passive consumers of "received" knowledge and dogma of all colors. The fix is to apply a fundamental correction in the way society has come to communally view risk and danger inherent in all aspects of life.

We also need to embrace risk. By this I don't necessarily mean taking up bungee jumping, although this could be an option. I mean stepping outside one's comfort zone. This is a cliché, a good one I think, but let me be more exact. To embrace risk is to engage in an activity not in keeping with one's self-defined or default identity. If a person is one of those naturally cerebral types, a risky activity might be learning to fix small engines or enrolling in a line dancing course. If a person is extroverted and always on the go, a risky activity might be to take up watercoloring or bird watching. There are universal fears, but very often fear is attached to a risk that operates at a very personal level.

A long time ago people built walled cities and forts to keep the things they feared—torture, rape, murder—at a safe distance. Today we build walls around ourselves and others under our influence in order to hedge our bets against threats so insub-

It is no coincidence that fear is flourishing in the age of emotion and intuition.

stantial and infinitesimally improbable they are effectively nonexistent. It is no coincidence that fear is flourishing in the age of emotion and intuition. Unfounded fears and worries are a direct consequence of emotional profligacy. Critical thinking is essential to reining in or understanding our emotions and breaking down those self-limiting walls people have built. Not only is critical thinking needed to rationally assess and understand risk, but accepting a certain amount of risk is a prerequisite for vigorous critical and creative thinking.

Assessing risk and understanding risk are two different mental tasks. Assessing risk usually involves the use of statistical methods to arrive at an estimate of the probability of an event—a sickness, an accident, hitting the lottery jackpot—occurring. Evaluating risk has largely been taken over by professionals armed with models and computers, and risk assessment and risk management are two burgeoning professions of our time. Scores of government agencies such as the Environmental Protection Agency and the Food and Drug Administration routinely conduct risk assessments in order to regulate, for instance, the emissions from a car's tailpipe, or types of materials allowed in food packaging. The overwhelming trend in this type of risk assessment over the past thirty years has been to reduce estimated risks to the public to lower and lower levels, often at a huge expense. (For instance, since air pollution regulations were passed in the 1970s, overall air quality has improved by 29 percent, even though U.S. population has increased by 36 percent and vehicle miles traveled increased by 143 percent.) Many people applaud this, insisting the cost is worth the benefit. But there is one whopper of a kicker, and that is that risk cannot be eliminated. At some completely arbitrary level, one part per million of a chemical, one chance in ten thousand of getting sick from a drug, we must cut and run and decide that "this" is an acceptable level of risk. We or, more exactly, government officials elected on our behalf, acknowledge that the benefits of doing something are worth some potential risks attached to the action.

Risk, therefore, is all around us, and while we may not be able to calculate it to the fifteenth decimal place, we need to understand it. When a person says, "the chances of getting hit by lightning are greater than the chances of winning the lottery," we understand intuitively that the probability of taking home the jackpot is very, very small. We know this because we know from experience that very few people get hit by lightning. Nonetheless, even though it is understood that winning is highly unlikely, many millions of people buy lottery tickets every week. Now consider the people in California locked up in their homes because of mountain lion sightings in the area. Wildlife experts say the hysteria is unjustified and the odds of getting killed in an attack are roughly the same as the odds of being struck by lightning. Same odds, totally different results. In one case, playing the lottery, the odds or risk has no influence over people's decisions; in another, the threat from a mountain lion, the same level of risk causes massive modification of people's behavior and lifestyle.

This is nonsensical. The common explanation for this discrepancy is that there is little downside (investment of a few dollars) to ignoring the small odds of winning the lottery, and a potentially huge upside, instant retirement. Paying heed to the remote chances of getting attacked by a mountain lion, on the other hand, provides a large potential upside (avoiding death) and a minor downside, confinement to one's house. Yet, another way of looking at it is that the downsides in both cases have been underestimated. In ignoring the small odds of winning the lottery, people throw away hundreds, if not thousands of dollars a year. If a person instead invested that money over the course of a thirty-year working career, he or she could have hundreds of thousands of dollars more to make early retirement an imminent possibility. On the other hand, in submitting to feelings of terror and radically modifying one's behavior to avoid the faint chance of being attacked by a mountain lion, one succumbs to a sort of voluntary prison of worry, doubt, and distraction that saps one's physical and intellectual energies. One sacrifices a part of one's life.

Traditionally, policymakers, companies, and individuals have been fixated on the social and economic costs associated with risk—for example, cleaning up a chemical spill.

Today, growing numbers of people realize there are profound psychic and social costs associated not only with risk, but with fear and the power it has over people's views, thinking, and behavior. Observing how, even in a relatively healthy economy, hardly a day passes without news of some dire financial indicator, writer Roger Lowenstein notes that "in limiting risk, people also miss the opportunity for gain." The principle can be applied generally to life, as well as the stock market. In a 2003 research paper, Matthew D. Adler at the University of Pennsylvania Law School proposed that regulatory agencies incorporate "fear assessment" into their analyses. Noting that fear and anxiety are welfare-reducing mental states, Adler writes, "I propose, concretely, that the methodology currently used to quantify and monetize light physical morbidities, such as headaches, coughs . . . should be extended to fear." He admits to being puzzled by "the virtual absence of economics scholarship on the pricing of fear and anxiety, by contrast with the vast literature in environmental economics on pricing other intangible benefits such as existence of species, wilderness preservation."

The proposal seems entirely reasonable. If scientists and regulators can use models to quantify and estimate human costs arising from changes to the physical environment, why not assess costs resulting from large-scale changes to the human psychological environment? Surely panic and fear have social and economic costs, as when people cancel vacation plans for fear of being bitten by a mosquito infected with the West Nile Virus. Perhaps if we attempt to quantify these costs we can better understand the sources of fear and seek to mitigate those sources, just as we seek to mitigate risk. If we can have experts in risk-management practices, why not professional fear-management analysts and consultants?

A current commercial for the ABC television show *Night Stalker* provides an ironic perspective on fear by asking, "What if everything we fear . . . is real?" In a way it is. Murder is real. Rape is real. Hurricanes and tsunamis are real. Even the possibility of getting attacked by a mountain lion is real. The sum totality of the things we have to fear has not really changed; our consciousness of them has increased. As a result, I believe, fear unbounded has become one of the most pernicious threats to the American way of life. The phenomenon isn't unique to American society—it's a worldwide trend. I'm not talking about security checks. I'm referring to an attitude that has sunk into our soul, which, by all outward appearances, is rapidly turning us into a society with zero tolerance for risk of any amount. The principle is manifesting itself both at a personal level, in the choices people make, and at the level of society and culture: My daughter's chemistry set has no chemicals. Today's typical playground is a padded and roped safe-trail with ramps and tight enclosures leading children from point A to point C with no chance they'll hang from or fall off at point B. No monkey bars, no high, fret-inducing slides. Small wonder kids prefer the virtual environment of a computer—at least you can take chances and puzzle your way out of tight jams in this created world. There can, in fact, be no adventures, intellectual or otherwise, without risk. As we systematically attempt to tune down risk, we also inadvertently begin to tune down the chance of achievement, progress, and discovery. As Virginia Postrel writes in her book *The Future and Its Enemies*:

> But in many areas of life, both trial and error—the freedom to experiment and the ability to fail—have been undermined by stasists uncomfortable with the inevitable risks such an evolutionary system entails. Disapproval of risk taking permeates our culture and shapes our law. Sometimes we forbid taking risks. Sometimes we spread the consequences from the risk taker to others. Either way, we squelch the learning that is essential to progress.

Because this outlook has become entrenched, the question of how to apply a fix or fixes is made more complicated. Tort reform and the reduction or elimination of lawyer contingency fees would certainly help stem the litigious strongarming producing risk-adverse policies and organizations. But ultimately the choices and corrections we make, if any, will work at a personal level. There are things we can do. In order to arrive at a more reasonable, realistic view of risk and danger, it seems we first need to confront the source or causes of exaggerated fear. This will allow us to see if or how we have erred in our views, and consider if there is any approach that will allow us to tune down our sensitivity to the risks inherent in life and modern society. Second, we need to understand *why* it's important to manage and control our outlook toward risk; to realize what we stand to gain by changing—namely, a mind cleared of needless distractions and a life that is more engaged, dynamic, and effective.

In September 2005 the public was hypnotized by graphic images of the carnage inflicted by Hurricane Katrina on the city of New Orleans. Single-word headlines "chaos" and "anarchy" were plastered in oversize print on the front of newspapers. News footage of people in shock, homeless, or trapped on their roofs above rising flood waters was being beamed around the world. Thousands were missing, with many of those believed to be dead. The catastrophe seemed a confirmation of everyone's deepest, darkest fears; an unsettling demonstration of the dark power of nature and tenuous character of not only life, but our security. As Katrina showed, nature is powerful and often unkind. But the catastrophe was ultimately set in motion, not merely by nature, but by the decisions of humans—for instance, the design of a system of levees capable of containing a tidal surge generated by a hurricane not in excess of a category 3 storm. Katrina was a category 4 storm. The risk was not unknown. An article published in *Scientific American* in 2001 called New Orleans "a disaster waiting to happen." The article told about modeling done by researchers at Louisiana State University predicting that a category 4 storm like Katrina crossing the Gulf of Mexico from the southeast could flood the city under twenty feet of water in thirty-three hours, which is pretty much exactly what happened. The level of risk was completely understood and the risk was "managed" at this level. In hindsight, of course, it seems obvious that the storm defenses of a city below sea level in an area frequented by giant tropical storms should be managed at a "worst-case scenario" level, sort of the way in which a bridge is engineered to withstand a maximum load, with a safety factor thrown in for good measure.

We generally don't worry when we drive over bridges. In the same way, a true understanding of what happened in New Orleans shouldn't make us more apprehensive about risks and dangers, it should make us less so. If there were no explanation, fear would be warranted. The reason we can put the vast majority of fears out of our mind is that humans have become adept at using critical thinking and ingenuity to anticipate, abate, and eliminate most risks. As New Orleans shows, errors in *judgment* can be made. But the disaster is also a demonstration and proof of this book's thesis: Critical thinking depends on analysis and logic, and *action*. It's a two-step process. Researchers, engineers, and government officials knew this could happen, and probably would happen, eventually. But all the thinking, modeling, and analysis aren't worth a damn unless acted upon. And this was a model based not on hosts of built-in, unproven assumptions and conjectures about the future, but one based on known, measurable events that happened quite frequently in the past. A breakdown in critical thinking, lack of a plan, wavering, indecisiveness, at a crucial moment, can have devastating consequences. People, managers, team leaders, organizations, and government officials have to think hard, and then put their thoughts into action.

Many fears, of course, are natural. For survival reasons, the human body is hardwired with a certain number of phobias—heights, snakes, and closed spaces are some of the more common things dreaded by people. But how do we "know" to fear public drinking water or DDT or bioengineered foods? The answer is that we learn these fears. As Richard Lovett reports in an article appearing in *Psychology Today*, "Experience and culture also teach us what to fear . . . we're more afraid of catastrophic events such as airplane crashes than of everyday risks like cancer. It's partly a matter of media coverage that makes the danger appear greater than it is . . . the result is a certain degree of illogical behavior." Lovett posits that this learning process has inclined us to be more fearful of man-made risks, such as pollution and terrorism, than of, say, snakes, because we rarely encounter snakes in modern life. In the case of anxiety about flying, fear of heights may combine with the memory of grisly descriptions of plane crashes to create this "illogical" emotional reaction. In the United States only one out of 1.6 million airline passengers die in accidents each year, compared to one death for every 6800 drivers in the same period.

The fear of the banned pesticide DDT is a good illustration of how our perception of the danger or risk of a man-made chemical is shaped by culture and learning. DDT was first used on a large scale during World War II to protect American troops from insect-borne diseases such as typhus and malaria. Testing on DDT conducted by the United States Public Health Service showed no serious human toxicity problems, and in this respect, the chemical was a vast improvement over arsenic-based pesticides, which were truly hazardous to humans. After the war DDT was used to eradicate malaria from the southern United States. The World Health Organization credits DDT with saving as many as 100 million lives—for instance, in 1943 Venezuela had over eight million cases of malaria; by 1958, after the use of DDT, the country reported only eight hundred. Unfortunately, DDT had an unanticipated side effect: In the 1960s researchers linked exposure to DDT with eggshell thinning in some bird species, such as eagles and falcons. This finding was documented in Rachel Carson's book *Silent Spring*, and in 1972 the U.S. EPA banned DDT. Carson is lauded, rightly, for helping to prevent the possible extinction of these magnificent birds of prey. However, Carson's declamations about DDT went beyond its effects on wildlife; she also argued the chemical was killing people. In an article, "Silent Spring at 40," published on Reasononline, Ronald Bailey observes, "Carson improperly cited cases of acute exposures to the chemical as proof of its cancer-causing ability. . . . The plain fact is that DDT has *never* been shown to be a human carcinogen even after four decades of intense scrutiny."

Silent Spring helped launch the modern environmental movement, but it also ushered in the practice of using wishy-washy science to make untenable claims about risks to health and the environment posed by human activity. It created the perception that the earth is literally stewing in poisons, and in particular inculcated a widespread fear of all technology—for instance, encouraging the belief that any man-made chemical is highly toxic or a potential carcinogen. The fears have no basis in reality. For example, Bruce Ames, a professor of cell and molecular biology at the University of California, Berkeley, has found that humans ingest about ten thousand times more natural pesticides (chemicals that plants produce naturally to thwart infestation), by weight, than man-made pesticides. Furthermore, in one study, twenty of forty-two plant toxins tested on laboratory animals were carcinogenic. Nonetheless, researchers have found eating fruits and vegetables is good for people. Ergo, plant toxins pose no health risk, and man-made pesticide residues, even less.

In 1999, Dr. Ames was awarded the National Medal of Science for his work. I am willing to bet at least 50 percent of Americans have heard of Rachel Carson or *Silent Spring*, whereas it would require fortunate circumstances (a biology symposium) to locate fifty people who have heard of Bruce Ames. Carson's precept, that of deadly chemicals invisibly poisoning the environment, is of course populist and plays better in the media. Ames's findings, which are upbeat and let chemical companies off the hook, do not draw as well. Not all environmental threats trumpeted by green groups and the media are bogus, of course. I am all for protecting the environment and I also have a background in science. I think I can stake a reasonable claim to objectivity. In my view, however, environmentalism, in the hands of well-meaning but misled or addled people, has become one of the fundamental sources in the propagation of irrational and unfounded fears in society. As well, it is not biased to say that the worst cases of unscientific, environmental extremism can be traced to people and organizations identified with the political left. The development is one of the most unfortunate developments in the history of critical thinking. As Bettina Lange and Gerard Strange observe in an article published in *Capital and Class*, "Recently it has often been environmental issues—rather than more 'traditional' labour or even, for that matter, feminist struggles—which have energized especially younger people into political activity, and this activity is more likely to be inspired by anarchism than Marxism." This is because even the great collectivist himself didn't dispute the primacy of either the needs of mankind or rational, critical thinking over emotion. Today, public belief in both of these premises is tenuous at best. In essence, the environmental movement, in the guise of imagined, statistically insignificant or unprovable risks, has politicized reason and science. Because the environment is "good," it has become politically incorrect to rationally question not only the science, but the costs of environmental extremism for the economy, society, or human psychology.

This self- or societal censure comes through in Barry Glassner's best-selling book, *The Culture of Fear*. Glassner boldly posits in the book's introduction that "false and overdrawn fears only cause hardship." He believes that "Americans are afraid of the wrong things." What are these things and how did we come to believe them? Glassner observes how a fixation on crime by local news stations around the country (captured by the producer's dictum "If it bleeds, it leads") has led many Americans to think crime is rampant, when statistics, such as youth homicide rates, show it has fallen dramatically. Glassner makes numerable insightful and entertaining observations about the fear industry, but as for taking the air out of the mother of all fears, the fear that started the contemporary fear epidemic, the fear that has driven a political wedge into reasoning and science, the fear, that is, that we are being destroyed by reckless environmental practices, Glassner assumes the mien of a Teddy bear with a popgun. He doesn't touch it, actually. There is not one mention of an environmental scare in his book. Obviously, Glassner thinks this is the right thing to be afraid of. This implies, at least at face value, that Glassner believes most environmental scares are real. Off the top of my head I can name four widely publicized, environmentally related health scares—the use of the pesticide Alar on apples, secondhand smoke, the effects of electromagnetic radiation from overhead power transmission lines, and the alleged toxicity of PCB chemicals used in some electronic equipment— that have never been validated by any peer-reviewed research.

Fear causes flaws in our perceptions, which leads to erroneous thinking and conclusions. For instance, a study conducted by the EPA found that the public's top environmentally related health concerns included radioactive waste, radiation from nuclear accidents, industrial pollution of waterways, and hazardous waste sites. Yet, when the EPA polled its own experts it got an entirely different list of concerns.

Radioactive waste and radiation from nuclear accidents were not even ranked, and some of the public's lowest concerns, for example indoor air pollution, were ranked "high" by experts. The EPA concluded that there was an extraordinary disparity between the views of the public and the views of its own experts.

Many fears, of course, are not based on evidence or rational methods. Rather than disregard these perceptions, some social scientists have argued that public policies and regulations with respect to risk should incorporate them. The gist of this argument appears to be that policy/law based strictly on science is "elitist." Paul Slovik, professor of psychology at the University of Oregon, urges sympathy with populist views, arguing that ordinary people are not irrational or confused, compared with experts, but possess a type of "rival rationality" worthy of respect. Risk, Slovik maintains, is not simply a matter of numbers, and a well-designed system of risk regulation should have democratic as well as technocratic elements. In other words, policy experts, lawyers, and government regulators should allow the public's intuitive, Blinklike judgments and fears about complex technological issues to prevail and guide their thinking in risk regulation. As Cass Sunstein suggests in his paper "Laws of Fear," the approach is tantamount to institutionalizing fantasy in law and jurisprudence:

Because of the predictable features of human cognition, people's intuitions are unreliable, and they are prone to blunder about facts. As we have seen, these blunders have harmful consequences for regulatory policy. To be effective, regulators

*must be aware of perceived risk, not only actual risk. But for
purposes of policy, what is most important, most of the time, is
actual risk rather than perceived risk.*

What ultimately counts is not whether a certain activity,
flying, for instance, is perceived as risky or dangerous because
it is dreaded, involuntary, or outside one's personal control;
what matters, at a both personal and societal level, is the probability of harm from that activity. If people based their decision to fly or not fly on their intuitive feelings, hardly anyone
would fly and the airlines would go broke. Most people are
able to overcome the intuitive fear of flying because of the
large amount of empirical evidence proving flying is safe. If
regulators insisted airlines use the public's intuitive gut feelings about flying as their guide for safety procedures, every
plane would receive a two-hundred-point inspection by a mechanic before flying, making today's gridlock at O'Hare look
like a feat of logistical efficiency. The same principles apply in
safeguarding people from terrorism. How much security is effective, and how much simply excess?

Perhaps all that some people need to overcome their fears
is a practical nuts-and-bolts primer to the universe of risk. In
this case I recommend *Risk: A Practical Guide for Deciding
What's Really Safe and What's Dangerous in the World Around
You,* by David Ropeik and George Gray. In order to become
risk takers and better thinkers, however, I think we ultimately
need to recognize the source of our magnified fears and suspi-
cions. In Chapter 6, I outlined the role the media play in creating fearful perceptions of the world. The media also provide
us with useful information and help keep government and

business honest, so we have to give them credit. Yet, whether they do so inadvertently or blatantly, the media are still the key source of all that feeds our anxiety. Glassner, as well as the previously mentioned book by Frank Furedi, supplies readers with numerous anecdotes and incisive examples of media machinations that can make us feel as if an axe murderer is hovering outside our door. But as mentioned earlier, in agreement with an assertion made by Furedi, the media's fixation on the apocryphal and the risky is a *symptom* of the problem, not its cause. One likely reason, in my view, for the increase in anxiety and panic over things that are not all that risky or important is that such anxiety has transformed into something similar to a "higher emotion," similar to guilt, trust, or despair (as opposed to primal, lower emotions such as anger or hair-raising fear resulting from, say, a charging pit bull). It is a learned response or social construct, picked up from the cues and expectations of others. Experts can talk about critical thinking and relative risk factors ad nauseam. Reasoning will have little influence over an emotional response so deep it has become similar to a belief.

The theory that many of our higher emotions are social constructions has philosophical roots that go back to Aristotle. The theory was more fully developed in the nineteenth and twentieth centuries by philosophers such as Ludwig Wittgenstein. In the book *The Myth of Irrationality* John Mc-Crone expounds the basic idea:

> An emotion like guilt, for example, is not inborn in a person but is learnt during childhood. In a child's early years, a parent stands over it and tells it off when it does something

wrong. . . . Later in life, when we have grown up and inter-
nalized our culture's code for what is right and wrong, we be-
come our own moral guardians. . . . The story is the same for
other higher emotions.

Why would people acquire fears about things, events, and circumstances that pose no proven, or infinitesimally small, risks to their well-being or the well-being of others? One reason could be that the fear is compatible with their beliefs, ideals, or ideology. They want to believe. Another reason could be simply social conditioning. When a neighbor expresses fear over the safety of a municipal water supply, appears to have a plausible argument, and backs up the argument with action by subscribing to bottled-water service, her action becomes a powerful model of normative behavior. Others can invest their own time to investigate whether her premise is valid or not, or they can simply accept that the premise is true with the logic that believing the water is unsafe *can't* harm them, but believing the water is safe *could* harm them. As the risks associated with technology and other complexities of modern life exceed the capability or will of many people to understand, fears and beliefs such as these have become default mental states, codes by which people conduct their behavior.

But there's hope and a possible fix. Just as a higher emotion, say distrust of people, has been learned, it can be unlearned. There are numerous examples of people overcoming all types of fears that have led to self-limiting or destructive behavior. The approach to unlearning acquired fears can be pos-

arguing against the mainstream, disposing of a murderous, treacherous dictator—then it becomes incumbent upon the party to "bring it," that is, employ the full package of the most technically sophisticated, clever, innovative, and energetic thinking. Research, strategic planning, debating and management skills, contingency plans, and feedback loops to incorporate new, incoming information must all come into play. More, newer information, in a situation of high risk, is not a source of stress or annoyance; it is the lifeblood of a method that stands at the pinnacle of human intellectual capability. Risk mandates responsibility. In order to succeed and lead, we need to recapture the risk-taking confidence that once defined America as a "can-do" society.

I AM NOT ADVOCATING that we all throw caution to the wind and live wild and recklessly in an effort to improve our mental prowess. As George Carlin once said, "I have lots of ideas. The problem is that most of them suck." There are loads of harebrained schemes out there and that they're risky doesn't mean a person's devoted concentration will make them work. An awareness of risk, and a desire to reduce it to its lowest realistic or feasible levels, is both logical and desirable, and has brought many social benefits. Seat belts have saved thousands of lives, and pollution laws such as the Clean Water Act have made America's waterways some of the cleanest in the world. Anticipating risks well into the long term is an essential feature of advanced, sophisticated analytical reasoning. As documented in Thomas Davenport's book *Thinking for a Living*, studies have found that although high performers take risks,

itive in nature, such as learning techniques to speak in public, or it can draw on the power of so-called negative capability— rejecting ideas and expectations imposed by others. My hope is that more of society will vigorously pursue these methods, as eliminating fear is one of the keys in repossessing control of one's thoughts, sense of curiosity and adventure, and a dynamic life of the mind.

The last point alludes to the "why" part of this theme, embracing risk, and in a sense is also the most potent fix for fearful, risk-averse behavior and outlooks: motivation. For it has been found that a fear-free mind is a better-working mind. Using magnetic resonance imagining (MRI) technology to watch and study human brains, researchers have discovered that emotions such as fear interfere with the mind's ability to focus and concentrate. "We've known for a long time that some people are more easily distracted and that emotions can play a big part in this," says Kevin S. LaBar, assistant professor at Duke University's Center for Cognitive Neuroscience. "Our study shows that two streams of processing take place in the brain, with attentional tasks and emotions moving in parallel before finally coming together." The people in the study were distracted in various ways, sometimes with an image likely to evoke an emotional response. The results confirm that emotions interfere with specific task-focused motor and reasoning skills.

Embracing risk also has another subtle but salutary effect on critical and creative thought processes. It creates an imperative to think well. If a person, organization, or government opts to take on a noble but risky venture—starting a company,

they characterize themselves as "calculated risk takers." These people carefully consider the pros and cons of investing their time in new projects or enterprises, but once they commit they have the ability to keep distractions at bay and master the domain of tasks required by the project.

I was once hired in a consultant capacity to help with the startup of new business, a small metal-plating operation. The owner, whom I'll call Ron, had secured a large loan against his house in order to buy the business. The venture was inherently risky for a number of reasons. Not only was Ron's personal wealth at stake, but the company's main customers were automotive manufacturers, businesses known for their volatility. Ron, who had a background in computers, had found a number of innovative ways of reducing his risk. He had to "win" every contract by quoting against competitors. The standard way of doing this was by roughly estimating, usually on a sheet of scratch paper, how much it cost, in terms of materials, labor, and so on, to produce a single part, then throwing in a certain percentage of profit. Ron had developed a program that allowed him to take into account a part's exact dimensions, thereby taking the guesswork out of how much material (metal) it would cost him to produce it. Ron was competitive and justly proud of his program, which gave him an edge on his rivals. "No one can touch me," he used to say, a wide grin on his face.

Risk, actual not perceived, is a reality. The challenge is not to ignore it, but to see it for what it is and address it. The most daunting barrier for most people is often not the risk or danger in itself. It is what the risk will entail. And what it will entail is effort, a mind that is firing on all its neurons. Accepting risk requires a mind that is unclouded by fears or preconceptions about the way the world works. It compels a person to leave his or her comfort zone, or create a new one. For many, this is asking too much.

The writer William Faulkner once said, "If I had to choose between pain and nothing, I would choose pain." To the best of my knowledge, Faulkner was not a masochist. He didn't literally mean physical pain or deprivation, although he did suffer his share of these. He meant struggle over mind-numbing complacency and pleasure seeking. Faulkner knew that it was only in struggle, through confrontation of one's fears and life's difficulties, that a person became fully human, alive, and growing.

Science has confirmed this growth to be factual, not merely figurative. In *How People Learn*, John Bransford and colleagues present evidence proving the mind literally expands when challenged. In one study, animals raised in complex environments were found to have a greater volume of capillaries per nerve cell, and therefore a greater supply of blood to the brain, than animals raised in caged, sterile environments. In another, animals presented with learning challenges formed greater number of synapses (nerve-to-nerve connections) in their brains than animals doing the rodent equivalent of watching television. One newer, important finding is that learning is an integrated process requiring all parts of the brain, and that learning, to be truly effective, seems to require an "active cycle." It is not enough to read. The best thinkers and students use the information they've learned to produce a functional result.

The finding implies, at least indirectly, a connection between thinking and physical health. Good, creative thinkers
tend to be fidgety people, full of nervous energy and curiosity.
By contrast, many people are lulled into a state of is-ness or
complacency by their routines and habits. It's not that they are
innately uncurious, slothful dullards. It's more likely they
have simply forgotten how to be curious. Because their jobs or
families require so much of their attention, they've actually
lost touch with the macroscopic, the big picture, the sense of
wonder and the indisputable fact that they, like every other
human being, have absolute free will. You really *can* do anything. Is-ness seems to be a universal default state of existence.
Europeans (and Canadians) who like to tut-tut Americans
about their narrow, provincial outlooks and lifestyles are unaware they are really living in a glass house. If anything, complacency, aversion to risk, and a "herd mentality" in these
societies are not just troubling trends, they are part and parcel
of a patriotic, national mind-set. So important is a sense of superiority to a fragile self-identity in these societies that many
people have shrunk their comfort zones to the size of pin-
holes. They do not want to remotely risk having their preconceptions debunked. At least the average American has a
fighting chance to extricate himself from a life of is-ness, as he
is not obliged to assume an air of perpetual smugness.

Americans also have the advantage of living in the most
prolifically dynamic society and economy ever created. It is a
society that (still) nominally rewards risk takers, inventors,
and clever, original thinking. As Virgina Postrel writes, it is
this "endless pursuit of knowledge—or of improved paper

clips, or new musical forms or better management practices—that delights dynamists (and) appalls the stasis-craving social critics who have shaped the Western *Zeitgeist* for decades."

American life is a continual clarion call inviting people into the arena.

Choose your weapon. Research has shown that material comfort alone does not ensure happiness. Is-ness is not freedom or release or fulfillment, it just is. To be truly happy a person needs to be engaged, using his or her mind. To be really happy a person needs to feel he or she has accomplished something. Just one act of taking control can expand your moral and intellectual horizons and make you a better critical and creative thinker. It doesn't need to be "intellectual." It could be something as simple as riding a bike to the store instead of driving. It could be stopping for a beer at a biker bar. By doing something completely out of sync with what we identify as our "character," we stimulate thought and ideas, rediscover plans and goals.

One extreme example of this is so-called self-experimentation. As documented in an article in the *New York Times Magazine*, one man has used self-experimentation to cure insomnia and lose weight. The idea, say writers Stephen J. Dubner and Steven D. Levitt, is for a person to try "a million solutions until he finds one that works." It took the man ten years of experimenting, but he eventually discovered that his morning insomnia could be cured if, the day before, "he got lots of morning light, skipped breakfast, and spent at least eight hours standing."

We've become a society preoccupied with protocol and politics; anxious about the way others "see us." On a comment page under an article about obesity posted on FreeRepublic .com, one person reflects on Americans' (and his) reluctance to walk: "I feel uncomfortable walking around my neighborhood to get exercise. I live in a very private neighborhood where there are no major streets. The nearest convenience store is two miles away. Therefore, many of my neighbors find it disquieting to see a man walking up and down their quiet streets." If his neighbors find it troubling to see him strolling alone around their peaceful little neighborhood, I wonder how they would feel if they saw him striding by in a cassock, or strutting in a drum major's hat, or playing the bagpipes. Maybe they would feel as the Irish felt when St. Patrick arrived and drove out the snakes. Maybe they would run out of their houses in their skivvies hoisting bottles of almond liqueur and singing the praises of buxom wenches and tight-assed sailors they have known.

We need to infuse a bit of the English "cheek" into our lifestyle. I don't mean copy the Brits, God forbid. America used to be about brashness; now it's about effete posing. The Brat Pack has been replaced by the Snack Pack, a lineup of cookie-cutter poster girls and poster boys with no discernible talent or distinguishable mannerisms other than perhaps where they lay stress in the phrase "And I was like, hello" during interviews with Regis and Oprah. Arnie and Trevino and Chi-Chi have given way to Tiger, Mickelson, and Vijay—great golfers, praise 'em, but about as fascinating as a fairway full of gorse and heather. Johnny Depp has perhaps singlehandedly rescued the possibility of producing challenging scripts in American cinema, but I'm afraid the only people still influenced by the performer with the most balls of her generation,

Madonna, are soccer moms and frequenters of retro gay night-
clubs.

I once had a teacher who described the way people were inflicted with "albedo" personalities. Albedo is a property of the
planets, the way they reflect sunlight into space. His point was
that some people are reflections of ideas, mannerisms, style,
and tastes, not sources. Increasingly it seems we are sitting in
an echo chamber listening to ourselves. Republican? That
side. Democrat? Over there. Discussion not allowed. Too
"risky." I inadvertently tested the thesis once while sitting with
a group of people, none of whom I knew, at a wedding recep-
tion. Introductions were made and conversation languished
politely on the weather, the state of this year's tomato crop,
and dogs. After a while, someone, noting I was an editor for a
business magazine, asked me if the economy would hold up.
I'm sure I rambled but I certainly meant no ill will in drawing
my analysis to a close by noting the obvious, namely, that globalism and the spread of free-market capitalism has been one of
the greatest single factors in improving living standards
around the world in history. Someone cleared his throat. For
a moment I thought the lady beside me, a retired school-
teacher, I believe, might plummet out of her chair onto the
hall's linoleum floor. She picked up her napkin and tried to
use it like a fan. Others at the table gazed mildly off into space.

WHEN THE PRIMARY PURSUIT in society becomes avoiding
risk, seeking one's own, and keeping one's head down, life inevitably resolves itself into a comforting numbness. Our
thoughts suffocate, the blood supply to our brains shrinks,

and we grow fewer not more synapses. Once again, *we* aren't compelled to do anything. *We* can just sit here and collectively allow our brains to shrivel and let the next generation deal with the consequences. However, I invite the reader to consider the benefits of putting on a beanie, grabbing a kazoo, and setting off on a scootering excursion through the streets of his or her peaceful, comfortable neighborhood.

Metaphorically speaking, of course.

CHAPTER 11

Hearing the Harmony of Reason: *Embracing Objectivity, Thinking Critically*

Problems cannot be solved by the same level of thinking that created them.

—ALBERT EINSTEIN

Both history and daily experience have confirmed time and again that critical thinking is a vastly superior method of solving problems and making decisions than an intuitive, random approach. It sometimes relies on number crunching and statistics, but the basic elements are the same for all the critical-thinking approaches used to write a report, figure ways to improve sales, or fix a jammed garage door. These elements are the use of empirical evidence (gathering data, knowledge), logical reasoning, and a skeptical attitude. Urging people to use their heads, think well, and be logical is a common refrain heard in society. Yet, the truth be told, hardly anyone has ever been taught what distinguishes good thinking from poor thinking. How do each of the three elements function and fit together to forward the process of critical thinking, which is characterized by careful analysis aimed at reaching an objective, well-founded judgment? It will be enlightening to examine these features in order to discover with fresh eyes exactly how each part works, where we can err, and why a sense of objectivity—the acceptance of a frame of reference (a reality) independent of one's beliefs, opinions, and feelings—is the glue that holds it all together.

THE FACTS, MA'AM, JUST THE FACTS (EMPIRICISM)

As I argued in Chapter Three, America was founded by people with an empirical outlook on life and society. Look at the facts. It isn't the way human nature might be that matters, it is the way human nature *is*. It isn't what a person says that counts, it is what a person *does*. Equipped with this pragmatic approach, America has become one of the most inventive, entrepreneurial, and productive societies of the modern era.

Empirical evidence is essential to good critical thinking and reliable knowledge. Before we can reach conclusions about anything we need to gather the facts. Empirical evidence is very often evidence that we can see, touch, hear, taste, or smell, but it can also be in the form of facts obtained from an authority, research papers, statistics, testimonies, and other information. Statistics can be cooked, made irrelevant, or be skewed by sampling methods, and depositions can be flawed and unreliable, so this type of secondary or received information is always suspect. Depending on the source, we can accept the reliability of much information, but in the Internet age, many if not most people have grown accustomed to letting others be their eyes and ears. There are obvious limits to the amount of time we can spend fact-checking received information, but whenever that information is strongly influencing important decisions (which include a person's views and beliefs), we need to ensure that the evidence is trustworthy. In most cases, the only person that can do this for you is you, yourself.

The evidence that we find with our senses is indisputable. It is not open to interpretation. The reason it is not open to questioning or invalidation is not that I or a higher authority says it is. It is that in a free society experience shows that such sensory experience is validated by *all* sentient, unimpaired human beings. When I say that a rose is a color associated with the word "red," and my neighbor says it is a different color, blue, I may be wrong. But when a million people confirm it is red, we will begin to scan the phone book to find help for our neighbor. One philosophical and sometimes legal counter-argument to universal objectivity is the common instance when two people observe the same thing and see it differently, for example, an accident in which one person says the driver ran the stop sign and another person says he saw the driver stop first. It is safe to assume these are technical glitches with observation (or memory), not evidence that objectivity is invented, a matter of viewpoint. It is similar to the replay problem in football—even though the referee was watching the play closely, the speed of the game makes it difficult to assess what

happened on any given play. The referee's view could be ob-
scured. In the case of an accident, precise observation is even
more problematic because witnesses are usually distracted.
The observation could be affected by sample size. If we
rounded up enough people who saw the accident, we should
begin to see some clear consensus on whether the driver
stopped or not. If there is no consensus, it only proves the limits of human perception. We know that the driver either
stopped or didn't stop.

This may seem like hair-splitting, but truth and objectivity
today often spin around some such semantics—"It depends on
what the meaning of the word 'is' is." Facts are not just unas-
sailable facts, measurable, observable events, words with precise definitions or data that mean exactly what they signify,
but political "texts" that need to be read and interpreted, so as
to conform to the way we want the world to be (more on this
later). Making accurate, empirical observations about the
world is in fact not simple or easy. Some people are better at it
than others, and to become really good requires training, sort
of the cerebral equivalent of abdominal crunches. One obvious rule of thumb is that emotions and other mental clutter
interfere with observations. This point is recurrently demonstrated to me when I am introduced to someone and immediately forget his or her name. What has happened is that I've
become momentarily self-conscious, not paying attention to
what is being said, but preoccupied with my own presentation.

The importance of empirical observation to thinking and
knowledge is illustrated in a fictional character, Sherlock

Holmes. Holmes is known by his fans around the world for his powerful deductive and analytical reasoning, but he is first and foremost a careful observer. In the novel *The Sign of Four*, Holmes observes that the ideal detective must have three qualities: the power of observation, the power of deduction, and knowledge. He reveals that he is an expert on tobacco ash, and can identify 140 forms of cigar, cigarette, and pipe-tobacco ash. Holmes tells Watson, "To the trained eye there is as much difference between the black ash of a Trichopoly and the white fluff of bird's-eye as there is between a cabbage and a potato."

The creator of Holmes, Sir Arthur Conan Doyle, appears to have learned about the importance of observation from an instructor, Dr. Joseph Bell, while attending the Edinburgh Medical School. Doyle was fascinated by Bell's powers of observation and deduction and frequently wrote down snippets of conversation between Bell and his patients. Another writer, Jack Kerouac, describes a game he and his friends would play in order to test their powers of observation. The idea was to re-member and re-create a setting—a room, a party, a restaurant—in exact detail. A person would have to describe the clothes everyone was wearing, objects in the room, aromas, the mannerisms and moods of the people, and so on. You don't have to be a detective or a writer to benefit from careful, fastidious observation, and Kerouac's sport seems like a fun, highly effective way to practice and hone one's powers of observation. Clear your head of immediate concerns and take a close look at the world around you. You'll be surprised at what you can see. In a rare Sherlockian moment, I walked into my in-laws' house one evening to pick up my daughter and inquired if she was done with her bath. "How did you know?" my mother-in-law asked. The upstairs bathroom window was steamed over, I replied smugly. More often than not my observational powers wane, rather than wax. "Did I notice the daffodils had bloomed in the back garden? That there was a new mat on the front step? That the Lichtenstein prints had been hung in the front hallway?" my wife asked. No, I was batting zero. This is more than just a sign of self-absorption and callousness. This is life, and I was missing it. Training yourself to observe not only enriches your thinking, it can enlarge your enjoyment of everything you take for granted.

USING YOUR HEAD,
NOT YOUR HEART (LOGICAL REASONING)

Critical thinking, the use of careful analysis and evaluation to arrive at sound judgments, whether it is done by a scientist or a mechanic, depends on logical reasoning. Before I raise any high expectations, however, I should give this disclaimer up front: I cannot explain, or teach a person, how to reason logically in a few paragraphs. There are entire university courses devoted to logic. But here is the basic principle: Logic is used to rationally establish a connection between what is known (evidence) and a claim or premise. Logic relies on *inferences*. An inference is an implicit or explicit step someone has taken in order to link the evidence with the claim. For example, the statement "Don't go swimming. The waves are big and there could be an undertow" contains several implicit, logical inferences. One inference is that the big waves are creating a dangerous undertow. Another inference is that a person could drown by swimming in these waves.

Another formal logic device is called a *syllogism*. A syllogism is composed of three statements: a major premise, a minor premise, and a conclusion. For instance, if the major premise is "Midwesterners are do-it-yourselfers," and the minor premise is "Troy is a midwesterner," then the conclusion is "Troy is a do-it-yourselfer."

The human brain appears to have a certain inherent ability to use logical inferences. Yet it is still a skill that must be practiced and learned. As Steven Schafersman, a geologist, writes in the book *An Introduction to Science:*

> I must point out that most individuals do not reason logically, because they have never learned how to do so. Logic is not an ability . . . that will gradually develop and improve on its own, but is a skill or discipline that must be learned within a formal educational environment.

Logic is fundamental to all formal fields of study, from medicine to accounting to plumbing. The power of logical deductive reasoning was really hammered home to me in one particular undergraduate science course I took long ago, organic chemistry. Organic chemistry, which is sometimes called the chemistry of life or "carbon" chemistry, is complex. Instead of dealing with molecules consisting of a few atoms, for instance, salt (one atom of sodium and one atom of chloride), organic chemistry describes the properties and reactions of molecules made up of dozens or thousands of atoms. Our bodies are composed of twenty types of organic molecules called amino acids, interspaced with some fat and lots of water, and fueled by carbohydrates. Protein, fat, carbohydrates, plants, trees, bacteria, viruses—all the building blocks of life and the seemingly infinite variety of life forms are a result of organic molecules and their interactions. Logical, scientific, rational methods are used to study and understand the organic basis of our body's functions, cure disease, and also synthesize man-made medicines, useful chemicals, plastic materials, and fibers.

My professor, a slightly built man with short, dark, matted hair, laid out the scope of the topic, readily acknowledging the challenges it would present to the understanding of us neophytes, in the very first class. "Organic chemistry is a vast, rich field of study that can only be mastered with a thorough knowledge of the first principles of molecular theory and the application of deductive, logical reasoning," were his approximate words to us. We could leave intuition at the door, for all the good it was going to do us in this class. We learned there is a tremendously significant spatial aspect to organic chemistry. Molecules assume different shapes—tetrahedrons, closed rings, kinked chains. The shapes of the molecules are in turn determined by the properties of each individual atom—for example, by how many other atoms it can combine with. (Carbon, say, can combine with a maximum of four other atoms.) When you bring these complex molecules together under the right conditions, called a "reaction," you don't get a hopelessly unfathomable mess, but beauty: The molecules combine with one another in precisely specific and predictable ways to produce things such as acetic acid (vinegar), alcohol, sugar, acetylsalicylic acid (aspirin), or nylon. Our exams often consisted entirely of questions asking us how we would make these molecules from scratch. Change the position of one atom and you get an entirely new molecule with completely different properties. And it is all, as our Poe-like professor foretold, explained using first principles and logical, deductive reasoning, and confirmed by experiment a million times over.

Professionals in various fields, tradespeople, and do-it-yourselfers can be as proficient in the basics of logical reasoning as a scientist. As with many things, we become better at it by doing it. It is a method, sort of like cooking, but the recipe depends on two essential ingredients, knowledge and objectivity. At some point in the logical chain of reasoning you have to have some special knowledge—that big waves can create an undertow, or that pentane is a five-carbon straight-chain hydrocarbon molecule.

Emotional knowledge is the much-hyped alternative to factual, empirical knowledge and objectivity. But it is one thing to say emotions play a role in helping us to learn, and another to say emotions are the same thing as knowledge and reasoning. The distinction is blurred, in part, apparently, because of misconceptions over the message of popular books such as Daniel Goleman's 1995 best seller, *Emotional Intelligence*. Goleman in fact defines emotional intelligence (EQ) as everything that is not IQ. Certainly it is important to be able to assess how other people feel or to be able to project confidence. These and other EQ attributes, Goleman argues, are just as important as or more important than hard intelligence in determining a person's success, happiness, and fulfillment. Yet at least one EQ attribute, the ability to regulate one's moods and keep distress from overwhelming one's thinking, appears to be crucial to critical thinking and its basic elements—observation, logical reasoning, and skepticism. As Schafersman writes:

> *Often the use of logical reasoning requires a struggle with the will, because logic sometimes forces one to deny one's emotions and face reality, and this is often painful. But remember this: emotions are not evidence, feelings are not facts, and subjective beliefs are not substantive beliefs.*

Recent research has confirmed it is not only possible to control our emotions, but healthy to do so. The research, led by Dr. Zindel Segal, professor of psychiatry and psychology at the University of Toronto, compared the brains of people who had recovered from depression using cognitive behavioral therapy with the brains of those who had used an antidepressant. The patients who had taken the drug showed changes in the more primal part of the brain, the limbic system, while the patients who had gone through therapy showed changes in the upper areas of the brain associated with higher thought. The study not only shows that people can feel better by changing the way they think, but, according to a colleague of Segal's, Dr. Adam Anderson, "empowers us as individuals to understand and regulate our own emotions." The discovery, in Anderson's view, is especially significant: "We're looking at untapped human potential."

The role emotions play in learning and reasoning is not

clearly understood. In one widely cited study, people with brain damage that impairs their ability to use emotion to make decisions did less well in discerning which decks of cards were "stacked," and lost more money than people with normal emotional function who were able to pay heed to their "gut feelings" about which decks contained better cards. First, I'm not sure the finding that people suffering from brain damage were less successful in a rigged game of chance proves anything. But the study also appears flawed by the built-in assumption that decision-making always relates to one's immediate self-interest, a sort of zero-sum game in which one stands to win or lose. More often than not the decisions we make or problems we solve do not result in instant feedback that will allow us to adjust our actions depending on whether we perceive harm or gain—for instance, the composition of a company report, or a decision to take a particular job. The consequences of these decisions, and whether they result in something good or bad, could be unknown for months, or even years. What possible role can gut feelings play in the quality of these decisions other than as an add-on—"I feel good about the report." The good feeling is most likely a result of doing one's homework, thinking hard, and sweating the details. Even more significant, as cited earlier, research has found that emotions actually interfere with the mind's ability to focus and perform a specific task-focused reasoning skill.

Emotions, especially in the way they appear to influence the formation of memories, appear to play a crucial role in how we acquire hard knowledge, but a lesser role in how well we use that knowledge to reason and solve problems. Clearheadedness is the most important attribute of sharp, logical thinking. Reasoning skills require knowledge—a hypothetical detective will need to know forensic evidence and how to interpret it before he can deduce who committed a crime; an engineer will need to know building codes and strengths of different materials before she can design a new high-rise. There is no quick and easy way to become better at logical reasoning—read, write, and take up math. Math is fun, to paraphrase an educational poster. In a world of increasing ambiguity and subjectivity, math gives a person concrete answers, tangible evidence of an objective world. There are scores of activity books, basic to advanced, for the lay mathematician. I also believe one introductory course in logic and the scientific method should be mandatory in all high schools. To accomplish this, educators could eliminate one gym class, on the logic that a healthy body requires a healthy mind.

SHOW ME THE MONEY (SKEPTICISM)

Just as the measure of good art is "willful suspension of disbelief," the gauge of good science is "willful suspension of belief." Skepticism, which can be defined simply as doubt in need of evidence, lies at the heart of critical thinking and the scientific method, its acclaimed, more formal cousin. Skepticism is sometimes confused with cynicism, which is really its polar opposite. Skepticism is an affirmation that there is truth and objectivity in the world; it's just hard to find. Cynicism is the view that truth is buried beneath a mound of lies. Cynicism is typified by the saying "Anyone can be bought." In the view of the cynic, society is corrupt, even if laughably so. The late rocker Frank Zappa was a classic cynic, as attested by his music, at least.

The concept of skepticism was taken to its most profound limits by the gadfly and peripatetic scholar Socrates, who argued (endlessly) that we cannot accept a fact, idea, or belief because it has come from a higher "authority." Using a method of debate (interrogation, really) named, fittingly, Socratic dialogue, Socrates showed that confused meanings, paltry evidence, and contradictions often lurked below the most common assumptions of people in Greek society. Socrates was interested in finding the true nature or meaning of ideals such as justice, equality, and the function of the state in people's lives. He was an absolute empiricist. For instance, he believed in equality of opportunity, but not equality of condition, saying the only way to determine if one person was better than another was by examination under strictly equal conditions. He demonstrated the importance of asking deep, probing questions, of taking nothing for granted, and he showed that even the well-educated or powerful could be bewildered and irrational. Socrates got under the skin of a lot of people and the Greeks gave him the long good-bye—a cup of hemlock.

The skeptical attitude has never been pursued with quite the same vigor since. Today, for reasons previously noted—PC, marketing culture, "stress"—we live, it seems, in the least skeptical of times. Taking things at "face value" is the common practice, if only because most people believe they do not have time to probe beneath the surface. But lack of skepticism has also worked itself into the mainstream outlook, even in people who consider themselves hard to convince. This gullibility trend, in my opinion, is seen in things such as the growth of the time-share business, wide acceptance of carbon-dioxide-induced global warming as fact, and the attempted debunking of evolution with pseudoscience.

Despite testimonies of aggravation and ample evidence that in many cases the cost of owning a time-share condominium or apartment far exceeds the actual value, thousands of people take up the offer of a get-away weekend, succumb to the sales pitch, and find they have paid a lot of money for an endless source of marital friction. In an exposé on the time-share business published in the *Dallas Observer*, a real estate agent referred to one time-share development as "essentially worthless." The view that the earth is warming because of man-made emissions is, as was said earlier, only a theory, and not a very good one, because, one, it can't be tested and, two, it doesn't explain all the facts—for instance, how the earth has been warming and cooling for millions of years before man arrived. Both evolution (the view that all life evolved from simple organic molecules over hundreds of millions of years) and "intelligent design" (the view that life is too complex to have been formed by random events) are theories, and neither is testable. However, evolution is confirmed by a fossil record that shows increasing complexity and diversity of life forms over time, whereas intelligent design is noteworthy for its complete lack of substantiating evidence.

Society stands to gain practically and philosophically from a more skeptical attitude about claims and received knowledge. One way of understanding why skepticism is important to truth and knowledge is to become better acquainted with the scientific method. The scientific method, like design of experiment, is an organized approach to applying critical thinking with the objective of reaching a general truth about the world and the things in it. It is based on evidence, not belief. The method, not the knowledge gained, is in fact what defines the practice of science. The first step of the scientific method is *observation*—not just any type of observation, but observation without bias. For a scientist, this is usually done by measuring something, say, temperature, heart rate, or the position of a planet, in exact terms. The next step involves asking a *question*. At a time when the earth, not the sun, was supposed to be at the center of the solar system, the fifteenth-century scholar Copernicus asked himself, "If the earth is in the center, why do some planets sometimes move east to west, and sometimes move from west to east?" The third step of the scientific method is to develop a *hypothesis,* or educated guess that will explain the question. Copernicus believed that his question about the planets could be explained if the sun, not the earth, were at the center of the solar system, with the planets moving around the sun in perfect circular orbits. The fourth step in the scientific method is to make *predictions* to test the hypothesis—if the planets move in circular orbits around the sun they should be in certain locations at certain times of the year with respect to the earth. The motion of planets observed from Earth will seem to "reverse" itself sometimes because the time it takes the earth to revolve around the sun differs from the time taken by the other planets. The fifth and final step is to conduct an *experiment* in order to confirm or refute the prediction. Copernicus measured the position of the planets and found that they were in the exact positions predicted by his theory—almost. Copernicus's model erred in subscribing circular orbits to the planets, when in fact the planets moved in elliptical orbits, a discovery made by Johannes Kepler about one hundred years later.

The beauty of science based on the scientific method is that unlike knowledge derived strictly from hearsay or dogma, science has the ability to self-correct and incorporate new evidence as it becomes available. For years scientists believed that all of space was permeated by an invisible substance, or "aether." When an experiment conducted by A. A. Michelson and E. W. Morley in the late nineteenth century found no evidence of aether, the theory was discarded. Rather than being a tool that only geniuses and nerds can understand and use, the scientific method offers a technique and a lesson of immense practical value. People, businesses, organizations, and governments that can incorporate new evidence and information into their thinking, tactics, and strategies will be more effective in making decisions and solving problems. They will be less rigid in their approaches and better able to adapt to changing circumstances.

The perceptions of Americans and citizens of other countries around the world can be shaped by skepticism, or lack of it. For instance, if I were to ask you to name the two top oil-producing countries in the world, you might say Saudi Arabia and . . . one of those other Middle Eastern countries. However, the second-largest oil producer in the world is the United States (tied with Russia),

> As measured by assaults per 100,000 people, the United Nations' perennial merit-badge winner Sweden has double the assaults of the United States, 667 versus 319.

which produces 7,698,000 barrels of oil each day, according to statistics compiled by the *Economist* magazine. Or, off the top of your head, name a country with one of the highest rates of serious assault? Surely the crime-ridden United States, the one the world saw on shameful display in the aftermath of Hurricane Katrina in New Orleans, would be at the top of the pack for this dubious honor. Yet, as measured by assaults per 100,000 people, the United Nations' perennial merit-badge winner Sweden has double the assaults of the United States, 667 versus 319. Or quick, name one or two countries that spend the most money on the military and defense—Michael Moore's warmongering United States is surely a chart-topper in this category. Yet, measured by defense spending as a percentage of GDP, the United States doesn't even crack the top forty. North Korea, at 25 percent, tops the list, and Cuba, Russia, and Egypt all divert more of their total economic output toward military spending than the United States. These statistics suggest we could use a good, healthy dose of skepticism in our outlooks, a resistance to believing what we hear, or in the case of Michael Moore's films, feel.

Certainly we have to take some things, observations, for instance, at face value. Extreme skepticism could lead one to a sort of emotional, intellectual gridlock in which a person doubts that he doubts. The philosopher Karl Popper, regarded by some as the high priest of the scientific method and its dictum of skepticism, held that the belief that all swans were white had to be qualified by the disclaimer "Subject to the sighting of a black swan." Today, more scientists are annoyed by Popper's hard line and argue that evidence of confirmation of a theory plays a more significant role in science than falsification. Extreme skepticism has also induced many brilliant people to utter some very silly things. Here's a brief sampling:

- "Heavier-than-air flying machines are impossible." (Lord Kelvin, British mathematician, ca. 1895)
- "There is not the slightest indication that nuclear energy will ever be obtainable." (Albert Einstein, 1932)
- "I think there is a world market for maybe five computers." (Thomas Watson, chairman of IBM, 1943)

At the time, these assessments probably seemed perfectly reasonable to the public and the majority of scientists. The true value of skepticism, however, is not in making assessments about what might or might not happen in the far future, it is in making judgments about what's taking place in the present. To practice skepticism at this level, you don't need a research lab or travel to a time-share sales meeting. Just turn on the television.

THE EFFECTIVENESS AND POWER of critical thinking and the scientific method in uncovering truth and solving complex problems has been proven again and again. Admittedly, famous scholars and scientists, from Pascal to Stephen Jay Gould, have waxed poetic about the role intuition, serendipity, and a Blinklike "aha" moment played in helping solve a problem or stumble on a discovery. My theory about this (although it may not be testable) is that great thinkers are themselves fascinated by this aspect of the human thought process because, first, it can't be totally "explained" and, second, they spend 99 percent of their time in classical critical mode. Intuition and all other types of inspiration are fine, but to have any value the insight or discovery still has to be testable or established. As I observed at the beginning, we normally have no interest in tracking how many of our intuitive insights end up crumpled and thrown into the wastebasket. I have several shelves of unpublished "aha" moments filed in my study at home. It is usually not some fanciful leap of thought that accounts for a great creative work, breakthrough discovery, or general success, but specific concrete knowledge, unending study, close empirical observation, high standards, fine attention to detail, logical analysis, and technical skill—Michelangelo's meticulous study of human anatomy, Newton's invention of differential calculus, Frank Lloyd Wright's "hands-on" education and apprenticeship with a renowned architect, a baseball manager's encyclopedic knowledge of statistics. In an article titled "Unleashing Creativity," Ulrich Kraft writes, "Various psychologists have floated different models of the creative process, but most involve an early 'preparation' phase. Preparation is difficult and time-consuming."

Despite shouldering the bulk of the workload that has produced humanity's most magnificent works of art and penetrating discoveries about the physical universe, critical and creative thinking and the scientific method are often quietly shunted into a corner of modern society, while emotion and intuition are placed on a pedestal and praised. Scholars don't talk about the power of scientific rationalism, but its limits. Distinguished university professors are browbeaten by guilt-mongering students and other faculty into a defensive stance about science for its ability to control nature. Feminists, environmentalists, and hosts of other disenfranchised groups disregard all the medical and everyday miracles worked by science and accuse rationalism of creating more problems than it solves, as well as imposing a white, male, Western value system on culture and society.

And we thought we were just using our heads. Yet, any intellectually satisfying and pragmatic solution to the decline of knowledge, reasoning, and thinking in society must ultimately address these criticisms.

At least part of the explanation for the tendency to shrug or damn reason and praise emotion and intuition appears to be human nature. In *The Myth of Irrationality*, John McCrone says the belief that we have a mysterious emotional and creative core is deep-rooted in the popular human psyche. McCrone argues the belief is wrong:

> *It is what we want to believe about ourselves rather than what evidence tells us. We like the idea that within us we harbor a secret well of power. It makes our lives seem more exciting—like living on the trembling lip of a volcano that might erupt any moment. . . . However, despite its undoubted allure, this belief in human irrationality is a myth.*

McCrone says the key to understanding the human mind is to view it as a social phenomenon. However, it is the same popular belief identified by McCrone that would seem to account for the "myth" that there is an actual alternative to reason—that is, the widespread belief that we can go about our business relying on instinct and snap judgments and do all right.

Another explanation for the appeal of emotion is society's egalitarian nature. Reason and critical thinking, because they often, but not always, are enhanced by at least some formal training, are seen by many people to be elitist, or to require special powers. At a mundane level, this view explains the faddish interest in books preaching the power of intuition— à la *Blink*. At its most political and socially subversive level, the egalitarian or anarchist instinct has paved the way for the postmodernist movement and its direct challenge to the central tenets of critical thinking and science: truth and objectivity.

Postmodernism has roots in the Dada craze of the 1920s and was fully developed by a number of French intellectuals, most notably Jacques Derrida and Michel Foucault. In contrast to the Enlightenment's quest for rational aesthetics, ethics, and knowledge, postmodernism is concerned with the "authenticity" of these ideals. The movement has developed a vocabulary of rhetoric to continually question and subvert that authority by a method called deconstruction. Postmodernists claim there is no such thing as universal truth or beauty, but only multiple, fragmented perspectives, which are themselves open to endless reinterpretation. From a postmodernist outlook, there is no point when a person can say, in absolute terms, "I know something."

It would be tempting, but naive, to write off this theory as intellectual mumbo jumbo. Yet, as detailed in books such as Allan Bloom's *The Closing of the American Mind*, postmodernism has become a strong influence in our universities and culture. Bloom writes, "There is one thing a professor can be absolutely certain of: Almost every student entering the university believes, or says he believes, that truth is relative." Many people believe the movement has hijacked university education and that its ultimate political intent is to limit free speech and kill open debate and expression of ideas. It has spread into our primary schools, where students are given worksheets requiring them to count the number of people in a story by gender and race, and in science classes, where teachers routinely build class discussions and projects around the evils of science and technology. By asserting that science is a sort of propaganda for the value system of a privileged elite, it has managed to politically taint reason and the scientific method. Since the sixties, when postmodernism fully bloomed, reason has been subliminally linked with the "establishment" and uncool. Ironically, postmodernism has drawn succor, at least in the public's imagination, from science itself, and physical laws such as relativity and the quantum uncertainty principle—both of which operate in realms far removed from, and inconsequential to, everyday human experience.

In practice and approach, however, postmodernism has nothing in common with science, a claim that is backed by noting that the "postmodernlike" quantum uncertainty principle, a feature of the subatomic world, has been confirmed by the scientific method to be "true" in absolute, nonconditional terms, a result disallowed by postmodernists. Also, the uncertainty principle doesn't apply to the macroscopic world of common experience where we can measure both the position and momentum of objects with complete accuracy, a feat confirmed every time we fly in an airplane. Nonetheless, postmodernists will apparently go to great lengths to scramble our common sense and shatter our "illusion" that we are seeing what we are seeing; that our senses and our experiments are for the most part giving us a completely correct depiction of the world as it is. In one famous tirade, an eminent postmodernist decreed that even the constancy of the speed of light was a human artifact or cultural value. Somewhere, Einstein was disturbed from his eternal rest by this one.

Emotion and fear cloud empirical observation. The fractured, "many-worlds" perspective of postmodernism, however, skews our *interpretation* of observations. It does this by creating a climate of confusion in which facts or data must first be reconciled with the projected feelings of others or with a universal "good." With this mind-set, seeking to find explanations for observations—say that young boys can be fidgety and disruptive, girls get lower scores in math, or only a small percentage of African-Americans read at a high level— invariably involves proposing convoluted political causes and fixes, rather than simple, practical ones. These data, these observations, our nonobjective society says, simply can't mean what they appear to mean. We demand an ill, a blame that works at some societal or psychological level, and then ask someone (usually the government) to cure it. Our denial of objectivity has a cost. With every drug or special program delivered up as a cure, we are defrauded into believing that the perfectly functioning, egalitarian society we desire is just around the corner. A state (or a drug), however, cannot teach a person to excel at reading or math or be socially adapted. The cognitive skills are too complex to be learned in an hour of instruction every day. The solutions to these and other problems can (obviously) be implemented only at cultural and personal levels.

Postmodernism is really nothing more than intellectual mischief making and nose tweaking, albeit with highly political objectives. A kid who blows up a mailbox with a cherry bomb is acting in accord with postmodernism's most profound principle—to raise havoc, to cause people who have been made comfortable by the fruits of reason and a rational life to be uncomfortable. Yet, through its political and subversive objectives, postmodernism requires our serious attention. Fortunately, its very premise is refuted by the logic and science it trivializes. For instance, postmodernists argue that science, critical thinking, and rationality embody the value system of white Western males, and therefore teaching and practicing the methods naturally lead to a society that devalues the ethics and outlooks of other cultures. First of all, the claim is not supported by the evidence—evidence of the use of logic and reason has been found in hosts of cultures, including the ancient Egyptian, Babylonian, and Mayan. Today, all races and genders are engaged in scientific research. Further, the claim that rationality is a derivative of white male values is itself racist and sexist. As writer Barbara Ehrenreich opines in an interview appearing in Z magazine, "I would not surrender to a more elite class or race the idea of rationality. Why cede them that? It's a very disturbing assumption." Finally, cognitive science has shown the human brain comes equipped to solve problems through the use of logical reasoning. That doesn't mean that everyone has the same ability to use logic, but certain innate language skills imply the human brain has a tendency to do so. As Steven Pinker writes in How the Mind Works, "Children use and, not, or and if, appropriately before they turn three. . . . Logical inferences are ubiquitous in human thought, particularly when we understand language." So, in summary, reasoning appears to have default values, but those values are universal to all cultures and genders; reasoning is elitist only in that its principles and practice are mastered better by some people than others—we are born with the rudiments of the ability to reason.

As for there being no universal standard for a thing such as truth or beauty, I have stood numerous times on Mallory Square in Key West watching the sunset with thousands of other people and I have never once heard anyone walk away uttering, "Man, that was ugly."

IN 1989 I STOOD in a packed conference room in Dallas and listened as Stanley Pons announced to a meeting of the American Chemical Society that he, along with his colleague Martin Fleischmann, had discovered a way of generating a sustained nuclear fusion reaction in a laboratory, something called cold fusion. Despite the fact that there was no known, feasible mechanism to explain cold fusion, despite the fact that the research had yet to be peer-reviewed or duplicated, as the presentation ended a room full of science-trained people rose and gave Pons a huge ovation for his remarkable discovery.

I trust these people have all taken the skeptical healing waters by now. In the time since this announcement, cold fusion has died a quiet death. Few chemists doubt what Pons and Fleischmann (two scientists with otherwise credible credentials) say happened in their experiment, happened. It's just that they, and others, couldn't make it happen again, at least not with any regularity. It was also clear that whatever the two scientists produced in their labs, it was not nuclear fusion. Cold fusion now lives in the ignominious purgatory of science called "artifacts." The tale of cold fusion also shows that neither professionally trained critical thinkers nor critical thinking itself are always perfect. Cold fusion reminds us that science and reason is done by humans, and that humans very often fuse their beliefs, biases, and egos into their thinking.

In his book *The Same and Not the Same*, Nobel laureate Roald Hoffmann observes that the irrational is often frightfully close to the surface in many scientists. Here are some comments one of Hoffmann's submitted papers received during the peer-review process (scientists comment on a paper anonymously through a third party):

I am not now and have never been an admirer of Hoffmann's efforts in the inorganic/organometallic field. To a bridge player, the sideline kibitzers, however intelligent, are of little interest. Hoffmann is very intelligent—but not intelligent to do anything positive. Kibitzing, however well done, soon becomes tiresome.

The human element in all thinking and science raises speculation about the limits of rational methods of thought. Philosophers and nonscientists argue the value of life often lies in its subjective context. Certainly not everything that happens in society is quantifiable, calculable, or predictable. This ambiguity is captured in an analysis published in the *Economist* in 2005: "It seems that every theory about how September 11 changed New Yorkers has an equally plausible rebuttal." Reality is messy, fuzzy. What sorts of insights, solutions, and verities can critical thinking provide for us? John Horgan, in his book *The End of Science*, argues that scientists are running low on the types of questions science and the human mind can actually answer. In Horgan's view modern science is becoming largely "ironic" science, which, "by raising unanswerable questions, reminds us that all our knowledge is half-knowledge; it reminds us of how little we know." Others, such as physicist Robert Laughlin, say it is not science that is coming to an end, but the reductionist, cause-and-effect view inherent in logical reasoning, which, he says, has created "the false ideology of human mastery of all things." In his book *A Different Universe*, Laughlin details how he and other scientists have begun to study nonlinear, "emergent" properties not predicted by standard models or theories.

We may or may not be running out of problems to solve in science, but we have no deficit of them in real life. Emergent properties could be an intriguing new area of study at the limits of science, but most of us are still bedeviled by imminent properties, the here and now. We could use some good, old-fashioned, clear, cause-and-effect reductionist critical thinking to solve the problems of foam flying off the space shuttle, figure out how to flood-proof New Orleans, help a large segment of our population learn to read better, manage companies in a global, knowledge-based economy, rebuild Iraq more effectively, address rising costs of health care, and generally help individual people reach their goals and enrich their lives.

Until someone comes up with a better way to solve these types of problems, the analytical, reductionist, scientific approach is the only game in town. The approach must wed evaluation, logic, and analysis with action; otherwise the entire exercise is useless. Considered by itself, the reductionist, scientific method is much more flexible, user-friendly, and ethical than is often supposed. Cold fusion, for all it tells us about the fallibility of science, also proves its fundamental strength—the ability to self-correct. Within days of Pons's announcement, scientists were attempting to duplicate the experiment without success, sending up the telltale red flags. Instead of being elitist, science and critical thinking based on observation, logical reasoning, and skepticism embody the highest ideals of democracy. The critical, rationalist approach is the front-line defense against dogma, bias, and superstition. People may try to use science to make outlandish claims, for instance the superiority of one race over another, but critical thought can organize a thorough examination of the facts and genetic evidence to disprove it. Horrible events like the Inquisition and the Holocaust were manifestations of the repression of open, rational inquiry by state power, fear, and hatred, not a consequence of rationalism. Science may be used to make bad things, such as nerve gas and nuclear bombs, but scientific rationalism, the process of thinking rationally, has generally shown a remarkable resilience to being co-opted by evil and crank causes.

When critical thinking does go awry as a method, it is because of things such as flawed observation (or incorrect data), faulty memory, or erroneous reasoning. Flaws in reasoning can usually be traced to lack of rigor in our logic due to an emotional appeal of some sort. Some of the fallacies, which can be categorized by type, are false cause, reckless generalization, false comparison, and the "slippery slope," summarized briefly below.

FALSE CAUSE

False-cause assumptions are a widespread source of errors in logical reasoning. One of the most common of false-cause errors is *post hoc* reasoning. *Post hoc* is extracted from a longer Latin phrase that when translated literally means "after this therefore because of this." *Post hoc* reasoning assumes that an event is caused by an event that preceded it. One example is: "The man committed murder after watching a television show depicting violent acts, therefore violence in television directed his behavior." A temporal association of one event to another does not prove a causal connection. Another variation, sometimes called single-cause fallacy, is frequently reported in the media, and is paraphrased in the following: "A study has found that people who eat fish live longer, therefore eating fish will make you live longer." There is rarely only one factor in a complex circumstance, such as a person's health, that accounts for the overall outcome—in this case lack of illness and longevity.

RECKLESS GENERALIZATION

A conclusion based on too few examples or an atypical example can lead to generalizations that have no basis in reality. For example, "I had an engine problem with my GM car. GM builds poor-quality vehicles." The American automotive industry has been under fire, so the logic may sound solid. Yet surveys of initial vehicle quality conducted by the company J. D. Powers shows that in recent years GM has been building some of the highest-quality vehicles on the market. Reckless generalizations can also lead to stereotyping and bias, as in, "Pedro was fired because he kept missing work. Hispanics are irresponsible." A larger sample size would no doubt disprove this prejudiced statement.

FALSE COMPARISON

A comparison between two things that are not alike in any important respect is illogical. The fallacy is often used as a rhetorical device, for political purposes, to sway people's feelings, as in "The senator comes from a rich, privileged background. He does not understand the needs of working people." If character traits were only a product of background, people who grew up in the city would not appreciate nature, and kids who were raised by poor, uneducated parents would never desire to go to college. Another false comparison is used in a disingenuous "what's good for the goose is good for the gander" manner, as in "Employee empowerment has made companies more efficient. If we gave more power to kids at home and in classrooms, they'd learn better." Workplace efficiency has little in common with teaching and raising children. Such reasoning is often insinuated, rather than stated directly.

THE SLIPPERY SLOPE

This sort of argument is frequently used to oppose change or taking risks. The slippery slope fallacy assumes, without evidence, that one event will lead inevitably to other events, usually with some undesirable outcome. Sometimes the argument is used to justify inefficiency or bureaucracy in a company or government by assuming the change will expose parties to new, uncontrollable risks, such as: "If we reduce the number of signatures required to allocate money for emergencies and disaster relief from five to one, money will be misappropriated." But here the logician really needs to look at the potentially huge gain, against the relatively small risk (with a system of checks and balances) of some minor loss. The fallacy is also frequently heard in other parts of the world these days in the following refrain: "The United States unilaterally invaded Iraq and is pursuing a unilateralist policy with the objective of world hegemony." While the U.S.-led invasion of Iraq did not have unanimous support of all the world's countries, it was not unilateralist, and consisted of a coalition of over thirty countries that voluntarily agreed to take part. Ridding a single country of a dictator, then allowing the country to write its own constitution and elect its own leaders, then leaving as soon as feasibly possible does not technically meet the definition of seeking hegemony.

FALLACIES IN REASONING and general errors in critical thinking are bound to happen and are not necessarily bad. They are an essential part of the trial-and-error process in learning how to think well. For instance, in 1911, Einstein attempted to calculate the amount by which a beam of light would be bent as it passed through the sun's gravitational field—his calculation was off by a factor of two. In *Einstein: A*

Relative History, Dr. Donald Goldsmith reports that events would show that Einstein's "attempt to grapple with the problems of explaining gravitation had led him into some useful errors."

Critical thinking, the practice of observing, evaluating, and making logical inferences in order to arrive at a sound judgment, does not always have to have a scientific or useful purpose. It can be used simply to dig into things to enhance one's awareness and discernment. Oh, the things I do not know: What makes a lager different from ale? What was the Beaux Arts movement? What does it mean to say a song or musician "swings"? How do you tell a well-made Persian rug?

The world is full of "silent" knowledge that will not reveal itself by itself but has to be tuned in and amplified by a curious, active brain. Critical thinking plays a vital role in filtering this knowledge from background noise and using it to inform and nurture one of the most eclectic human capacities, "taste" and discernment. Taste is often called critical knowledge and those who employ it critics. But taste, which is a refined understanding of why and how things work the way they do, also seems to be an essential ingredient in the creativity of creative people. Here, for example, is guitarist Pat Metheny's assessment of the style of pianist Paul Bley in the song "All the Things You Are," during an interview that appeared in the *New York Times:* "His relationship to time is the best sort of pushing and pulling; wrestling with it and at the same time, phrase by phrase, making these interesting connections between bass and drums, making it seem like it's a little bit on top, and then now it's a little bit behind." Metheny's trained ear is able to discern things in music that most of us miss.

Life, for whatever reason, allows very little stasis. Like much else, the brain is either growing or it is wasting. Numerous brain-imaging studies have shown that people who are mentally active are significantly less likely to suffer senility, and that the earlier the brain is engaged the better. The mental calisthenics can vary—learning a second language, doing crosswords, playing a musical instrument, woodworking, reading, writing—but the net effect is largely the same: a brain that knows more and thinks better.

Reading and writing are especially important to critical thinking, as cognitive scientists have long recognized that language is the key to all higher thought. Thought power is basically as good as the quality of the language in which it is expressed. Writing is critical thought in action, and to that end the introduction of a written essay requirement on the SAT is a positive development. The explosion of e-mail is a double-edged sword for writing skills: On the one hand, it means more people are using the written word to communicate than at any time in history; on the other, the automatic, conversational style of e-mail does not lend itself to nuanced thought or rigorous prose. Memory is another key component for good critical thinking, because it doesn't matter how much you know if you can't remember it. Writers such as Charles Dickens and Jack Kerouac seem to have had a photographic memory that was at least in part related to their power of meticulous observation. One memory game we play in our house is a well-known card game called I Spy. A hundred cards are laid face down on the floor in ten rows of ten cards each. Each card has a picture—a guitar, a fish, a clown—and each picture a double. The goal is to find the cards with the same image, which you then get to keep, and to acquire the most cards to win the game. If you turn over the clown card, for instance, the trick is to remember where the other clown card is that someone turned over four turns earlier. As neither my wife nor I have ever beaten our children, the results definitively prove that, at least in our house, memory is a function of age. Studies have shown that a better diet and more exercise also sharpen memory, so I'm hoping with a little effort I can avoid the slippery slope.

CRITICAL THINKING, the scientific method, rationalism—these are all slightly different terms for a rigorous approach drawing on knowledge and observation to make logical inferences leading to sound judgments, good decisions, and the recovery of truth. The approach has been used to make revolutionary, nonintuitive discoveries about the physical universe, plan and execute monumental works of art, and improve efficiencies, yields, productivity, and winning percentages across hundreds of different fields and professions. Special knowledge or advanced analytical methods are sometimes, but not always, needed to maximize the technique's effectiveness. Logical reasoning lies at its core, and history and psychology show that logical reasoning is innate to the human brain and universal to all cultures. The method can err, but in time usually self-corrects. People can improve their critical thinking by working to improve their memory, becoming better observers, learning as much as they can, and being skeptical. Yet, if we allow our society and law to continue to be informed by subjectivity rather than objectivity, with the insistence that the world is composed of a system of isolated truths unique to each individual or group identity, then we have no hope of using reason to solve any problem, or of ever agreeing on anything substantial. We will have succeeded in extinguishing the efficacy of our highest power and therefore, logically, we will have succeeded in extinguishing ourselves.

CHAPTER 12

How to Save Civilization in One Easy Step

George Reynolds knows how to fix problems. As director of industry and university initiatives at Northrop Grumman, Reynolds has troubleshot his way through dozens of projects that have helped save the aerospace and defense contractor millions of dollars by eliminating waste and redundancy. In almost every case, he notes, the biggest hurdle was not technical but managerial—changing dysfunctional habits and ways of thinking that had become institutionalized and caused the problems in the first place. "Everyone is for progress; no one is for change," Reynolds notes wryly.

Today, America is in a similar circumstance. The biggest puzzle is not solving and fixing problems, per se, it is fixing the thinking that causes problems. Certainly, in any specific situation—declining student performance, poor emergency response, lack of anticipation or originality in fighting the war on terrorism—flawed logic or scarce data could be the direct source of error. But the complexity and severity of degree of these afflictions suggest an intellectual malaise consisting of more than one part—not merely, at all times, a breakdown in thinking, but often a disconnect between thinking and action; a disjunction between plan and execution, between intent and result.

There are undoubtedly many alternative explanations for failures to properly carry out what otherwise might pass for sound thinking, or to fail to think at all, but I believe the simplest, most all-inclusive account is this: the widespread acceptance of a Blinklike mind-set. It is this diminishment of power once accorded to critical thinking and reason, the loss of the ability of reason to influence people, policy, and institutions, that is leading to a decline of good outcomes in America and Western civilization as a whole. It is *the* central challenge of our time to change this mind-set.

The task involves nothing less than willfully changing a pattern of thinking that has institutionalized emotion, dogma, political machinations, false science, aversion to risk, and guilt in place of empiricism, objectivity, and reason. The stakes are huge—nothing less than our standard of living, national security, and the possibility of raising the quality of life in other parts of the world. With no objective standard or framework as a point of reference, this mode of thought is creating a society in its image and likeness—a loose association of island universes, each governed by its own set of self-reflecting "truths," each capable of talking and communicating only with itself, each asserting its right to self-esteem and to act as its own judge and arbiter, producing the equivalent of moral and intellectual gridlock. In his book *From Dawn to Decadence, 500 Years of West-*

ern *Cultural Life*, Jacques Barzun observes that, in these modern conditions, no matter how sound a specific proposal might be, "Not two, but three or four groups, organized or impromptu, are ready with contrary reasons" to resist it. Needless to say, the possibility of accomplishing anything in such a society is severely restricted. Barzun believes this condition promotes "the impulse to primitivism," an outlook openly hostile to the conditions of modern life and things as they are, and one in perpetual search of causes to promote—fighting nuclear power, land mines, pro- or antiabortion. As a result, "Institutions function painfully. Repetition and frustration are inevitable."

In an article titled "How Civilizations Fall" appearing in the *New Criterion*, Kenneth Minogue, a professor of political science at the London School of Economics, argues that the division between barbarism and civilization has been blurred by a subjectivity and egalitarianism encouraged by the West's own political and social institutions. Minogue writes:

> *In the past, civilization was a sensibility shared by a class of people, while barbarism would be found not only in tribes beyond the frontier, but also in the slaves and the servile within the realms of civilization itself. In modern liberal democracies, this clear distinction between a culture and a class has disappeared. Everyone is touched by the higher forms of culture. Schooling, museums and the media are available to all. But barbarism remains an active force in modern societies, partly in gracelessness and ignorance, and partly in a loss of cultural coherence found among those who mistake a few years at an institution of higher learning for education itself.*

The barbarians really are dining with us. Minogue supposes that this nonelite, distinguished, it would seem, only by their utter lack of ideas, talent, and originality, have used the privileges of Western democratic society to usurp power with the intention, at best, of reconfiguring it to serve their interests, at worst, to destroy it. Minogue posits that radical feminism in particular has weakened, perhaps fatally, the ethical and intellectual principles upon which Western civilization has been able to grow and flourish. But it seems just as plausible that these principles are being undermined by radical environmentalism, or radical multiculturalism, or radical fearmongering. What gives these various movements any credence in the first place is a mode of thinking that accepts propositions based on emotion, subjectivity, and predetermined ideology.

Our marketing culture not only encourages subjectivity, it directs it. Marketers want us to feel we're all special, "individuals," and at the same time no different. Differences—that is, real differences between people—are a big problem for advertisers because they break up the audience and lower potential revenue. For marketers, an ideal world would be one in which men like the same things as women, and women like the same things as men. Movie and television show producers desire to depict a completely egalitarian and nearly androgynous society where women are tough and adventurous and men sensitive and passive. The Holy Grail is a "crossover" smash, a movie, a show, a story that appeals to all genders, ethnic groups, and ages. Before having won a tournament, teenage golfer Michelle Wie has probably received more daily newspaper coverage in last three years than Jack Nicklaus did in his entire career. Why? Because she has played in a couple of tournaments against men. Wie, for her age, is a very good golfer, and the story has obvious appeal. But there are hundreds of young male amateur golfers as good as or better than Wie who have never received a single line of publicity in *USA Today*.

This rise of subjectivity, and the patterns of fragmentation it has imposed on American life, explains a number of political and social trends. First, it accounts for the fact that the country's "social capital," that is, membership in nonreligious voluntary associations, has been declining for a number of years: Island universes seek only themselves. Second, it accounts for the increased marginalization of critical thinking and reason, and the rise of image and materialism, as the standard for a meaningful or successful life. When logic and reason appear to have little influence on outcomes or decisions in the workplace, home, and society, people naturally begin to wonder, "Why bother?" Emotional, subjective decision-making becomes a meme, a self-reinforcing trend. When I asked a person whose intelligence I respect why he supports the Kyoto protocols to reduce carbon dioxide (a nonpollutant) emissions at a cost of billions of dollars, when most scientists acknowledge that the reductions will have no impact on the earth's climate, he replied, "Reagan once said bird poop, not pollution, was making lakes acidic, so I decided then it's all a matter of what you want to believe."

Far from being the exception, such outlooks have become the norm, pointing to a collapse of the belief in human reason as a way to solve problems, guide progress, and intelligently argue toward degrees of civility. Of course, some lakes in the eastern United States were turning acidic not from bird poop, but from sulfur dioxide and nitrogen dioxide emissions (released from coal-burning power plants), which were then finding their way into the rain and soil (emissions which have been significantly reduced since 1990). But because of one unsophisticated instance of intellectual conceit, this person, like many others, has received a profound psychological wound that will not allow him to trust the powers of his own mind. One more island universe has been created in an ocean across which no bridge of reason can be built.

The fragmentation caused by the banishment of reason in public life seems to be fueling an ever-accelerating vicious cycle: Critical thinking falls into disuse or becomes afflicted with fallacies, and when it is used it is often ignored or discredited, which causes it to fall into further decline. Today, as historian James Harvey Robinson once noted, "Most of our so-called reasoning consists in finding arguments for going on believing as we already do." Ironically, a society of island universes, each with staunch, unshakable, but essentially unexamined beliefs, is not creating diversity, it is producing uniformity. Because the uncritical, incurious mind is not creative, there is over time a leveling off of knowledge, ideas, and attitudes. We are what we think, the saying goes, and, as it takes in thinner and thinner slices of the world, uncritical thought becomes shallower and shallower. It spews platitudes, mouths the received half-wisdoms and biases of others, and is unable to express nuance. The precipitous deterioration of American literary and social criticism is not a consequence of a lack of talented writers and scholars, it is the upshot of a lack of an audience. The preponderance of how-to books is a direct result of the market demand produced by the retreat of the shallow mind from understanding, discretion, and taste, toward the level playing field, the instant reward, and the quick fix.

Such a society, over time, invariably becomes more and more high-maintenance, service-intensive. It is no coincidence that there has been a continual expansion of government in the lives of Americans, despite a quarter-century of half-serious attempts to reduce it, and a strong, popular consensus to tackle the job: Subjective belief is not equipped to engage the world; it lends itself to being taken care of. As we draw into our island universes, avoiding risk, anxious to preserve our belief systems at any cost, sensitive to the way others perceive us, restraining the number and types of our associations as free men and women, the informal systems upon which civil, public life depend begin to wither. A cohesion that would normally arise from social, civic, commercial, and intellectual intercourse must be imposed by rules. In this fragmented, Hobbesian society of our own making, the call goes out for grander plans, further studies, more oversight, and additional programs. We concede the act of governing to specialists and institutions.

Butler Shaffer, a professor of law at the Southwestern University School of Law, analyzes the harmful effects of state and bureaucratic growth on advanced societies in an article called "The Decline and Fall of a Civilization." Shaffer writes:

> *The problem with all of this, as historians advise us, is that the institutionalization of the systems that produce the values upon which a civilization depends, ultimately bring about the*

> *destruction of that civilization. Arnold Toynbee observed that*
> *a civilization begins to break down when there is "a loss of cre-*
> *ative power in the souls of creative individuals," and, in time,*
> *the "differentiation and diversity that characterized a dy-*
> *namic civilization, is replaced by 'a tendency towards stan-*
> *dardization and uniformity.' "*

Why do bureaucracy and, more specifically, institutional-ization of values cause a society to decay? In a nutshell, be-cause creative and productive societies are dynamic societies, capable of adapting to complex, changing conditions. Even in the era of the Roman Empire, the world was never pre-dictable; it is far less so now. In a global society structured on instant, widespread communication of knowledge, informa-tion, trends, and events move too fast for institutions to model and predict. Yet, as a lumbering response to declining primary education, global terrorism, or hurricane prepared-ness and relief demonstrate, America, the very symbol of ini-tiative and individual responsibility, has become paralyzed by the illusion that institutions, not people, solve problems. A so-ciety bogged down in a quagmire of rules, regulations, com-mittees, and departments, all ruled over as fiefdoms by little emperors and empresses, is a "can't do" society.

Because modern American society has an apparent ra-tional structure—plans, systems, models—some critics have ar-gued that its flaws and problems are caused by reason itself. According to this theory, the inherent limits of the rational method cause it to begin to work against itself. Others, such as writer John Ralston Saul, have expanded the theme into a blanket condemnation of reason and science as the root cause of every atrocity and ill that has befallen the West in the last five hundred years. In his book *Voltaire's Bastards*, Saul writes, "The twentieth century, which has seen the final victory of pure reason in power, has also seen unprecedented unleashings of violence and of power deformed. It is hard for example, to avoid noticing that the murder of six million Jews was a perfectly rational act." The book is a frightfully long-winded compendium of similar obtuse rhetoric, unsubstantiated by any evidence or logic. Indeed, far from being rational, the Holocaust was the very epitome of madness. It was not a product of reason or logic or evidence, but a result of delusion, hysteria, mass hypnosis, and a murderous thirst to exact revenge on a scapegoat. Saul naively equates a state and how it comes into being and functions with reason. But a state functions for and through power, not reason, with its main objective being self-preservation. Its purpose is to exert authority and maintain order. Any self-referential system, such as a state, is generally not structured or politically inclined to use the elements of critical thinking (evidence, logic, skepticism) to discover, for instance, that an opposing system or political party has a good idea for reducing the budget deficit or improving literacy. This is why Americans have traditionally feared growth in state power and wrote a constitution originally intended to rein it in.

What the Framers did not anticipate is that empiricism would be replaced by feelings, that reason and logic would be supplanted by subjectivity, and that society would come to attach less importance to measurable deeds and work and more to image and perception. By placing feelings on equal footing with intellect and reason, one automatically tilts a society away from freedom, objectivity, and reason, toward dependence on institutions, acceptance of government intrusion, and standards based on subjective criteria. It is the direction in which the United States has been sliding for the better part of a century. Academics and intellectuals are usually far removed from experiencing the effects of a society configured to the demands of virtue, rather than the demands of reason. Universal justice is always a moving standard. How much money is the physical and psychological damage resulting from spilled coffee worth? Five million dollars? A hundred million dollars? To what degree do we manage the risk that someone will be harmed by a certain activity—one chance in a thousand, or one chance in a million? If Johnny, Alicia, or José can't read, whose fault is it? Does being inclusive and multicultural mean we give equal weight to all ideas? The chairman of the English department at Pennsylvania State University once remarked, "I would bet that Alice's Walker's *The Color Purple* is taught more in English departments today than all of Shakespeare's plays combined." How do we foster creativity and accomplishment in a society in which standards are nonexistent or relative? In the 1980s I witnessed the human resources director at a large automotive plant inform a young man that he would not get a position in the skilled trades, even though his test scores were higher than those of several people who had been accepted—the company had to hire a woman and a minority. That young man walked out of the office angry, distraught, another island universe.

Once walked down, the road of subjectivity and feelings leads not to a better society, but to an increasingly dysfunctional one, with an ever greater dependency on institutions, government programs, lawyers, therapy, and received knowledge, superstition, and dogma. It doesn't produce a more "just" world, but a more alienated and demoralized one. While reason can err or be used to justify injustice, reason also depends on an ordered social context, law, and some limitations on freedom. Reason, in essence, comes prepackaged with ethics. Free people employing critical thinking in pursuit of their self-interest are naturally pursuing "the world they want." They are also building a "just" society in which people are held accountable for their actions, and in which their self-interest has value only in relation to everyone's mutual interest. Managers at today's companies display a concrete understanding of how reason and the pursuit of self-interest advance the betterment of the whole when they aspire to make their organizations "lean." The predominant business model of the day is based on lean principles, paring out hierarchy, decentralizing, and creating independently operating plants or divisions with total accountability for product or service design, sales, and production. One company, for example, Magna International, Inc., has set the standard in the automotive business for the successful use of a rational, lean approach that hands over to employees both high levels of responsibility and potential reward.

IN PONDERING THE MIRACLE of the American economy, an article in the *Economist* ponders "how much better a country as successful as this might do if it really tried."

The question contains a compliment but also implies a potentially grave assertion, one increasingly mused over by people around the world and by some Americans. Does "not doing better" also mean "in decline"? I do not need, here, to make a prolonged case for the American Empire. It is self-apparent. The sheer wealth of the United States is prodigious and possibly historically unprecedented. Economists at a Swedish think tank, Timbro, found that if Europe were part of the United States, only Luxembourg could equal the richest of the fifty American states in gross domestic product per capita. Americans need not take umbrage at scrutiny eager to detect the first signs of a hint of a slide. This watchful curiosity is not motivated as much by envy as it is by precedent and empirical evidence. Science and psychology have confirmed that nothing alive exists in a state of stasis. A lilac bush, a salmon, a person, a civilization is either moving upward to some organic, physiological, intellectual, or cultural apex or it is moving downward. Sometimes the movements, as with the stock market, can be infinitesimal, and thus hardly noticed. Sometimes there can be a number of small, multiple peaks and valleys. Over time, however, the trend plays itself out. History, of course, confirms this: All great civilizations, empires, kingdoms eventually deteriorate, although their influence can still be profound for a long time after their peak. While the rise of a particular civilization, say the British Empire, can take place over hundreds of years, its actual peak, in terms of the full realization and extent of its power, creativity, and influence, is often far less than that, sometimes less than one hundred years, and many historians believe the causes for decline settle into the culture long before the first noticeable signs of weakening make their appearance.

Speculation about the causes of decline in civilization is not in any way scientific, but one of the most common explanations invoked by historians is a cycle of growing vigor and gradual decay. As summarized by historian James Anthony Froude, "Virtue and truth produced strength, strength dominion, dominion riches, riches luxury and luxury weakness and collapse—the fatal sequence repeated so often." The Roman Empire, which flourished from roughly 27 B.C. to 300 C.E., appears to have followed the pattern of the cycle precisely, although weakness may have been brought on by more than mere luxury. A shrinking population made it more difficult to recruit men for the army and collect taxes from its citizens. Decline was hastened by incompetent and dissolute leadership. The stench of decay eventually reached the barbarians, who invaded Rome in 410 C.E. The impetus for the decline of other civilizations has been attributed to specific events. The Han Dynasty of China (206 B.C. to 9 C.E.), for example, appears to have been undone by a popular revolt over landlord exploitation. A more befuddling but politically correct view of history proposed by author Jared Diamond seems to be the historical counterpart to *Blink*: The rise and fall of civilizations is caused by circumstance, environment, and random, chance events.

Another vein of thought in the theory of collapse focuses less on macroscopic causes and pure luck and instead affixes responsibility for decline to changes in the psychology of a civilization's population. It is not luxury, or corruption, or invasion per se that ultimately threatens and weakens a society, but moral decline, spiritual decline, ennui, or some sort of intellectual lethargy. This, it seems, more exactly describes the situation in the United States today.

The most significant change in America over the past two

hundred years has not been political, or economic, or even philosophical—it has been psychological. Subjectivity and emotion have displaced empirical evidence, reasoning, and skepticism as the basis for the nation's outlook on life, law, and the pursuit of happiness. This has resulted in an epidemic of intellectual *disengagement.* Why be curious about the world and what goes on in it when "that" world couldn't possibly have any relevance to my life? "It's all a matter of what you choose to believe," goes the common refrain, encapsulating the capitulation of reason to emotion and intuition. But it would be one thing if such an outlook led merely to relativity of values or beliefs. Instead, the trend is also leading to relativity in people's judgment, inability to make sound decisions, lack of imagination and creativity, and loss of willpower. As a result, today many people's interests are chiefly defined by their causes, one of the chief ones being their self, their identity, their culture.

In his book *The Clash of Civilizations,* Samuel Huntington reports on the threat that fixation on cultural identity and separateness poses to the American political system.

> *The Founding Fathers saw diversity as a reality and as a problem: hence the national motto,* e pluribus unum, *chosen by a committee of the Continental Congress. . . . Later political leaders who also were fearful of the dangers of racial, sectional, ethnic, economic and cultural diversity . . . responded to the call of "bring us together," and made the promotion of national unity their central responsibility. "The one absolutely certain way of bringing this nation to ruin, of preventing all possibility of its continuing as a nation at all," warned*

Theodore Roosevelt, "would be to permit it to become a tangle of squabbling nationalities." In the 1990s, however, the leaders of the United States have not only permitted that but assiduously promoted the diversity rather than the unity of the people they govern.

Island universes, as I've noted, are high-maintenance, requiring ever greater amounts of government and personal service, assistance, and advice. Psychologist and author Rollo May believes one sure sign that American society is in decline is its increasing dependency on therapy.

At the beginning of an age (civilization) there are no psychotherapists. But at the end of an age—every age through history has been the same—every other person becomes a therapist, because there are no ways of ministering to people in need, and they form long lines to the psychotherapist's office. I think it's a sign of the decadence of our age, rather than a sign of our great intelligence. . . . Almost every other person in California is a psychotherapist.

Therapy may be needed by some people, but when an entire population is under therapy it is a sign that it is an indulgence that has become for most people the study of the self, the study of one's own subjectivity. Such a study is seen as necessary in a universe with no truth where self-knowledge is the only knowledge. Yet, over a protracted period of time, which is typical for many therapy sessions these days, such an activity detracts from the productivity and creativity of society. In historical terms, a civilization will decline when it diverts more and more intellectual capital to preoccupations that essentially draw off existing wealth and innovation, while adding nothing in return. Therapy, in today's business lingo, is "noncore."

There appears to be no great amount of research on the role subjectivity has played in decline of great ages, civilizations, and nations. Still, it is clear there must be a connection. Objectivity is rooted in the outside world, its physical laws, the functioning of society, the practical needs of human beings; subjectivity is fixed in the self, the contemplation of consciousness and the meaning of its own emotional states. It is objectivity that motivated human beings to measure the world with science and mathematics, invent language, make tools and pottery, build aqueducts, and create sculpture and painting. All dynamic, creative civilizations are fundamentally objective. Objectivity makes reason and critical thinking possible, an insight that the ancient Greeks used to form a new type of society, a democracy. The significance of objectivity to Greek democracy, and democracy in general, is made clear by Charles Van Doren, in a passage from his book A *History of Knowledge.*

> In short, there was suddenly a new thing in the world, which the Greeks called episteme, *and we call science. Organized knowledge. Public knowledge, based on principles that could be periodically reviewed and tested—and questioned—by all. . . . There were enormous consequences. First the idea grew that there was only one truth, not many truths,*

about anything: men might disagree, but if they did, then some must be right and others wrong.

The idea that "some must be right and others wrong" does not jibe with modern multiculturalism, radical feminism, or extreme, nonscientific environmentalism. But objectivity and reason are universal. Subjectivity has grown at the expense of objectivity, it would seem, because subjectivity has become the equivalent of a quick fix—a means to right perceived past wrongs, to avoid risk of future wrongs, and generally to make life easier. If you can't bring people up to educational standards, then lower the standards. If people are going to protest outside your office, it doesn't matter what the science says, if you don't pass an expensive new regulation, you will have egg on your face. Subjectivity has become the instrument of choice for political subversion, expedience, and atonement. In its ability to instill the powerfully debilitating forces of guilt and self-hatred into society, subjectivity appears to be a feature of declining and declined civilizations. As Niall Ferguson documents in his book *Empire*, "When I got to Oxford in 1982 the Empire was no longer even funny. In those days the Oxford Union still debated solemn motions like 'This House Regrets Colonization.' " Yet, clearly, as Ferguson argues, with appropriate prostration of course, the British Empire of the nineteenth and early twentieth centuries did much that was good.

YET IN ONE SENSE, America has time, location, and even history on its side. Aside from dependence on foreign oil, the country has no fundamental weaknesses arising from geography, ethnic rivalries and hatreds fueled by historical cycles of violence, welfare-state mentality, or structurally unreformable government. Its top-tier universities and research facilities are second to none. It is abundant in water, land, natural resources, and capital and is a country that has been run on innovation and free enterprise since its founding. As Huntington observes, "The overriding lesson of the history of civilizations, however, is that many things are probable but nothing is inevitable." America also has incentive in the form of grand, new opportunities.

The world is changing, and Americans have traditionally been able to adapt to change better than most. Some scholars and writers believe the terrorist attacks of 9/11 marked a turning point in history, one that debunks the notion, first put forth by philosopher Oswald Spengler, that all civilizations eventually collapse into universal states. In modern times Spengler's view has been reinterpreted to mean that globalism and electronic information will turn the world into a monoculture, with the only differences being the efficiency and execution of a country's or region's market economy. Instead, it is clear that vast social, cultural, political, and economic differences remain between nations and regions around the world. The world may not be as flat as many, such as Thomas Friedman, suppose. In this environment, ideas, and more important, ideas in action, rather than military might or sheer industrial-style economic muscle, will play the most decisive role in influencing international relations, the spread of democracy, and the success of business ventures. America's future influence in this realm of geopolitics will largely depend on its intellectual capacities and its ability to logically communicate ideas to a diverse global audience, much of which genuinely want to like America. Critical thinking, and specific intellectual skill sets, will obviously be needed for American businesses to compete effectively in this environment, as well as for the U.S. government to thaw out and improve relations with traditional allies and convince emerging countries that democracy is in *their* best interest.

A simple demonstration of this point is the war on terror and the war in Iraq, both of which have been hampered by a severe deficit of Arabic linguists. One can extend the principle even further to conjecture how much better our relations with our allies and nominal strategic partners would be if we had not only a large diplomatic corps, but a body of citizens fluent in German, French, Chinese, or Russian. Things really do get lost in translation. But just as important is what a mother language symbolizes to a country—the embodiment of its history and culture. Americans have been spoiled by the universality of English, but the simple ability to speak another's tongue can accomplish as much as or more than millions in foreign aid or rounds of shuttle diplomacy.

Critical thinking, and more specifically, critical thinking that is better implemented, is also needed at home to address lingering problems in education, urban decay, personal health, and racial disparity in reading, writing, and other essential job-life skills. The importance of applied critical thinking is driven home by acknowledging that pragmatic, effective solutions for these and other complex problems simply cannot be expected to be provided by the government. There is no empirical evidence that any government, anywhere, can do anything more than offer Band-Aid fixes to large problems such as these. The solutions, especially in a country founded on the principles of liberty and individual responsibility, must ultimately come from the people.

The bigger question that looms is how does America change from being a society run by emotion, ideology, and political expediency to being one run by reason and logic? In previous chapters I suggested specific fixes—a return to active parental mentoring and guidance, an acceptance of risk and change as a means of stretching people's minds and finding fulfillment, a pursuit of the study of the elements of critical thinking and an understanding that there is an objective truth outside ourselves. These actions will enhance the importance people attach to knowledge and allow them to practice the art of making inferences and judgments supported by observations and data. Some institutional changes would also further the cause of critical thinking. One report compiled by a team of international scientists, "Statistics, Science and Public Policy," urges government to make better use of scientists in shaping public policy. The recommendations contained in the report make perfect sense in light of the anomalies and costs that have been introduced into society through ill-conceived policy and law. Pork-barrel projects, bureaucratic redundancy, environmental and safety overkill, tort law, affirmative action programs, and biased or blatantly false reporting in the media have understandably instilled in the public's mind a grave doubt that objectivity and truth still exist. Ongoing reform in laws and institutions is absolutely required to restore confidence that we live in a rational world governed by a rational set of laws that apply equally to all people.

But the biggest change will be philosophical. It is one thing to ask to a person to read. It is quite a different thing to create and live in conditions in which reading is seen as important and essential. For this, the objectives of learning must be more than acquiring the ability to recite the state capitals or calculate the circumference of a circle. For this, learning must be seen as essential to the way a society functions, through the application and *acceptance* of critical thinking and logic as the way to solve problems, make decisions, and determine policy. As author Chester Barnard puts it, "The most interesting and astounding contradiction in life is to me the constant insistence by nearly all people upon 'logic' . . . on the one hand, and on the other their inability to display it, and their unwillingness to accept it when displayed by others." If a family, business, or government does not accept or act on evidence of facts and the conclusions logically inferred from them, then all the declamations about the importance of learning ring hollow. People can learn vocationally, to ready themselves and their children to master tasks needed to do certain jobs. Under conditions in which subjectivity and emotion reign, there is diminished motivation to take up the challenge of broad, lifelong learning that leads to the development of good critical thinking.

I say "diminished motivation" because I believe that learning is its own reward, one that immeasurably adds to the quality and fulfillment of one's life. I am certainly not the exception. There appears to be a growing, pent-up demand for knowledge and ideas in Ameri-

Best-selling books such as *The Kite Runner* and *John Adams* suggest that Americans are reading more than just steamy romance novels and spy thrillers.

can public life. Americans rank fourth in the world in money spent on books per capita, and the popularity of such best-selling books such as *The Kite Runner* and *John Adams* suggests that Americans are reading more than just steamy romance novels and spy thrillers. The assumption that Americans will pay to see only witless, dialogue-challenged action movies full of violence and special effects is a myth. The top two all-time movies in the United States in terms of gross revenue are *Titanic* and *Star Wars*, hardly the stuff of the shoot-'em-up crowd. In a PBS interview, author Gregg Easterbrook says he sees signs of a shift of values in many parts of American society:

> One theory that I want to throw out is that we're in a period of transition from materialistic want to meaning want. . . . I think people have gained a second interest in really wanting to feel that their lives have meaning or value. It's common sense now that you know I live in a nice house, have a comfortable car, my kids are going to college, but what does my life mean? What's the purpose of my life? I think it's much more common to think that today and it's a healthy sign that people think this obviously.

A trend backing up Easterbrook's observation is the growth of "Socrates cafés," which are weekly, informal gatherings dedicated to philosophical discussion and inquiry. The concept of Socrates cafés grew out of Chris Phillips's book with the same title, and there are now about 150 of them around the world, most in the United States. At one meeting at a café in Seattle, people debated questions such as "To what

extent is the media responsible for trash culture?" and "What place should music have in your life?" according to an article in the *Seattle Post-Intelligencer.* "It's one thing to just offer an opinion," said one participant. "At a Socrates café we have to say why we have the opinion."

Objectivity, reasoning, and empirical evidence were the basis of the great philosopher's method. The cafés are a wonderful development because in all walks of life there needs to be a clearer demonstration and firsthand experience of the immense usefulness and ability of critical thinking to probe the world and solve practical problems.

One way of directly experiencing the power of critical thinking is, not surprisingly, to immerse oneself in the reading or writing of criticism. By criticism I mean a reasoned evaluation of a work, an issue, an event, an organization, or a whole society. Criticism was once widely written and read in small journals and magazines. Some of those publications are still in circulation, but they are not widely read, and today the only exposure most people get to criticism is through a book review or restaurant review in a newspaper.

Criticism should strive first to raise our consciousness, rather than our conscience or feelings, in the mode of Michael Moore. There is a reason Moore always wears a ballcap. He is a big kid with a slingshot in his back pocket picking off large, easy targets. His method of making movies is highly subjective. Moore has already come to his conclusions before he starts filming. His method requires that some facts be selected and some facts be rejected. One can only assume his work appeals to a certain group of people, not merely for its politics, but also for the way it portrays on film their own selective perception of life and society.

THE GREAT TIDE of emotion and snap judgments sweeping across the country seems to push and pull people onto two opposing shores: Either everything is right about the country, or everything is wrong. Neither side is objective or constructive. However, when it comes to transmitting its message to the public, the body of evidence shows—whether it's in the subject matter of movies, or stories covered by the media, or actually implemented public policy and law—that the everything-is-wrong side generally has the upper hand. Many people from other countries whose only perception of United States comes from Hollywood and the media actually believe Americans live in a sort of Uganda-style state in which a tiny percentage of people live in mansions and the rest of us reside in shanty-towns, ghettos, and trailers. The impulse to guilt and self-loathing has become so fashionable that some people have attempted to formalize the sentiment in, of all places, the rebuilding project at Ground Zero. One feature of the rebuilding project, the International Freedom Center and Drawing Center, has been designed and unveiled as "part of a lasting tribute to freedom," according to New York governor George Pataki. A relative of one of the victims of 9/11 says, however, that the Freedom Center would be "a high tech, multi-media tutorial about man's inhumanity to man," according to an article published in the *Wall Street Journal*. The relative, Debra Burlingame, added that building this over Ground Zero would be like "creating a 'Museum of Tolerance' over the sunken graves of the USS *Arizona.*" The committee overseeing the design of the Freedom Center is reevaluating its plans.

It would be great if restoring objectivity and the relevance of critical thinking to American society were as simple as asking people to let go of their personal fetishes, hurts, angers, and all manner of emotional extravagances; to accept personal responsibility for their situation, even if that means allowing that someone or something at some time treated them contemptuously or unfairly. The problem, I believe, is not that people can't or won't change. The problem is that large numbers of people—trial lawyers, bureaucrats, corporations, feminists, minorities, activists—have benefited from the institutionalization of subjectivity. The departure from science, the politicization of decision making, the elimination of standards, and the complicity of the media with the fear industry are phenomena that did not spontaneously sprout from the American cultural soil. They are the result of systematically applied political pressure and the realization that in most cases there are votes, jobs, and lots of money to be gained from all this wishy-washiness.

But there is, I would argue, much, much more to gain in the short and long term, for all Americans, by breaking up this forty-year romance with subjective idealism and returning to this country's empirical, objective roots.

- *Health/fulfillment:* A life built around subjective feelings is usually filled with anxiety and unwarranted fears. A mind intrigued by the objective world, one able to ask questions and solve problems, is no fail-safe against physical and mental deterioration, but evidence shows a strong correlation between knowledge and intelligence, and success and longevity.

- *National security:* We knew where bin Laden and al Qaeda were for many years. We knew they were planning an attack. A better-thought-out strategy and the *will* to implement it could possibly have prevented 9/11.

- *Money:* The potential flooding problems in New Orleans resulting from a direct hit of a major storm had been known and studied for years. A fix would have cost several billion dollars. A conservative estimate for the cost of rebuilding New Orleans is currently in the range of $70 billion to $200 billion.

- *Economic growth:* As the question was posed by the *Economist,* how much better could America do if it really tried? Sharp and professional on the surface, many American companies are nonetheless afflicted with the same "can't do" mentality and bureaucracy seen in various levels of society and government. Growth and profits have slowed at many American corporations as product lines have matured and offshore competition has increased. Better critical thinkers graduating from all the country's universities, not just the elite schools, are needed to spur new cycles of innovation and challenge all the old assumptions about doing business, most of which no longer apply in a global knowledge economy.

- *Foreign relations:* As Stephen Walt asserts in his book *Taming American Power,* the fact that many countries prefer, grudgingly, American world dominance over the alternatives doesn't mean America can simply ask other countries to entrust themselves to its power. America needs to be persuasive, and to do this will take more than a second language, as much as that would help. Americans need to learn more about the history and culture of other peoples and countries, not to "celebrate" diversity, but to specifically understand how and why the world works. The nation needs to have diplomats who can anticipate the standard anti-American propaganda and debate on their feet. For example, in a meeting with Undersecretary of State for Public Diplomacy Karen Hughes, one Saudi Arabian woman asserted that America had become a right-wing country in which criticism of the government was suppressed, according to an article in the *New York Times*. Ms. Hughes replied, "I have to say I wish that was sometimes true, but it's not." Clever, but Hughes's response needed to cite empirical evidence. Had the Saudi woman heard of Michael Moore's *Fahrenheit 911*? Did she know of the outpouring of criticism from the media directed at the government in the aftermath of Hurricane Katrina?

I am not suggesting that a return to objectivity and better critical thinking can provide clear-cut answers to every question. We do not live in a black-and-white world, and truth itself is often fuzzy. But when one is in want of answers, there is no alternative. Neither are any of the potential benefits listed here of the low-hanging-fruit variety. The perks of objectivity and critical thinking will require effort and the incorporation of a new paradigm into American public life and into its educational system. Beginning in elementary school, we need to place a greater emphasis on both the study of world history, geography, and politics and the development of critical- and creative-thinking skills. This latter "module" of education would consist of generic, non-math-oriented problem solving, writing essays and reviews, and the practice of rhetoric and debate. This style of traditional "liberal" education, as Professor William B. Allen observes, will equip students with the skills they need for life *and* work. Allen writes, "A liberal education will develop students' skills in speaking, writing, thinking critically, and reasoning ethically, along with other skills that employers across many job sectors say are essential."

Perhaps all great civilizations do inevitably decline. As it is America's apparent destiny, however, to be the caretaker of the values of liberty, true freedom, and objectivity inherited from the Western European Enlightenment, I believe it is imperative that the country do all it can to stave off the moral and mental complacency that comes with success and affluence. All the more so because the true meaning of our historical experience, etched into the founding of the republic, is progress. To settle for less, to arbitrarily limit the potential of human beings in the name of safety or egalitarianism or some other ideology, is to erode the case for popular government, and likewise embolden the case for tryanny. To avert this, America needs to engage the world, and itself, by reengaging with its vital and substantial intellectual energies. Individual Americans must rediscover, and assert, their revolutionary spirit. This spirit was, and always has been, the courage to use one's intelligence.

Notes

Chapter 1

Page

6   "Thinking Critically about Critical Thinking," John Bardi, self-published, 1.

6   OECD/PISA 2003 database, 33.

7   National Assessment of Educational Progress 2003 results, *U.S. News & World Report*, Nov. 24, 2003, 12.

7   Bob Lutz, from speech at the Society of Automotive Engineers World Congress, April 12, 2005.

8   "Writing: A Ticket to Work . . . or a Ticket Out," National Commission on Writing, *New York Times*, Brent Staples, May 15, 2005.

8   M. Gladwell, *Blink: The Power of Thinking Without Thinking*, 2005, introduction (Little Brown and Co.).

28 "Four Places Where the System Broke Down," *Time*, Sept. 19, 2005, 16–23.

31 G. Holton, "Einstein and the Cultural Roots of Modern Science," *Daedalus*, Winter 1998, 14.

32 B. Russell (1917), *A Free Man's Worship* (London: Unwin Paperbacks).

Chapter 2

36   Bert James Loewenberg (1972), *American Thought in American History*, 14 (New York: Simon & Schuster).

37   William Graham Sumner, www.criticalthinking.org.

37   R. Ruggerio (2003), *Beyond Feelings: A Guide to Critical Thinking*, 21–22 (McGraw-Hill Higher Education).

40   Enterprise Value Stream Mapping citation, *Canadian Plastics*, Feb. 2005, 15.

42   University of California, Berkeley, *International Journal of Behavioral Research*, 2004.

43   Time Americans Spend Reading, NPD Group, Port Washington, N.Y.

44   National Institute for Literacy, "Reading Facts," www.nifl.gov.

44   D. A. Norman (1993), *Things That Make Us Smart*, 15 (Perseus Books).

47   CNN/USA Today poll, *USA Today*, June 23, 2005, D1.

48   R. Krevolin, *Scriptwriting Secrets*, May 2002, 14.

48   C. White (2003), *The Middle Mind*, 44 (HarperSanFrancisco).

54   D. Mamet, *New York Times*, Feb. 13, 2005, OpEd Section, 15.

54   University College, London (cited study), James Shreeve, *National Geographic*, March 2005, 16.

56   J. McKenzie, www.fno.org.

Chapter 3

59   C. De Waal (2005), *On Pragmatism*, 15 (Thomson Learning Inc.).

60   "It depends on what the meaning of the word 'is' is." Starr Grand Jury Investigation Report, footnote 1, 128.

63   B. Carey, *New York Times*, July 3, 2005, Section 4, 3.

65   U.S. productivity statistics, United States Department of Labor, Bureau of Labor Statistics, "Revised Data for 2003."

65   "Have the courage to use your own intelligence!" Frederique

Krupa, "History of Design from the Enlightenment to the In-dustrial Revolution," www.translucency.com.

65 "Originality is not the prime factor, effectiveness is." Quoted in Neil Genzlinger's review, "They Made America," by Harold Evans, *New York Times Book Review*, Jan. 23, 2005, 14.

67 "We're actually training our engineers to be managers." SAE World Congress, April 12, 2005.

72 "Customers are becoming more diverse." Ibid.

74 R. Hofstadter (1962), *Anti-Intellectualism in American Life*, 25–50 (New York: Vintage).

76 "What people resent out there are those in the blue states think-ing they're smarter." Quoted in *Reasononline*, "Intellectual War-fare," Cathy Young, May 2002.

79 "I pay no attention to what I have been taught." Quoted in *American History in American Thought*, Bert James Loewenberg, 261.

80 Ibid., 93.

81 Ibid., 90.

81 T. J. DiLorenzo (2004), *How Capitalism Saved America*, Ch. 7 (Crown Publishing Group).

83 "The genuine liberty on which America is founded is totally and entirely a New System of Things." Quoted in *American His-tory in American Thought*, Bert James Loewenberg, 141.

83 "The revolution was fought with words." Ibid., 166.

84 "The first King of England." Ibid., 170.

Chapter 4

87 L. Diller (1999), *Running on Ritalin*, Ch. 1 (New York: Bantam Books).

88 Note on adverse reactions to Ritalin, "Ritalin is Poison," The DeWeese Report, FreeRepublic.com, 4.

89 Statistics on ADD prevalence, Reuters Limited, Sept. 2, 2005, yahoo.com.

90   "A study published in the Journal of American College Health." *Orlando Sentinel*, "Report: Students use ADD pills as study aid," David Damron, Jan. 26, 2005, www.messenger-inquirer.com.

90   Market for Ritalin and other ADD-controlling drugs. "Celgene grows to No. 9 biotech company on once-loathed drug," Linda Johnson, Associated Press, April 24, 2005.

91   "The low level of intellectual effort was shocking." Quoted in *A Dose of Sanity*, Dr. Sidney Walker, 22 (New York: Wiley & Sons, 1996).

91   "To read about the evolution of the DSM." Ibid., 20.

92   "The visceral dislike of medicine." Ibid., 18.

93   C. Hoff Summers (2001), *The War Against Boys*, 46 (New York: Simon & Shuster).

93   "As yet no distinctive pathology." Quoted in "ADD/ADHD: The Designer Disease," By Tim O'Shea. 1999, www.chiro.org.

95   S. Satel and C. Hoff Summers (2005), *One Nation Under Therapy* (New York: St. Martin's Press).

96   G. Easterbrook (2003), *The Progress Paradox* (New York: Random House Publishing Group).

96   *The Social Importance of Self-Esteem*, National Association for Self-Esteem.

97   "One study conducted by a group of University of Iowa researchers." R. Baumeister, J. D. Campbell, J. I. Kreuger, and K. D. Vohs, ScientificAmerican.com, Dec. 20, 2004.

97   J. Tierney, "When Every Child Is Good Enough," *New York Times*, Nov. 21, 2004, Week in Review, 1.

98   M. Barone (2004), *Hard America, Soft America* (Crown Forum).

98   L. Diller (1999), *Running on Ritalin*, Ch. 1 (New York: Bantam Books).

Chapter 5

102   Larry Summers's speech, quoted in "Dear Ellen: or Sexual
       Correctness at Harvard," Ruth R. Wisse, *Commentary*, April
       2005, 32.

102   G. Will, "History, Hubris and Harvard," *Jewish World Review*,
       May 19, 2005.

103   R. Wisse, "Dear Ellen: or Sexual Correctness at Harvard," *Com-
       mentary*, April 2005, 32.

103   L. Chavez, "Bias doesn't explain gap in math, science skills,"
       Creators Syndicate, Los Angeles, Calif.

104   The College Board, 2004 Advance Placement Test.

105   J. Eccles, "Why Women Shy Away from Careers in Science,"
       University of Michigan News Service, April 7, 2005.

105   D. Falk, *The Walrus*, June 2005, 60.

105   R. Wisse, "Dear Ellen: or Sexual Correctness at Harvard," *Com-
       mentary*, April 2005, 33.

107   Forest Products Laboratory, brochure titled "Performance Engi-
       neered Composites Research," Madison, Wisc.

108   S. Cavanagh, "Educators Revisit Girls' Loss of Math, Science
       Interest," *Education Week*, May 4, 2005, Issue 34, 6.

109   S. Johnson (2004), *Mind Wide Open*, 14 (New York: Scribner).

109   W. Farrell, taken from interview in the *New York Times*,
       C. Deutsch, Feb. 27, 2005, BU 7.

114   Prof. R. Sander, *Stanford Law Review*, study cited in the *New York
       Times*, A. Liptak, "For Blacks in Law School, Can Less Be
       More," Feb. 13, 2005, Week in Review, 3.

115   J. McWhorter, *Losing the Race: Self Sabotage in Black America*,
       cited in "The Distortion of Affirmative Action," George Will,
       townhall.com, *Washington Post Writers Group*, March 1,
       2001.

115   National Assessment of Educational Progress (1999), cited on
       National Institute for Literacy's "Reading Facts," www.nifl.gov.

117   S. Mnookin (2004), *Hard News: The Scandals at the New York*

Times and Their Meaning for American Media, xvi (New York: Random House).

118   Ibid., 140–200.

118   Ibid., xvii.

119   Ibid., 188.

120   FrontPageMagazine.com, interview conducted by Jamie Glazov, Oct. 5, 2004.

123   Chuck Hagel, *New York Times Magazine*, July 3, 2005, 17.

123   T. Franks, with M. McConnell (2004), *American Soldier* (Regan-Books).

123   Y. Bodansky (2004), *The Secret History of the Iraq War*, 490 (ReganBooks).

Chapter 6

126   Lewis Lapham interview, conducted by Casey Walker, *Wild Duck Review*, Feb. 16, 2000, MediaChannel.org.

130   N. Chomsky, E. Herman (1988), *Manufacturing Consent* (New York: Pantheon).

130   R. McChesney (1997), *Corporate Media and the Threat to Democracy* (Seven Stories Press).

133   S. Brownback, *USA Today* (Society for the Advancement of Education), LookSmart's FindArticles, Nov. 2000.

134   S. McClellan, "Fox Breaks Prime-Time Record," *Adweek*, Sept. 12, 2005.

135   Lewis Lapham interview, conducted by Casey Walker, *Wild Duck Review*, Feb. 16, 2000, MediaChannel.org.

138   A. Huxley (1942), *Brave New World Revisited*, pp. 35–36 (New York: Harper Perennial Modern Classics).

139   K. Dixon, "Obesity Costs Soar Tenfold to $36.5 Billion on U.S," *Reuters Ltd.*, June 27, 2005.

140   University of California, Berkeley, *International Journal of Behavioral Research*, 2004.

143   J. Miller, "Light Show," *Sound on Sound*, Feb. 1994, soundon sound.com.

143   B. B. Hargus, interview with Robert Moog, originally published in online magazine, *Perfect Sound Forever*, March 1997.

143   G. J. MacDonald, "Contrarian Finding: Computers are a drag on learning," *Christian Science Monitor*, online edition, Dec. 6, 2004.

144   K. Forsyth, "Computers in Our Schools, Too Much, Too Soon," from daviswaldorf.org, Feb. 17, 2005.

146   C. Stoll (1995), *Silicon Snake Oil*, 133 (New York: Doubleday).

146   J. Gleick (2002), *What Just Happened: A Chronicle from the Information Frontier*, 269 (New York: Pantheon).

146   FMarketer, "Stop the Presses," WebMetro.com, May 9, 2005.

147   Journalism.org, "The State of the News Media 2004."

150   NASA Near Earth Object News Archives, http://neo.jpl.nasa .gov/news.

151   B. Radford, "Ringing False Alarms," *Skeptical Inquirer*, March/ April 2005, 34.

152   G. Browning, "How to Exaggerate," *Guardian*, Aug. 14, 2004, guardian.co.uk.

153   Michael R. LeGault, "How Ideas Are Like Viruses," *National Post*, April 4, 2000, A17.

155   F. Furedi (2005), *Culture of Fear*, ix (Continuum).

156   E. Waugh, (1938), *Scoop*, Introduction (Penguin Books).

157   Pew Research Center for the People and the Press, "News Audiences Increasingly Polarized," June 2004.

Chapter 7

160   D. Breashears (1999), *High Exposure*, 58 (New York: Simon and Schuster).

161   S. Sheperd (2003), *Who's in Charge?*, 14 (Rainbow Books).

162   Blogger notes, trivialbutimportant.blogspot.com, Oct. 28, 2004.

163   Blogger notes, secraterri.com, May 4, 1999.

164   *Time*, June 6, 1983, summary taken from stress.org.

164   *Prevention* magazine survey, summary taken from stress.org.

164   National Institute for Occupational Safety and Health, "Stress at Work," DHHS (NIOSH) Pub. No. 99–101, cdc.gov.niosh/stresswk.html.

166   S. Sheperd (2003), *Who's in Charge?*, 9 (Rainbow Books).

168   National Institute for Occupational Safety and Health, "Stress at Work," DHHS (NIOSH) Pub. No. 99–101, cdc.gov.niosh/stresswk.html.

169   International Labor Organization, "Key Indicators of the Labor Market 2001–2002, ILO Press Release, Aug. 31, 2001.

169   *The Economist*, March 5, 2005, 30.

170   C. McGrath, "No Rest for the Weary," *New York Times Magazine*, July 3, 2005, 15.

171   Rollo May, interviewed by Jeffery Mishlove, from the *Thinking Allowed* series, intuition.org.

172   S. Sheperd (2003), *Who's in Charge?*, 58 (Rainbow Books).

172   S. Johnson (2004), *Mind Wide Open*, 2 (New York: Scribner).

174   D. Kirsh, "A Few Thoughts on Cognitive Overload," icl-server.ucsd.edu, 2000, 2.

175   K. Maclay, "University of California, Berkeley Professors Measure Exploding World Production of New Information," UC press release, Oct. 18, 2000.

175   K. Miller (2004), *Surviving Information Overload* (Zondervan).

176   D. Shenk (1999), *Data Smog*, 91, (HarperEdge).

177   N. Chad, "Information Overload," *Washington Post*, Feb. 28, 2005, D2.

178   L. Lessig, J. C. Herz, quoted in *Code and Other Laws of Cyberspace*, 25, (Basic Books).

179   K. Miller, M. Davis, quoted in *Surviving Information Overload*, 20, (Zondervan).

179   P. Forbes, book review of J. Gleick's *Faster*, published in *The Guardian*, Dec. 11, 1999.

179   L. Rosen, M. Weil, contextmag.com.

180   L. Lessig, *Code and Other Laws of Cyberspace*, 25, (Basic Books).

180   P. Magee, *Brain Dancing*, 1996, 7 (BrainDance.com).

181   D. Breashears (1999), *High Exposure*, 185 (New York: Simon and Schuster).

Chapter 8

186   Washington State Internet Classroom, "World Civilization."

187   *Wikipedia*, "Pythagoras," en.wikipedia.org.

189   D. Goldsmith, R. Libbon (2005), "Einstein: A Relative History," Ch. 3 (iBooks, Inc.).

191   T. Gobble (2004), *Nicholas Copernicus and the Founding of Modern Astronomy* (Morgan Reynolds).

193   K. Easter, "The Universality of Shakespeare," *The Paper Store, Enterprises, Inc.*, May 2005, 9.

194   B. Meyer (2000), *The Golden Thread*, 316 (HarperFlamingo-Canada).

194   K. Easter, "The University of Shakespeare," *The Paper Store, Enterprises, Inc.*, May 2005, 3.

195   H. Evans, "The Spark of Genius," *U.S. News & World Report*, Oct. 11, 2004, 44.

199   D. Berlinski (2000), *Newton's Gift*, 93 (New York: The Free Press).

201   J. Glenn (1996), *Scientific Genius: The Twenty Greatest Minds*, 74–79 (Saraband Inc.).

202   S. Jones (1999), *Darwin's Ghost: The Origin of Species Updated*, xxi (Doubleday Canada).

208   K. Devlin, "Witten at 50," *Mathematical Association of America*, July/August, maa.org/devlin.

209   M. R. LeGault, "Additional Universes Postulated," *National Post*, Feb. 17, 2001, A1.

209   Public Broadcasting System, *Nova*, "The Elegant Universe," interview conducted by Joe McMaster, July 2003.

Chapter 9

215   L. Greenfield, *Fast Forward: Growing Up in the Shadow of Hollywood*, 49, 38 (Chronicle Books).

216   Ibid., 4.

217   A. Hulbert (2003), *Raising America: Experts, Parents and a Century of Advice about Children*, 365 (New York: Alfred A. Knopf).

218   Reuters news release, "Kids More Spoiled Than a Decade Ago," July 2001.

222   CNN *Talkback Live*, aired July 31, 2001, cnnstudentnews.cnn .com.

224   L. Hoke, "Teaching Millennials: Do We Need a Paradigm Shift," Eastern Economics Association Meeting, New York, 2004, 6.

224   Ibid., 6

225   R. Keegan (1994), *In Over Our Heads: The Mental Demands of Modern Life*, 79 (Harvard University Press).

226   "National Playday 2001: Facts and Statistics," playday.org.uk.

226   J. Almon, "The Vital Role of Play in Childhood," Waldorf Early Childhood Association of North America, waldorfearly childhood.org.

226   B. Furlow, "Play's the Thing," *New Scientist*, nethappenings .com, 3.

228   "Outtakes from Cosby's Speech to NAACP," *Washington Post*, "Reliable Source," May 23, 2005, rosenblog.com.

229   D. Brooks, "How to Reinvent the GOP," *New York Times Magazine*, Aug. 29, 2004, 37.

229   N. Asimov, Caroline Hoxby report "How Important Are Schools in Determining Achievement," cited in "Hakuta Ar-

gues Teachers of English Learners Unqualified," *San Francisco Chronicle*, May 5, 2003, A1.

230   P. Leman; T. Kragh-Muller, "Parenting Style as a Context for Moral Legitimacy: Children's Perceptions of the Reasons Behind Adult Moral Rules," Dept. of Psychology, Goldsmiths College, University of London, UK.

235   T. Lewin, "Young Students Are New Focus for Big Donors," *New York Times*, Aug. 21, 2005, A15.

237   "Why Johnny Can't Add," pims.math.ca/education/2004.

237   B. Stein, "How to Ruin American Enterprise," Dec. 23, 2002, Forbes.com.

238   T. Lewin, "Young Students Are New Focus for Big Donors," *New York Times*, Aug. 21, 2005, A15.

239   C. Reid-Wallace, quoted in *Habits of Mind*, by B. Allen and C. Allan (2004), 29 (Transaction Publishers).

240   Ibid., 23.

240   R. Bennett, "The Extreme Family," *Mossback Culture*, Cosby Show dialogue, May 26, 2002, mossback.org.

241   C. Argyris, "Empowerment: The Emperor's New Clothes," *Harvard Business Review*, May–June 1998, 98.

241   N. Gibbs, "Parents Behaving Badly," *Time*, Feb. 21, 2005, 42.

243   S. Johnson (2005), *Everything Bad Is Good for You* (Riverhead).

Chapter 10

247   G. Rivlin, "In California Enclave, Cougars Keep the People at Bay," *New York Times*, Aug. 28, 2005, A10.

249   Alabama Policy Institute, "Environmental Indicators," alabamapolicyinstitute.org.

251   M. Adler, "Fear Assessment: Cost-Benefit Analysis and the Pricing of Fear and Anxiety," U. of Penn.; *Institute for Law & Econ. Research Paper 03–28*, Nov. 2003, 1.

253   V. Postrel (1998), *The Future and Its Enemies*, 71 (New York: The Free Press).

255   M. Fischetti, "Drowning New Orleans," *Scientific American*, Oct. 2001, 78.

256   R. Lovett, "Fact versus Fear: We Worry Too Much about Man-Made Catastrophe," *Psychology Today*, May–June 2003, find articles.com.

257   R. Bailey, "Silent Spring at 40," *Reasononline*, June 12, 2002, 7.

258   E. Garfield, "Man-Made and Natural Carcinogens—Putting Risks in Perspective," *Veterinary and Human Toxicology*, 31 (6), 589–90, 1989.

259   B. Lange and G. Strange, "Environmental Politics: Analysis and Alternatives," *Capital & Class*, Autumn 2000, findarticles.com.

259   B. Glasner (1999), *The Culture of Fear*, xv (New York: Basic Books).

261   C. R. Sunstein, "The Laws of Fear," *University of Chicago Law School, John M. Olin Law & Economics*, working paper No. 128, June 16, 2001, 1.

262   Ibid., 35.

263   J. McCrone (1993), *The Myth of Irrationality*, 250 (Carroll & Graf).

265   "MRI Studies Provide New Insight Into How Emotions Interfere With Staying Focused," Duke University Press Release, Aug. 20, 2002.

266   T. H. Davenport (2005), *Thinking for a Living*, 150 (Harvard Business School Press).

268   J. Bransford, A. Brown, and R. Cocking (2000), *How People Learn*, Ch. 5 (National Academy Press).

269   V. Postrel (1998), *The Future and Its Enemies*, 70 (New York: The Free Press).

270   S. J. Dubner and S. D. Levitt, "Does the Truth Lie Within," *New York Times Magazine*, Sept. 11, 2005, 20.

271   Freerepublic.com/forum, posted Feb. 11, 2001.

Chapter 11

278   A. C. Doyle (1903), *The Sign of Four*, Ch. 1 (James Askew and Son).

280   S. D. Schafersman, *An Introduction to Science*, Miami University, Ohio, Jan. 1997, 4, muohio.edu.

283   Ibid., 4.

284   Megan Aston, "What Makes Us Happy," *University of Toronto Magazine*, Spring 2005, 23.

287   A. Pitluk, "Unfair Share," dallasobserver.com, Jan. 25, 2001, 5.

290   *The Economist Pocket World in Figures*, 2005 Ed., 54, 92, 101 (Profile Books Ltd.).

292   U. Kraft, "Unleashing Creativity," *Scientific American Mind*, Vol. 16, No. 1, 17.

293   J. McCrone (1993), *The Myth of Irrationality*, 2 (Carroll & Graf Publishers Inc.).

294   A. Bloom (1988), *The Closing of the American Mind* (Simon & Schuster).

297   Barbara Ehrenreich, interviewed on zmag.org, 4.

297   A. Lerner and S. Pinker, quoted in "Using Our Brains: What Cognitive Science Tells Us About Teaching Problem Solving and Professional Responsibility," University of Pennsylvania Law School, 3.

299   R. Hoffman (1995), *The Same and Not the Same*, 83 (Columbia University Press).

299   *The Economist*, "After the Fall," Feb. 19, 2005, 7.

300   J. Horgan (1996), *The End of Science* (Addison Wesley).

300   K. Davidson, review of *A Different Universe*, by Robert Laughlin, *New York Times Book Review*, June 19, 2005, 19.

305   D. Goldsmith and R. Libbon (2005), *Einstein: A Relative History*, 84 (iBooks, Inc.).

305   Ben Ratliff, "Pat Metheny: An Idealist Reconnects With His Mentors," *New York Times*, Feb. 25, 2005, B1.

Chapter 12

311   J. Barzun (2000), *From Dawn to Decadence, 500 Year of Western Cultural Life,* xxi (Perennial).

311   K. Minogue, "How Civilizations Fall," *New Criterion,* April 2001, www.newcriterion.com, 2.

315   B. Shaffer, "The Decline and Fall of a Civilization," *Free Republic,* freerepublic.com, Dec. 10, 2001, 2.

317   J. R. Saul (1993), *Voltaire's Bastards: The Dictatorship of Reason in the West,* 16 (Penguin Books).

318   Closson, "Politically Correct Education," www.leaderu.com, 1992, 2.

319   *The Economist,* "Damaged Goods," May 21, 2005, 11.

320   *Wall Street Journal,* "Europe vs. America," editorial page, June 20, 2004.

320   K. Minogue, "The Idea of Decline in Western Civilization," *National Interest,* Summer 1997, findarticles.com.

322   S. Huntington (1996), *The Clash of Civilizations,* Ch. 12, 4 (New York: Simon and Schuster).

323   Rollo May, interviewed by Jeffery Mishlove, from the *Thinking Allowed* series, intuition.org, 2.

324   C. Van Doren (1991), *A History of Knowledge,* 57 (Ballantine Books).

325   N. Ferguson (2002), *Empire: The Rise and Demise of the British World Order and the Lessons for Global Power,* xvii (Allan Lane).

326   S. Huntington (1996), *The Clash of Civilizations,* Ch. 12, 2 (Simon and Schuster).

328   *Statistics, Science and Public Policy: Recommendations for Government and the Scientific Community,* A. M. Herzberg and I. Krupka, eds. (1998), Queens University, Canada.

329   C. Barnard, cited in *Beyond Feelings, A Guide to Critical Thinking,* 2004, 15 (McGraw-Hill).

330   G. Easterbrook, interviewed by B. Wattenberg, *PBS Think Tank,* aired Feb. 20, 2003, p. 6 of transcript.

331   C. Goodnow, "Socrates Cafes Dish Up Intellectual Nourishment," *Seattle Post-Intelligencer,* Feb. 21, 2004, lifestyle section, seattlepi.com.

332   D. W. Dunlap, "Freedom Center at 9/11 Site, a Lofty Idea Gives Way to Realities on Ground," *Wall Street Journal,* Sept. 25, 2005, 25.

334   S. M. Walt (2005), *Taming American Power* (W.W. Norton).

335   S. R. Weisman, "Saudi Women Have Message for U.S. Envoy," *New York Times,* Sept. 28, 2005, A1.

336   W. B. Allen and C. M. Allen (2004) *Habits of Mind,* 23 (Transaction Publishers).

Acknowledgments

This book is the result of a lifetime spent trying to alleviate my ignorance. As such, I am not certain that the chain of credits of those who supported and assisted this challenging endeavor—leading to the end product, this book—has a definite beginning, so I will invoke author's privilege and "air it out."

My parents, together with my sisters Dawn and Sandy, and my deceased sister, Linda, along with their families, have been an endless source of inspiration, debate, love, laughter, and moral support throughout the years and the long, formative stage of this work. As well, I would be remiss if I did not mention the type of subtle, but geological-timescale backing supplied by close friends, in my case Michael Lowe, Michael Schaefer, Bob Cardinal, Gary Stroutsos, and Tom O'Brien, whose skepticism, struggles against "the good night," and talents for literal translation of experience have kept me on my toes and egged on my search for truth. A special note of thanks goes to my good friend Jeff Cianci for the "Miami Years," (yes, they played an important part in this book) and for coming through with a key contact that set this whole project in motion.

ACKNOWLEDGMENTS

There are no known words that can express the depth of my gratitude to my agent, Nina Collins. She not only believed in this book from the get-go, but provided astute technical advice in helping to formulate the proposal and some of the book's stylistic and structural nuances. Her assistant, Matthew Elblonk, also played a major role in bringing the proposal to fruition. I am also hugely indebted to both Louise Burke and Mary Matalin for being the formidable driving forces behind this new Simon and Schuster imprint, Threshold Editions; and I am honored and thrilled that *Think!* is the first book in an exciting new venture that seems destined to shake up the American cultural and political scene.

My editor, Kevin Smith, has played a vital, indispensable role in the development of the book's style and structure. Kevin's perceptive feel for narrative and tone of language kept my writing from straying down many a tempting but dubious path. I am also grateful to Kevin's assistant, Joshua Martino, for providing an added level of quality control through his solid, professional support in various forms. I'd also like to thank copy editor Sean Devlin and production editor Al Madocs for thoroughly weeding my prose of errors, both large and microscopic.

I consider myself extremely fortunate to have "discovered" Christine Honeyman shortly before setting out to write this book. Time and time again, Christine's research turned up valuable reports, statistics, and other information that gives the book, I believe, its foundation on evidence, not merely my imagination. I also cannot miss this opportunity to thank my longtime associate editor, Cindy Macdonald, at whose knee I learned much about the importance of clarity and accuracy.

Finally, I'd like to give my profuse and loving thanks to my wife, Anneli, and daughters, Kristen and Katherine, for their unwavering, cheerful, enthusiastic support of this work, and for their tolerance of my neglect.